SRI LANKA
From Dominion to Republic

SRI LANKA
FROM DOMINION TO REPUBLIC
(A study of the changing relations with the United Kingdom)

Dr. (Miss) Lucy M. Jacob

NATIONAL - DELHI

NATIONAL PUBLISHING HOUSE
23, Darya Ganj, Delhi-110006 (India)

Overseas Distributors
BOOKS FROM INDIA
32, Coptic Street
Opp. The British Museum
London, W.C. 1 (U.K.)

© Dr. (Miss) Lucy M. Jacob

First Published : *1973*

Printed in India at Saraswati Printing Press, Delhi-110053 and Published by National Publishing House, 23, Darya Ganj, Delhi-110006

To
My Beloved Parents

PREFACE

Sri Lanka, a small island, is one of the Asian countries to attain independence after the World War II. Besides her strategically important position in the Indian Ocean, she is also the focal point on the trade route between the East and the West. Obviously these considerations made the UK virtually interested in Sri Lanka. Non-availability of a comprehensive work on the subject prompted me to undertake the present study.

While the book was still in the press a new constitution declaring Ceylon the Republic of Sri Lanka was promulgated. Hence both the names—Ceylon and Sri Lanka—have been used interchangeably.

This book attempts to unfold various aspects of Ceylon's relations with the UK since her independence in 1948. Providing a historical setting against which Ceylon's relations with the UK should be analysed, the study highlights the motivations underlying Colombo's relations with White Hall under the UNP regime. While examining the context of the Agreements pertaining to Defence and External Affairs, the study explains the nature of Ceylon's Commonwealth connections and analyses her stand on some of the foreign policy issues and their implications on Ceylon-UK relations. The study also attempts to examine the domestic compulsions of Ceylonese non-alignment and to correlate them with the UK in the political as well as constitutional spheres. Focussing on the Ceylon-UK economic relations, the study makes a significant point that bilateral economic and political interactions need not converge. It also attempts to review the Ceylon-UK socio-cultural relations. The study builds up a theme of continuity and change in Ceylon-UK relations during the UNP-Bandaranaike eras in socio-politico-economic fields.

Substantially based on a doctoral thesis on Ceylon-UK relations covering the period 1948-65, submitted to the University of Rajasthan in 1970, the post-script reviewing briefly the major developments in Sri Lanka-UK relations since 1965, has been added in the book to bring the developments up-to-date.

Observations and conclusions in the study have been based on primary and secondary sources accessible both in Ceylon and the UK. Further, the arguments at some places have been strengthened by what I could gather from interviews during my field trip to Ceylon and the UK in 1965-66. Interviewing prominent leaders and statesmen from the island such as Dudley Senanayake, the then Prime Minister of Ceylon, Mrs. Sirimavo Bandaranaike, the then Leader of the Opposition in Ceylon Parliament and the present Prime Minister of Ceylon, J.R. Jayawardane, the then Minister of State and Parliamentary Secretary to the Prime Minister, John Kotelwala, the former Prime Minister of Ceylon; and the British officials and unofficials who had intimate knowledge of the Ceylon affairs like S.A. Pakeman, the then Secretary to the Commonwealth Parliamentary Association, Lord Soulbury, the former Governor-General of Ceylon and the architect of the Ceylon constitution which held good for over two decades since independence, was a rewarding experience. This is reflected throughout the study.

I express my profound sense of gratitude to my supervisor Dr. S.P. Varma, Professor and Head of the Department of Political Science, University of Rajasthan, who guided and encouraged me at every stage of the work. For their guidance and invaluable suggestions, I am thankful to Prof. Hugh Tinker, School of Oriental and African Studies, London University, Dr. S.U. Kodikara, University of Ceylon, and Prof. W. Howard Wriggins of the University of Columbia. I owe a debt of gratitude to Dr. (Mrs.) Urmilla Phadnis, School of International Studies, Jawaharlal Nehru University, New Delhi for her invaluable help and encouragement throughout.

I am deeply grateful to the British Council for the award of a Travel Grant under the Commonwealth Inter-University Scheme which enabled me to plan my field trip to the UK.

I record with great pleasure the facilities offered to me by the staff of the combined library of Indian Council of World Affairs and School of International Studies, New Delhi and of the various libraries in the UK and Sri Lanka in the preparation of this book and I acknowledge my immense gratitude to all of them.

My thanks are also due to the Indian Council of Social Science Research, New Delhi whose financial help facilitated the publication of this book. However, I am exclusively responsible for the opinion expressed and the conclusions reached.

It is a pleasure to express my gratitude to several friends and colleagues who have helped in various ways in the process of bringing out this book. Last but not the least, I am thankful to Shri Virendra Narain, Research Associate, Department of Political Science, Rajasthan University for helping me in proof-reading.

L.M. Jacob

CONTENTS

Preface		vii
Key to Abbreviations		xii
1.	The Setting	1
2.	The UNP Regime and the Whitehall	21
3.	Non-aligned Ceylon and the United Kingdom	64
4.	Economic Relations	104
5.	Socio-cultural Relations	146
6.	Conclusion	164
7.	Post-Script : Major Developments in Sri Lanka-UK Relations since 1965	172

Appendices

I.	United Kingdom-Ceylon Defence Agreement 1947	195
II.	United Kingdom-Ceylon External Affairs Agreement 1947	197
III.	Exchange of Letters between the Government of Ceylon and the Government of the United Kingdom Service Establishments in Ceylon 1957	200
IV.	Repatriation of UK Capital from Ceylon	212
V.	Ceylon's Trade with the UK 1948-1970	213
VI.	Number of Students who entered the various London External Examinations (1) 1949-1963	214
VII.	Number of Ceylonese Students in the Universities of the UK 1948-1970	215
Select Bibliography		216
Index		237

KEY TO ABBREVIATIONS

Ceylon H.R. Deb.	=	Ceylon House of Representatives Debate
Ceylon S. Deb.	=	Ceylon Senate Debates
Ceylon S.C. Deb.	=	Ceylon State Council Debates
Cmd.	=	Command Papers
CP	=	Communist Party
F.P.	=	Federal Party
GAOR	=	Official Records of the General Assembly of the United Nations
IBRD	=	International Bank of Reconstruction
IMF	=	International Monetary Fund
LSSP	=	Lanka Sama Samaja Party
MEP	=	Mahajana Eksath Peramuna
RIIA Documents	=	Royal Institute of International Affairs Documents
SLFP	=	Sri Lanka Freedom Party
SLFSP	=	Sri Lanka Freedom Socialist Party
TC	=	Tamil Congress
UNP	=	United National Party

1
THE SETTING

Ceylon, an island in the Indian Ocean, off the southern coast of India, with an area of 25,332 square miles is roughly of the same size as Tasmania or the Irish Republic and a little more than one-quarter of the United Kingdom. This island, though small, is yet an important country in South Asia by virtue of its unrivalled geo-strategic value in the Indian Ocean. South Asia has been the classic home of Western imperialism. The impact of the West on South Asia was affected by the duration, intensity, and policies of Western rule. Ceylon experienced Western rule, longer than any other Asian country, under three successive European colonial powers—the Portuguese (1505-1656), the Dutch (1656-1796), and the British (1796-1948)—each of whom ruled the island in succession for about a century and a half.[1] During the Portuguese and the Dutch era, the Kingdom of Kandy maintained itself in the mountainous interior of the country. It was left to the British to destroy the last vestige of independence in the country and unify the entire island under a single government after several centuries.

The early Contacts

Though the British contacts with Ceylon go as far back as 1589,[2] the conquest of the coastal areas of Ceylon was carried out by the British in 1796 which marked the end of a century and a half of the Dutch rule in Ceylon. At first Ceylon was administered from Madras, for the Imperial government could not take over the island under its direct control, as the East India Company had some claim to the revenue and trade of Ceylon after the occupation was carried out by their forces. But an attempt to apply the Madras revenue system and the employment of a host of Malabar officers in Ceylon led to a rebellion in 1797. Consequently, in 1798 the Imperial Government placed the island under a dual control whereby the Company was to keep control of the collection of revenue and of commerce, and the Crown officials were to control the general administration.

The difficulties attendant on such a system of administration, with divided loyalty and responsibility between the Crown and the East India Company, compelled the British Government to take over full administration of the island.[3] On 1 January 1802 Ceylon was made a crown colony[4] and remained so till 4 February 1948.

The Kandyan conquest and the unification of the Island

The British, however, secured full control of the island only in 1815 when certain Kandyan chiefs deposed their king, Sri Wickrama Rajasingha, with the aid of the British. In an agreement signed with the chiefs, the British promised to honour the national religion as well as to protect the "ancient privileges and powers" of the indigenous bureaucracy.[5] Thus ended the kingdom of Kandy which had survived the Portuguese and Dutch occupation in Ceylon.

Even though the whole island was brought under the British Government, the status of the Kandyan chiefs and people vis-a-vis the Crown was maintained by the provisions of the convention of 1815. But an insurrection which broke out shortly after, and was suppressed by the British, reflected the uneasiness of the Kandyan chiefs vis-a-vis the administration of the new regime. This led to the proclamation of 1818, according to which the powers of the chiefs were curtailed and the dominion of the Kandyan provinces was vested in His Majesty subject to the condition of maintaining the laws, institutions, and the customs of the country.[6] Nevertheless the Government of Ceylon was occasionally troubled by popular uprisings in 1820, 1823, 1824, 1842 and 1848.[7] The 1818 reforms which brought a change in the social order of the Kandyans lasted without substantial changes till 1833 when the Kandyan Provinces were administratively united with the Maritime Provinces.

From a Crown colony to an independent Dominion 1802-1948

The real story of British relations with Ceylon starts from the establishment of the Crown colony, the administration of which was directed from Downing Street. The form of government for Ceylon, though designated a 'colony', was not of the traditional indirect method[8] but that of direct rule as worked out in India. Their conception was that of "an autocracy, an avowedly benevolent one, running the country on humane principles and acceptable to the people by reason of the advantages which it brought to them."[9] Accordingly, a highly centralized system of administration replaced the one which was personal and feudal. The Governor was vested with complete executive and legislative powers, assisted by an advisory council. In his discretionary powers, he was answerable only to the Secretary of State and through him to the British Parliament. In other words, as Tennent has observed, "In a Crown colony such as Ceylon... the powers of the Governor constitute a paternal despotism, modified only by the distant authority of the Queen."[10] Before long, many complaints against the arbitrary rule of the Governor had already reached the Home Government. Meanwhile, a radical change took place in the political, social, and economic life of Britain due to the great developments in the early nineteenth century like the Industrial Revolution and the evangelical movements. The British policies were also influenced by the views of utilitarians and liberals like Jeremy Bentham, Adam Smith, James Mill, and others who succeeded in creating an indifference towards traditional values,—autocratic form of government, doctrinal system of mercantilism, slavery etc.[11] It was in 1820s that these new conceptions were influencing the British colonial policy and that the Colebrooke-Cameron Commission was sent out to examine the entire administration of Ceylon. Its report was accepted in 1833 by the Colonial government.

In 1833, consequent to the Colebrooke Reforms, a unified system of administration was organised for the first time for the whole island. Despite the many criticisms raised against these reforms it is a landmark in the history of Ceylon as it contributed to the constitutional advancement of the island. The most important changes made were : the introduction of an Executive Council of Senior Officials to assist the Governor, and a Legislative Council including both officials and nominated non-officials to ensure free discussion of public questions and the enactment of laws.[12]

Towards the close of the century an entirely new class emerged in the political life of the island as a result of the general prosperity of the country and the expansion of educational facilities. The new middle class, mainly concentrated in urban areas and educated in British political ideas, refused to be satisfied with its lot. Hence, there was a continuous demand from it for a substantial reform of the Legislative Council as the British middle class had done in 1832 in its own country.[13] But the British authorities did not sympathise with these aspirations of a handful of Ceylonese politicians, who represented only a small privileged class. But continuous agitation for reforms by the leaders of the new middle class resulted in the passing of the Crewe-McCallum Reforms which took them a step forward in the constitutional development of Ceylon. The concessions granted by these reforms, though not very far-reaching, were vital in the sense that the national-minded educated middle class had won the first round in their campaign for further self-government. They succeeded in getting for the first time the right to elect one member to the Legislative Council and in increasing the number of unofficial members from 8 to 10.[14]

These reforms served only as an 'appetizer' to the politically conscious Ceylonese. The nationalist movement, which had its genesis with the rise of the middle class, gained added momentum in the years of the First World War. The religio-communal conflict between the Sinhalese and the Muslims in 1915 roused the national feeling due to the repressive measures with which it was suppressed by the Government. In 1917, the Ceylon Reform League was formed, and this was developed further into the Ceylon National Congress in 1919. With the declaration of the Montague-Chelmsford Report of 1918 in India,[15] the Ceylonese leaders who expected similar treatment for Ceylon also at the hands of the Imperial government, continued the agitation for reform with a new vigour.

In response to these demands, for the first time an unofficial majority was provided by the Order-in-Council of 1920.[16] This was an attempt to introduce "balanced representation"—a system in which no community could have had a majority in the Legislative Council unless it had the support of the officials.[17] The Ceylonese leaders, who were not satisfied with the 1920 compromise, obtained another amendment of the Constitution in 1924 which conceded for the first time, the principle of representative government.[18] Though this Constitution was intended to lead the way to ultimate self-government, its working proved "an unqualified failure" as there was divorce of power from responsibility. Nevertheless it continued to exist until 1931 when it was replaced by the Donoughmore Constitution.

The principal changes made by the Donoughmore Constitution were : the transference of a large measure of ministerial, executive and administrative responsibility to the elected representatives in the new State Council ; the introduction of adult suffrage without property, income or education tests, for the first time, in any British colony; and the establishment of the Executive Committee system whereby each member of the Legislature shared in departmental administration. Last but not least, the abolition of communal representation was perhaps its most important contribution to the unity and harmony of the Ceylonese. The introduction of the Donoughmore Constitution not only marked a further important step towards self-government for the people of Ceylon, but was also important in the history of British Imperial self-government in that "it was the first attempt to apply the machinery of democratic and responsible government to a non-European country."[19]

The Constitution, however, could be said to be only a 'half-way house' as it fell short of complete self-rule.[20] Hence it resulted in a renewed agitation by the Ceylonese for self-government. But the outbreak and continuance of the Second World War necessitated the postponement of all considerations of constitutional changes till the end of the War. However, in 1943, to win the loyalty of the Ceylonese in a deteriorating world situation, the Imperial Government was forced to make the declaration that "the post-war re-examination of the reform of the Ceylon Constitution... will be directed towards the grant to Ceylon by Order of His Majesty in Council, of full responsible Government under the Crown in all matters of internal civil administration." The declaration also added that the Ministers could, in the meantime, draft their own constitutional scheme which would be duly examined by a Commission or Conference and duly accepted, if approved by three-quarters of all the Members of the State Council of Ceylon.[21] But even before the end of the hostilities, the process of reform was set in motion in 1944 by appointing the Soulbury Commission to examine the draft of the Ministers of the State Council and also to recommend a constitution for Ceylon. This roused the grouse of the Ceylonese leaders like D. S. Senanayake and Dudley Senanayake,[22] who, during the course of the Debate in the State Council in 1944 on the Introduction of the Constitution Bill, spelt out the characteristic change of attitude in the British policy and viewed with suspicion the intentions of the Imperial Government in sending the Commission on the pretext of examining vested interests as well as interests of various communities, which was a complete departure from the original Declaration.[23] Though none of the Ministers gave evidence before the Commissioners, the Commission's report, based on the Ministers' Draft, was overwhelmingly accepted by the State Council.[24] The Ceylon Order-in-Council of 1946 (the Soulbury Constitution) which came into force in 1946 granted full responsible government in all matters of internal administration while the Imperial Government retained the defence, external affairs and power of reservation on certain kinds of bills.[25]

Though the Soulbury Constitution was accepted without much ado, negotiations for a further advance towards Dominion Status had been initiated by the Ceylonese leaders before it came into operation. Fortunately for the Ceylonese, the political climate in Britain had taken a turn for the better.

Two important events accentuated the agitation of the Ceylonese. The first was the Labour Party's succession to the helm of affairs after the 1945 general election in Britain,[26] and the second was the British government's decision to grant independence to India and Burma which made it difficult for Britain to deny some measure of freedom to Ceylon any longer.[27] Moreover, unlike India, Ceylon's willing co-operation and loyalty to the British Commonwealth throughout the Second World War[28] and her experience in internal self-Government since 1931 stood to her credit in making the Imperial Government realise the inevitability of granting independence to Ceylon.

But the British Government could not balance all these factors in favour of Ceylon against her own strategic interests,[29] the claims of the minorities[30] in the island, and her obligations towards the Public Services.[31] At the same time, it was quite clear to them that Ceylon was not in any case going to remain a colony for a very long time and these issues would arise on the grant of independence at any time. Hence they were convinced that it would be wise to grant Ceylon full independence with minimum of trouble and maximum of friendly feelings. But as the negotiations went on, it was feared by the Ceylonese leaders, who were conscious of Ceylon's strategic position in the Indian Ocean, and her inability to defend herself, that this strategic weakness would be used as an argument against the granting of independence. So, D. S. Senanayake, to make it easier for the British Government to contemplate the immediate grant of Dominion status, agreed to sign suitable agreements on defence and external affairs.[32] In the subsequent announcement made by Creech Jones (the then Secretary of State for the colonies) in the House of Commons on 18 June 1947, it was made clear that the agreements to be concluded on terms satisfactory to His Majesty's Government and the Ceylon Government which would assume office under the new constitution, were a condition precedent to the grant of a fully responsible status within the British Commonwealth of Nations.[33] While discussions were going on between His Majesty's Government and Sir Oliver Goonetilleke[34] who was negotiating the last instalment of freedom in London as a representative of D. S. Senanayake, some misgivings arose about the use of the term 'Dominion Status' the status Senanayake had sought in August 1945 and February 1947. Some sections of opinion both in India and Ceylon argued that 'Dominion Status' was something inferior to independence. This led Sir Oliver to choose the expression "fully responsible status within the Commonwealth." But, as Senanayake was not quite happy about the phraseology used, he cabled the Secretary of State that "independence" be substituted for "Dominion Status." Although assured by the Secretary of State that the "status" meant what was generally understood by "Dominion Status," the term "independence" was used in the legislation conferring independence on Ceylon. Moreover, "none of the Ceylon documents uses the term 'Dominion', though the status which they confer is clearly the same as that of Canada, Australia, New Zealand and the Union of South Africa."[35]

The next step was the negotiation and the drafting of the three Agreements[36]—the Defence Agreement, the External Affairs Agreement and the agreement relating to Public Service—which were to be concluded between the two independent governments. The Defence Agreement made provision for mutual military assistance, use of Ceylon bases for that purpose and British help in training the Ceylonese armed forces.[37] The External Affairs Agreement defined Ceylon's position as a sovereign independent member of the British Commonwealth of Nations.[38]

By an Agreement on Public Officers, which was only a repetition of the undertaking already given in the new constitution, the British government transferred to the Ceylon government, the responsibility to pay the salaries, pensions etc. of the officers of the Public Services, particularly the European officers who were appointed by or on behalf of the Secretary of State for the colonies towards whom he had a special responsibility.[39] But, as Sir Ivor Jennings has pointed out, Ceylon's obligations under the agreement were not towards the officers of the Public Services but towards the United Kingdom Government and it was the responsibility of the United Kingdom Government to state a case before an international tribunal if the agreement was not carried out.[40]

At the time the terms of the agreements were being negotiated by both the Governments, the general elections for the first House of Representatives of Ceylon (as provided in the Soulbury Constitution which necessitated a parliamentary majority to make the government function)[41] was conducted, in which the United National Party (UNP) under the leadership of D. S. Senanayake emerged as the strongest party. The UNP was a hastily formed party under the leadership of D. S. Senanayake to contest the general elections. It was essentially a 'centre' grouping, composed of most of the retiring Ministers and members of the old State Council who belonged to some political organizations like the Ceylon National Congress, the Sinhala Mahasabha, and the Ceylon Muslim League.[42] The members who were returned in the election belonged to the Westernised, English educated, land-owning class. The opposition political parties were either 'left-wing'[43] whom people feared more than they loved the UNP or too weak to win against the UNP. Another reason for which the UNP was favoured was that the leaders of the party were 'tried politicians' who had gained experience as the junior partners in ruling Ceylon in the pre-independence years. It was obvious that in the general election the people voted for individuals and not for the party. Notwithstanding all these advantages in the UNP's favour, particularly the one like Senanayake's leadership, it could emerge only as the largest single party securing only 42 out of 95 seats. Nevertheless, the UNP formed the first national government with the help of the nominated members and several independents.[44]

With a responsible government formed, the new Cabinet formally approved of the drafts of the three agreements which were signed in Colombo on 11 November 1947 by Sir Henry Moore, the then Governor of Ceylon on behalf of the UK, and by D. S. Senanayake on behalf of Ceylon.[45] Soon after these necessary agreements were concluded, the Ceylon Independence Bill to confer upon Ceylon fully responsible status within the British Commonwealth of Nations was presented in the British House of Commons on 13 November 1947,[46] and was simultaneously published in Ceylon. Though the Opposition raised some misapprehensions, the bill was unanimously passed in the UK Parliament.

In Ceylon, though no legislative action was taken, a Motion expressing satisfaction at the negotiations for the attainment of its independence was introduced in the Ceylon Parliament on 1 December 1947.[47] The grant of independence became suspect in some quarters because of the Defence agreement. During the debate in the House of Representatives, the party in power was vehemently criticised by the Opposition for having subordinated Ceylon's interests to those of Britain and for having accepted a 'fake independence' by signing the Agreements. Throughout the debates in the Ceylon legislature on the Governor's Throne speech (on 25 November 1947) and on the Agreements, these doubts persisted especially in the ranks of the Left-wing in the Opposition. Nevertheless, after a three-day debate the Motion was passed by a very substantial majority.[48]

The Ceylon Independence Act 1947— "an Act to make provision for, and in connexion with, the attainment, by Ceylon of fully responsible status within the British Commonwealth of Nations"—received the Royal assent on 10 December 1947 and was to come into operation on a day to be appointed and by His Majesty by Order-in-Council.[49] This Act did not could not in itself confer independence on Ceylon as it was a composite operation which required a change in the law of the UK, the law of Ceylon and the relations between Ceylon and the UK. Hence, to provide a fully self-governing status was necessary that a new Order-in-Council had to be passed to remove from the existing constitution [Ceylon (Constitution) Order-in-Council 1946] all limitations[50] which were inconsistent with the independence of Ceylon within the Commonwealth. This was effected by the Ceylon Independence Order-in-Council passed on 19 December to come into operation on the 'appointed day'. As agreed to by both the governments, the appointed day was fixed as 4 February 1948, according to the Ceylon Independence (commencement) Order-in-Council, 1947 passed on 19 December 1947. On 4 February 1948, when the provisions of the five documents—the Ceylon Independence Order-in-Council 1947, the Ceylon Independence Act 1947, the Defence Agreement, the External Affairs Agreement, and the Public Officers Agreement—came into force, Ceylon became a complete, self-governing Dominion within the British Commonwealth of Nations.

THE SETTING

Socio-Economic changes during the British Rule

Till the end of the Dutch domination in 1796, which marked the end of an era in Ceylon's history, the economic structure of the island was essentially agrarian, the basis being paddy cultivation. The cultivation was not done for the market but for domestic consumption and the system of exchange was that of barter.[51] The chief source of revenue was trade in cinnamon, which after the British occupation of the Maritime Provinces in 1796 was taken over by the East India Company which retained it till 1821. There was very little of internal trade, and the foreign trade was a government monopoly. Thus the economic structure which existed in the pre-colonial feudal Ceylon, remained unaltered even in 1815 when the whole island was brought under the control of the British administration.

Under the Governorship of Sir Edward Banes (1819-20) the economic system of the island underwent a radical change with the development of modern means of communication.[52] The plantation industry, especially coffee which the Dutch had abandoned in 1739, was revived by the British. Initially it was started purely as a private enterprise. In 1833, the Colebrooke-Cameron Report removed the shackles that were placed on the economic progress of the island and opened the way for the economic exploitation of the country.[53] Thus, it can be said that Colebrooke reforms formed a landmark in the economic history of the island, as they marked the transformation of an agrarian economy, a heritage from the pre-colonial feudal Ceylon, into a plantation economy, a product of the 19th century British policy, which had its impact on the whole social structure of the island as well.

The opening of the plantation industry brought in its train many problems like the scarcity of land, the shortage of labour, the increase of population, lack of communication, and lack of capital. Even though the forest lands were converted to plantation, because of the large-scale commercialised production of plantation crops there was still scarcity of land suitable for plantation.

Another difficulty which the planters had to face was the insufficiency of adequate labour to work in the plantations. This situation was created partly by the abolition of *Rajakariya*,[54] partly by the peasants' attachment to the soil and indifference to the 'cash nexus', and partly due to the location of plantation in uninhabited areas. This problem was solved by the immigration of the Indian labour. The influx of workers from India resulted in the increase of population and produced a large landless working class[55] which became a fundamental problem of the economy of Ceylon.

As the plantation was being developed on a commercial line, roads and railways had to be multiplied to keep pace with the transport. With the improvement in the communication system much of the barriers like the rural isolation, geographical remoteness etc. were automatically lifted up exposing the people to the new values of life which commercialism created.

Closely connected with these technical problems was the problem of the lack of capital investment. The indigenous people of Ceylon were unable to contribute either capital or manpower to the new development. Hence the plantation economy of Ceylon was built upon the basis of an alliance of British capital and Indian Tamil labour. It was the stationed military and civil service which pioneered the plantation enterprise with their small capital and influence with the government. The government was 'capital-shy' with regard to large-scale investment in the industry. But by 1840 a large number of 'small capitalists' and small investors with loans provided by the agency houses in Colombo or London entered the industry.[56] As these British-owned banks and agency houses were reluctant to give credit to the Ceylonese, the estate owners were mostly British.

After the coffee crash in 1847, with the revival of the industry in the fifties coffee was exported to almost all the countries at the highest prices in the markets of the world.[57] But when the coffee industry declined rapidly due to blight between the years 1871-1906, it was replaced by the "new plantations" like cinchona, tea, rubber and coconut. For the sale of the products of these plantations, the planters had to depend almost exclusively on foreign markets. Thus the economy of the island was susceptible to fluctuations in crops.

The growth of plantations gave an impetus to the development of both internal and external trade. As the British were the imperial masters in colonial Ceylon, much of her trade (both imports and exports) was with the British countries. Between the years 1938-47, the average percentage of Ceylon's export to the British countries amounted to 64.07 out of which 41.71 was to the United Kingdom itself, and 35.92 to other countries. The average percentage of Ceylon's imports from British countries amounted to 70.8, out of which 13.07 was from the UK and 28.21 from other countries.[58] Thus, on the eve of independence, the economy of Ceylon was "a poorly developed and narrow-based agricultural export economy."[59] The three main industries—tea, rubber and coconut—mainly owned by the Europeans and cultivated by Indian labour were overwhelmingly export industries, which accounted for nearly half of the national income. Since the main products were mainly produced for export, the country had to import two-thirds of its food, nearly all of its textiles, and all of its fuel.

The development of the plantation system on capitalistic lines had its impact on the indigenous society as well. The most noteworthy social change was the startling rise of a prosperous native middle class who were educated on English lines anxious to secure a large share in the government. This class consisted of planters, traders, doctors, teachers, government servants, transport agents and businessmen from all races and castes.[60] It was this group which acquired political consciousness and led various movements that heralded the growth of a national independence movement.

Education as a catalyst for Change

In the beginning of the British occupation of Ceylon, the Dutch system of education which had provided some instruction in Sinhalese and Tamil was continued. Nevertheless the British, who were determined that education offered should be essentially Christian in character, encouraged the existing missionary schools with meagre grants.[61] The liberal attitude of the British encouraged many more missions[62] to come to the island and education was left in their hands. The Colebrooke reforms brought in far reaching changes in the educational policy of the government. It recommended the abolition of schools in local languages and the establishment of English schools with the idea that a knowledge of English was a necessity if Ceylon were to transform herself from a feudal into a commercial society.⁶³ Another recommendation of the Commission that the management of education be entrusted to the School Commission consisting of Anglican clergy and government officials strengthened missionary influence in the state control of education.⁶⁴

In the latter part of the 19th century, with the expansion of government activities and economic development of the country, the policy of increasing the number of English schools and encouraging them to adopt the Cambridge system of examination was followed.⁶⁵ The curriculum of English schools, in which Western classics, history and literature were included, was oriented towards Western culture. By promoting the growth of English language schools, the government also facilitated the transmission to the Ceylonese of the writings of the English social and political thinkers like Bernard Shaw, H. G. Wells, G. D. H. Cole, Harold Laski whose work had a deep influence on modern Ceylonese trends of thought. This resulted in the development of increased social awareness among the local population which led in turn to the growth of a Sinhalese nationalist movement. This movement was stimulated by the inspiration derived from contact with democratic movements in Europe and with constitutional developments within the British Empire, particularly the movement towards self-government in India.

But during this period little attention was paid to the vernacular schools as a knowledge of Sinhalese and Tamil did not take students very far. The English schools also almost ignored the culture of the people by not teaching Buddhism or Hinduism.⁶⁶ The minority who could afford higher education, confined themselves to English studies as education in English was regarded as an investment for a better career.⁶⁷ Moreover, the coffee industry stimulated a great demand for English speaking employees.

Along with the neglect of language there began the degeneration of the cultural elements intimately woven into the pattern of the life of the people. The result of these developments was the emergence of a class of Westernized Ceylonese⁶⁸ who were cut off from the mass of people and grew farther away from the people in the villages. In other words English education added new kinds of cultural differentiation to the older divisions in the society.

These Western-educated elite got access to the coveted posts in Civil Service[69] professions, business and politics. Hence during this period, this educated minority dominated the political and economic life of the towns and cities. Animated by the progressive and liberal ideas of Europe acquired through the medium of English, they led the movement for a series of constitutional reforms which finally led to complete independence. It was these Western-oriented, English-educated, intellectuals who effected the transfer of power from the British on the eve of independence and held cabinet positions until they were unseated in the 1956 general elections which marked the first break in the political monopoly of the Westernized elite.

Hence, when Ceylon became a complete self-governing Dominion within the British Commonwealth of Nations on 4 February 1948 the British tutelage of Ceylon which lasted a century and a half came to an end. This newly won freedom appeared to underline the achievements of the British period: economic prosperity, educational development, establishment of law and order, and the growth of a sound political system with a respect for those values which make democratic government possible in a community of several minorities of different races and religions.

Though the British heritage in Ceylon was undoubtedly a valuable one, it also left behind many problems for future governments of independent Ceylon. Progressive and liberal outlook, introduced by the British into the medieval society of Ceylon, affected only a small section of the population which emerged as a privileged and dominant class in the political life of the island. The dual educational structure—English medium schools in the cities and vernacular medium schools in the villages—also created social and cultural divisions. In the economic sphere, Ceylon was left with an agricultural economy as a result of which she had to depend on world markets for imports of essential goods for some time to come. The devolution of power and responsibility by His Majesty's Government to the elected representatives of the people of Ceylon had been effected so smoothly and sympathetically that there was hardly any evidence of a sense of triumph over the newly won freedom.

NOTES

1. Almond and Coleman, *The Politics of the Developing Areas* (Princeton, 1960), p. 163.

2. Master Ralph Fetch, a merchant of London who longed to secure for Great Britain a participation in the gorgeous trade of the East, visited Ceylon in 1589. Sir, J. Emerson Tennett, *Ceylon*, (London, 1860), Vol. 2, p. 63.

3. Frederic North was appointed as the first Governor of Ceylon. The instructions defining his powers and duties "were the result of a compromise, by which he was responsible to the King, through the Secretary of State, for the government of the territory, but was required to act under the directions of the Company, especially in commercial and financial matters". Sir Charles Jafferies, *Ceylon—The Path to Independence* (London, 1962), p. 17.

4. Sydney D. Bailey, *Ceylon* (New York, 1962), p. 73.

5. Tennent, *n.* 2, p. 90.

6. Report of Lieutenant-Colonel Colebrook upon the Administration of the Government of Ceylon to the Rt. Hon. Viscount Goderich, (London), 24 December 1831, p. 32.

7. Lennox A. Mills, *Ceylon under the British Rule 1795-1932* (Colombo, 1964), pp. 164-5.

8. The traditional form of government was parliamentary and representatives of the people were associated with the Governor in his executive and legislative functions, as in the West Indian Settlement Colonies. Jafferies, *n.* 3, p. 19.

9. *Ibid.*

10. Tennent, *n.* 2, p. 167.

11. G. C. Mendis (ed.), *The Colebrooke-Cameron Papers*, Vol. 1 (London, 1956), p. XXXI.

12. H. A. J. Hulugalle, *Ceylon*, (Colombo, 1957), p. 40.

13. G. C. Mendis, *Ceylon : Today and Yesterday* (Colombo, second edition, 1957), p. 82.

14. A. J. Wilson, "The Crewe-McCallum Reforms, 1912-1921". *The Ceylon Journal of Historical and Social Studies* (Peradeniya), Vol. 2., p. 114

15. "The policy of His Majesty's Government... is that of the increasing association of Indians in every branch of the administration and the gradual development of self-governing institutions with a view to the progressive realization of responsible government

in India as an integral part of the British Empire." *Report on Indian Constitutional Reform* (Calcutta, 1918), p. 1.

16. There were 14 officials and 23 unofficial members, though 12 were elected. Sir Ivor Jennings, "Nationalism and Political Development in Ceylon", *The Ceylon Historical Journal* (Dehiwala), Vol. 3, p. 75.

17. *Ibid.*, p. 198.

18. In the Legislative Council of 49 members, 34 were elected, 3 nominated by the Governor to represent special interests, and 12 officials appointed : Jennings, *n.* 16, p. 76.

19. W. R. Brock, *Britain and the Dominion* (Cambridge, 1951), p. 450.

20. Though the measure of autonomy provided under the Donoughmore scheme was indeed very large, still important subjects like those under the purview of Officers of State and particularly those in relation to the Public Services were reserved. Sir Charles Collins, *Public Administration in Ceylon*, (London, 1951), p. 139.

21. Report of the Commission on Constitutional Reform. *Cmd* 6677, (London, 1945), p. 27.

22. D. S. Senanayake was the leader of the State Council of Ceylon since 1943 after Sir Baron Jayatillaka. Dudley Senanayake, son of D. S. Senanayake, was a Member of the Executive Committee for Agriculture and Lands.

23. Ceylon, *S. C. Deb.*, Vol. 2, 1944, cols. 2638-40 and col. 2671.

24. The White Paper of 31 October 1945 was passed in the State Council by 51 with 3 dissentients. *Ibid.*, vol. 2, 1945, col. 7102.

25. *Cmd.*, 6677, p. 115.

26. The importance of the Labour Party coming into power lay in the fact that the declared policy of the Labour Party had been the freeing of colonial peoples and "anti-imperialism". S. A. Pakeman, *Ceylon* (London, 1964), p. 152.

27. *Ibid.* Also see Sir Charles Jefferies, '*O. E. G.*' *A Biography of Sir Earnest Goonetilleke*, (London, 1969), p. 87.

28. The Indian Leaders' non-cooperation, civil disobedience and even collaboration of the Indian troops captured by the Japanese, with the enemy during the World War II, were in contrast to Ceylon's loyalty towards the Allies. Pakeman, *n.* 26, p. 152.

29. "Ceylon, from her geographical position, was the nodal strategic point of what was still the British Empire in Asia." *Ibid.*, p. 154.

30. Though the Soulbury Constitution had included all the possible protective provisions, the British Government was conscious of the claims of the minorities in Ceylon as her people had not as yet shown signs of luring together as one nation. Jefferies, *n*. 3, p. 115.

31. The British Government feared that an independent Ceylon Government could repudiate the provision in the Soulbury Constitution concerning its liability to pay compensation or pensions to retired officers, who did not wish to stay on under the new conditions. *Ibid.*, p. 116.

32. Sir Charles Jefferies, *Transfer of Power* (London, 1960), p. 63.

33. U. K., *H. C. Deb.* series 5, Vol. 438, 1947, col. 2015.

34. Sir Oliver Goonetilleke, who worked along with Senanayake was the Financial Secretary to the Government of Ceylon, (one of the three Officers of State) and the first and the only Ceylonese to be so appointed. Pakeman, *n*. 26, p. 154.

35. Sir Ivor Jennings, *The Constitution of Ceylon* (London, 1949), p. 16.

36. Even though D. S. Senanayake offered to sign only two agreements—on defence and external affairs—the British Government insisted on and obtained an agreement on Public Services also. Pakeman, *n*. 26, p. 156.

37. "Proposals for conferring on Ceylon full responsible status within the British Commonwealth of Nations", *Cmd.*, 7257, (London, 1947), pp. 2-3. For the text of the Agreement see Appendix I.

38. *Cmd.*, 7257, p. 3. For the text of the Agreement see also Appendix II. The Defence Agreement and the External Affairs Agreement are discussed in great detail in Chapter Two.

39. *Cmd.*, 7257, p. 4.

40. Jennings, *n*. 35, pp. 278-79.

41. It is relevant to note that under the Donoughmore Constitution, despite the introduction of universal sufferage, no party system was required to make the Government function.

42. Ceylon National Congress was an association founded in 1919 on the model of the Indian National Congress; the Sinhala Maha Sabha was founded in 1937 by S.W.R.D. Bandaranayake and represented Sinhalese and Buddhist interests; Ceylon Muslim League was founded in 1924 to foster inter-communal harmony in Ceylon. The UNP was loosely knitted to accommodate members of other political organizations which existed prior to the formation of the UNP. It also provided for the retention of their affiliation to their parties. W. Howard Wriggins, *Ceylon : Dilemmas of a New Nation* (Princeton, 1960), pp. 106-9.

THE SETTING

43. The Lanka Sama Samaja Party (LSSP) was led by Dr. N. M. Perera, the Bolshevik-Leninist Party by Dr. Coluin R de Silva, and the Communist Party by Dr. S. A. Wickremasinghe.
44. I. D. S. Weerawardena, *Ceylon General Election 1956* (Colombo, 1961), p. 46.
45. *Cmd.*, 7257 (London, 1947), pp. 2-4.
46. U. K., *H. C. Deb.*, Vol. 444, 1947, col. 557.
47. Ceylon, *H. R. Deb.*, Vol. 1, 1947, col. 437.
48. *Ibid.*, col. 739.
49. U. K., *H. C. Deb.*, Vol. 445, 1947, col. 1041.
50. These limitations are dealt with in great detail in Jennings, n. 35, pp. 20-41.
51. S. G. Perera, *A History of Ceylon for Schools* (4th edition, Colombo, 1946), Part I, p. 147.
52. A. B. Perera, "Plantation Economy and Colonial Policy in Ceylon", *Ceylon Historical Journal*, Vol. 1, p. 51.
53. "In trade it marked the virtual end of monopolies and restrictions, with the way cleared for a big expansion of agricultural and trading operations and openings for the investment of private capital." Collins, n. 20, p. 70.
54. *Rajakariya* in Ceylon involved the performance of two classes of duties : (a) unpaid services rendered by people for the repair and maintenance of the paths and bridges in their district, and (b) services performed in respect of lands held, varying according to the caste of persons who performed them. G. C. Mendis, *Ceylon under the British* (Colombo, 1952), p. 46.
55. I. H. Vanden Driesen, "Some Trends in The Economic History of Ceylon in The Modern Period", *Ceylon Journal of Historical and Social Studies*, Vol. 3, pp. 7-8.
56. *Ibid.*, pp. 13-14.
57. Perera, n. 51, p. 55.
58. Department of Census and Statistics, *Statistical Abstract of Ceylon*, 1949, (Colombo).
59. The reasons for characterising the Ceylon's economy thus are : (1) the producing industries were very small in number and low in productivity due to inadequate capital; (2) it was an undiversified economy depending entirely on agriculture; (3) it was predominantly an export economy; (4) the foreign capital, nearly 85 per cent of it was held in its productive agricultural sector. *Ceylon Daily News*, 18 December 1947.
60. Mendis, n. 54, p. 7.

61. Hulugalle, *n.* 12, pp. 33-34.
62. The London Missionary Society came in 1805, the Baptists in 1812, the Wesleyan Methodists in 1814, and the Church Mission in 1818. Even a non-British body, the American Missionary Society, was allowed to settle in Jaffna, if not in Colombo, in 1813. S. Arasaratnam, *Ceylon* (New Jersey, 1964), p. 154.
63. Mendis, *n.* 54, p. 61.
64. Arasaratnam, *n.* 62, p. 157.
65. In 1880, the Cambridge examinations were introduced in Ceylon. Their adoption by the English schools was encouraged by awarding the university scholarships on the results of the Cambridge Senior Examination, and by throwing the scholarships open to general competition instead of confining them as hitherto to the pupils of the Colombo Academy. 21 candidates took these examinations in 1880, and in 1890, the number rose to 223. Mendis, *n.* 54, p. 128.
66. Buddhism was closely interwoven with the culture of the Sinhalese, and Hinduism with the Tamils.
67. There were vast avenues for employment. Plantations were being opened, trade and commerce were being developed, and government services were being expanded. The one requirement for any of these positions was the knowledge of English. Mendis, *n.* 58, p. 163.
68. "The westernized Ceylonese class were holding either government posts or making profits from coconuts or coffee. They wore European clothes, ate European food, worshipping (often) in Christian churches and above all spoke English." Sir Ivor Jennings, *The Economy of Ceylon* (London, 2nd edition, 1951), p. 11.
69. One-third of the posts in the Civil Service was reserved for the Ceylonese in 1919 and this was gradually increased to two-thirds in 1938 in which year all future recruitment was restricted to the Ceylonese. Leonard Woolf, *Diaries in Ceylon 1908-1911 and Stories from the East* (London, 1963), p. xxv.

2
THE UNP REGIME
AND THE WHITEHALL

Unlike other countries in Asia which won independence after World War II after decades of struggle against colonial power, the manner in which Ceylon attained her independence was the most striking symbol of the goodwill which marked the relations between the Imperial Government and the Government and people of Ceylon in the pre-independence period. Among the Asian dependencies Ceylon had enjoyed the most benevolent aspects of colonial rule. Ceylon was granted constitutional reforms which almost kept pace with nationalist demands. Hence, unlike other colonies, Ceylon never had, in any event, any emotional antagonism towards her former colonial power. That Ceylon achieved independence without violence or animosity against British imperialism, as compared with the more turbulent experience of many other colonies is very significant. A sense of gratification for the smooth and cordial transfer of power to Ceylon and the hope that both countries would consolidate and perpetuate the cordial friendship and mutual understanding underlined official as well as unofficial statements made in both Ceylon and the UK. Sir Oliver Goonetilleke expressed this sentiment thus :

> We ask you to think of Ceylon as a little bit of England to look to us with confidence because the collaboration between Britain and Ceylon will be so strong and because you are dealing with men whose word is their bond. If ever another war should break out, Ceylon will rival Australia as the first Dominion to rally to the side of the Mother Country. The regard which the people of Ceylon have for the British is due to their high status of administration and justice and fairplay.[1]

In the UK the same sentiment was expressed by D. R. Rees-William, the then Under-Secretary of State for the colonies, during the second reading of the Ceylon Independence Bill in the House of Commons. "The Ceylon Government," he declared, "is as anxious for the protection of the Common wealth interests as we are. They will not take any action which would in any way cripple or interfere with the general interests of Commonwealth."[2] After the second reading of the Ceylon Independence Bill in the House of the Commons the *Ceylon Daily News*, one of the leading newspapers of Ceylon, stated in its editorial :

> The fact that not a single dissentient voice was raised against the Independence Bill during its second reading in the House of Commons indicates that the British people have the utmost confidence in the ability of Ceylon to use this new freedom wisely.... The goodwill and friendship which British statesmen of all shades of opinion have shown, should always be a source of encouragement to a country which is setting out on the new and arduous enterprise of governing itself.[3]

In his message to the people of Ceylon on the first Independence Day, D. S. Senanayake, the Prime Minister of Ceylon, reiterated this sentiment when he declared,

> whatever disagreements we may have had with the British in the past, we are grateful for their goodwill and cooperation which have culminated in our freedom. The seed of voluntary renunciation which they have sown will grow into a stately tree of mutual and perpetual friendship.[4]

In Ceylon, the United National Party (UNP), which took over power from the British, represented a thin layer of conservative and highly westernized elite who had had intimate knowledge of the West and its traditions through education abroad either in the imperial capitals or in institutions established in western traditions elsewhere. Moreover, the administrative experience which these western-educated had during the colonial administration, made them fairly integrated in the British system of administration. With this historical association with the colonial power, it was but natural that D. S. Senanayake desired to have closer ties with Britain, once it was known to him that the British Government had decided to grant freedom to Ceylon. This he was able to do by signing Defence and External Affairs Agreements with the British, by continuing to have a political system on the British pattern and by accepting the membership of the Commonwealth of Nations. An attempt will be made in this chapter to examine the implications of the Defence and External Affairs Agreements for Ceylon-UK relations as well as the pattern of constitutional relationship that Ceylon maintained an assessment of the extent to which the UK policy influenced, if at all, the foreign policy orientation of Ceylon particularly in relation to some of the international issues in which both the countries were involved will be made.

The Defence Agreement

As a statesman with far-sighted political vision, D. S. Senanayake was aware of the fact that the security of his country was primarily conditioned by her geographical situation. Ceylon is the focal point in the Indian Ocean of the trade routes linking East and West. This strategical importance of Ceylon in the Indian Ocean was emphasized by Senanayake in his statement on defence in the House of Representatives : "We are in a specially dangerous position because we are in one of the strategic highways of the world. The country which captures Ceylon could dominate the Indian Ocean."[5] It is true of all self-governing nations that they must provide for their own defence, and also the maintenance of their external relations. But when Senanayake became the Prime Minister, he found himself the leader of a nation that had neither defence forces of its own nor the means to provide them. This was perhaps the reason that made him declare on one occasion in the House of Representatives : "I cannot accept the responsibility of being the Minister of Defence unless I am provided with the means of Defence."[6] Considering the size of the country, her strategically vulnerable position and her limited resources, he argued, she could not afford to cherish her newly won freedom in isolation and also without the protection of a great power. For Ceylon it was impossible to defend herself on her own. In Senanayake's opinion, there was only one country with sufficient interest in their defence at her own expense and that country was Great Britain.[7] It was in this context that he entered into an agreement with Britain, a country which had been associated with her for almost a century and a half, whose ways of government she had accepted and who was helping her to attain freedom and whose interest it was to see that Ceylon remained free. He was aware of the fact that in Ceylon's security was great Britain's security because Great Britain had to keep the Indian Ocean open to her ships and aircrafts in order to carry out the East-West trade.[8]

The basis of the Defence Agreement, thus, was a mutually 'enlightened self-interest'. Clause I of the agreement provided for the mutual military assistance but only to the extent of their mutual interest to do so, and the forces to be stationed would be such as might be mutually agreed.[9] For this purpose it was provided under Clause II, that the UK would be granted such bases and facilities as might be agreed upon. Under Clause III the Government of the UK would furnish the Government of Ceylon military assistance necessary for the training and development of Ceylonese armed forces.[10] Justifying the defence agreement in a covering memorandum issued after the signing of the agreement, D. S. Senanayake emphasized the fact that

> we can discover nothing irrevocable or coercive about this agreement. If a future Government feels that it does not require assistance it will be under no obligation to receive it. The Government can decide for itself whether any British forces should be stationed in Ceylon or not, and what bases, if any, should be provided for them.[11]

This view was confirmed by Sir Oliver Goonetilleke, the then

Home Minister, when he said in a press conference that the agreement was in the mutual interest of the two parties. He further clarified that there were no secret agreements nor was there any time-limit to the Defence Agreement. If either party decided at any time that it was not in its interests, the agreement could then be terminated.[12]

Because of the Defence Agreement Ceylon felt more secure as the continued stationing of naval and air bases assured constant British interest in the island's security. The Defence Agreement differentiated Ceylon from the other Dominions of the Commonwealth by providing specifically for mutual military assistance, the use of bases, and for the training of Ceylon's armed forces. Mansergh has pointed out this difference when he wrote :

> Though not new in principle, so comprehensive a defence agreement does in practice afford a more clearly defined basis for co-operation, not merely in defence but also in foreign policy, than exists among the older Dominions. The foundations of Commonwealth co-operation, some part of the obligation each partner incurs, are here set out in a way that may well provide a useful and valuable precedent.[13]

Again, though the Agreement was set out to state the basis for co-operation between the UK and the older Dominions, in Ceylon's case the position was that the UK would maintain bases at her own expense whereas the older Dominions provided the bases at their own expense as in the case of Halifax and Esquimalt in Canada and Simontown in South Africa respectively.[14]

The Defence Agreement was subjected to vehement criticism both inside and outside the Parliament. The left-wing Opposition in the Parliament charged the Government for having acquiesced to the colonial pressure and having accepted a 'fake' independence. Some critics feared that there might be some secret agreements giving her certain bases to the British. Speaking at a rally, Dr. N. M. Perera, the leader of the Lanka Sama Samaja Party (LSSP), viewed "Ceylon's independence and the Agreement as a shady transaction which was nothing less than bartering away of the country."[15] D. S. Senanayake attempted to allay these apprehensions by categorically stating in the House :

> There are no secret agreements or informal undertakings.... There is no question of giving bases to any one.... They were only to be given when it became necessary in our own interests and after entering into an agreement.... The only Agreement we have entered into is one enabling us to come to some agreement in the future.[16]

Justifying the necessity for such an agreement with Britain he told the House :

> I like to keep my connections with Britain.... As far as I am concerned I cannot think of a better and a safer friend for Ceylon than Britain. I would ask my friends to look round the world and see for themselves whether there is anyone else who can be of better use to us and of greater help to us than Britain.[17]

In its editorial the *Ceylon Daily News* endorsed D. S. Senanayake's views :

> Let those who would criticize the agreements look around and see whence Ceylon can look for help in time of trouble. Can it be had on better terms from a country which may be interested in dominating Ceylon than from one which has voluntarily and handsomely yielded its power and renounced its authority.... The agreements entered into between Ceylon and the UK are therefore vital to Ceylon even if they were not to the protecting power. Only an inveterate enemy of stable government, peaceful development and the security of the State will dare obstruct them.[18]

The Defence Agreement was continued by the next two UNP Prime Ministers, Dudley Senanayake and Sir John Kotelawala. The Agreement was always called in question as long as the UNP Government was in power. One of the Ceylon newspapers, *The Morning Times*, in its editorial, "British bases in Ceylon" called on the Government to review the question of Ceylon bases by warning that the Government must beware of being inveigled into a position in which bases in Ceylon could be used in power-bloc warfare.[19] The Ceylonese Press made a demand that in view of the gravity of the international situation the Ceylon Government should categorically tell the Government of the UK that air bases in Ceylon should not be used in the event of a world war.[20] Following the demand made in the Ceylonese Press, Suntharalingam, an Independent Member of the Ceylon House of Representatives, gave notice of a no-confidence motion to the Government "for its failure to terminate the Defence Agreement with Britain."[21]

On his return to Colombo on 18 February 1955 after attending the Commonwealth Prime Ministers' Conference, Sir John Kotelawala retorted when his attention was drawn to the no-confidence motion to be moved in the Parliament by the Opposition :

> There is no defence agreement with Britain as such. What we and Britain have agreed to is that Britain would come to our assistance when asked, by mutual consent. We have every right to tell them they should quit our bases. In the event of war we can ask Britain to man these bases if we were in the thick of war. If, on the other hand, we decide to keep away from the war, we can very well tell them that they cannot use our bases. We are complete masters of our bases and we have every right to tell them to vacate our bases when we desire.[22]

The Colombo Municipal Council passed a resolution on 13 May by a majority of one vote, calling on the Government to terminate its Defence Agreement with Britain.[23] Referring to this demand, Sir John reiterated his strong feeling about Ceylon's link with Britain when he said : "It is difficult for Ceylon to do away with the Englishman completely. We simply cannot live without them because of the fact that we will be utterly helpless the moment we do so. The day Ceylon did away with England it would go under India."[24]

Thus, throughout the UNP regime (1948-56), Ceylon was associated with the UK through the Defence Agreement. Though the agreement was not abrogated, one of its important provisions became ineffective after 1957.

The External Affairs Agreement

This Agreement placed Ceylon in the position of other

members of the British Commonwealth making it obligatory to adopt and follow the resolutions of past Imperial Conferences. It also provided that both Ceylon and the UK were to be mutually represented by the High Commissioners in both the countries and Britain undertook to extend support to Ceylon's membership of the United Nations and its other specialised agencies. By Clause II of the agreement Ceylon undertook to observe the same practice and principles as were then observed by the Members of the Commonwealth in regard to external affairs in general and to the communication of information and consultation in particular.[25] This brought her into the system of intra-Commonwealth consultation. The Commonwealth practice of consultation on all important world problems leaving each government to make its own decision was stressed when in 1950 the Commonwealth Foreign Ministers at their conference considered the question of the recognition of Communist China as well as the future relations of the Commonwealth countries with her[26] although four countries—Great Britain, India, Ceylon and Pakistan—had already announced their recognition. The intra-Commonwealth consultation and co-operation was carried out through different institutions : the High Commissioners Office and the Commonwealth Relations Office.

As in the case of other Commonwealth countries Ceylon appointed its High Commissioners, as distinguished from Ambassadors, and maintained a clear tie with the ex-colonial country.[27] Apart from this, the Commonwealth Relations Office, by transmitting varied information on every subject of mutual interest—foreign affairs, economic development, military co-operation and the like, not only acted as disseminator of information but also facilitated exchange of views between members of the Commonwealth.[28]

In addition to these permanent institutions through which communication and consultation was carried out, there were the periodic Commonwealth Ministers' Conferences—Commonwealth Prime Ministers' Conference, Commonwealth Foreign Ministers' Conference, Commonwealth Finance Ministers' Conference etc.

These conferences and exchanges of information not only enabled Ceylonese statesmen to obtain a clear picture of varied but inter-related problems and policies of the Commonwealth countries in general, and the UK in particular, but also tended, in view of the nature of the relationship to influence Ceylon's policy decisions. Thus, in the case of the recognition of the Communist China, for example, Ceylon was merely following the British lead on the question as the subject had already been discussed at a meeting of the Commonwealth High Commissioners' conference in London in which the Commonwealth representatives were informed about the British decision to grant recognition to China.[29]

Ceylon's representation in foreign countries was also defined by the Clause IV of the Agreement by which the UK Government would represent Ceylon's interests in the various capitals of the world through her representatives if so requested by the Government of Ceylon.[30] Unlike India which had diplomatic representatives in nearly fifty countries immediately after her independence, Ceylon was represented only in eight countries.[31] This limited representation was not only due to financial consideration but also because of the diplomatic arrangement she had with the UK under the Clause IV of the Agreement. This provision was made use of by Ceylon on a number of occasions. In countries where Ceylon did not have a diplomatic or consular representative, she utilized the good offices of consular representatives of the UK Government or of other Commonwealth Governments to issue visas on her behalf.[32] In 1948, a Payments Agreement between Ceylon (along with the UK and other sterling area countries) and Japan was effected as a result of negotiations by the UK representatives in Tokyo with the Supreme Commander of the Allied Powers in Japan.[33] In 1949, soon after her decision to recognize the Peking regime, the Government of Ceylon asked the British Government, who had a Consul-General in Peking to forward a note according her recognition to Peking.[34] In 1949, at a meeting between the sterling area and Japan for the conclusion of a trade pact, negotiations on behalf of Ceylon were conducted by the UK delegation with the assistance of J. H. Jinadasa, the Deputy Commissioner of Co-operative Development of Ceylon.[35]

The Agreement not only gave Ceylon the full status of a Dominion but also altered her inferior position in international affairs. Her equal status with the other Dominions was accepted when she signed, as an independent and separate signatory, the Final Act of the Conference on Trade and Employment at Havana on 24 March 1948.[36] This independent status of Ceylon, though recognised by the 1948 Commonwealth Premiers' Conference as equal to the status of other fellow members who had already become members of the UNO, was frequently challenged by the USSR till 1955 in the United Nations as and when her application for the membership of the UNO came up.

It might be stated that the two Agreements did not specifically mention Ceylon's right to declare war and make peace, as the UK had accepted the Balfour Declaration which recognised the individual responsibility of the Dominions in those matters.[37] However, so far as Ceylon is concerned, the executive matters such as declaration of war and making of peace etc. are vested in the Queen who, under Section 4 of the Constitution, acts on the advice of the Ceylon Government. This could mean that Ceylon would not be obliged to declare war when the UK was at war. Finally, as the membership of the Commonwealth of Nations was postulated in both the Agreements[38] one might infer that the membership was a condition precedent to the Agreements.

The nature of Constitutional and Commonwealth connection between Ceylon and the UK

Though the British Government offered equal membership of the Commonwealth to all the four countries—Burma, India, Pakistan and Ceylon—at the time of the grant of independence, every country reacted differently to this offer. Burma opted for complete separation from the Commonwealth. India accepted membership but soon thereafter established a republic within the Commonwealth, an act which effected a noticeable change in the complexion of the Commonwealth. Pakistan accepted membership on the original basis but was inclined to follow the example of India. Ceylon readily assumed the membership of the Commonwealth on the original basis. Her desire to be in the Commonwealth arose out of D. S. Senanayake's belief that such a relationship would help preserve the country's newly won freedom. Ceylon was not in a position to safeguard her security alone; hence she chose to do it in co-operation with the Commonwealth. To D. S. Senanayake, Commonwealth ties meant a counterforce against India. Visualising a distant future when India under a different leadership might become aggressive,[39] he felt that in such a situation, though the Commonwealth was not in itself a safeguard against the conflict among members, Ceylon would be more safer because of her association with the Commonwealth. This feeling was voiced when he said in Bombay on his way from London : "Ceylon will remain in the Commonwealth of Nations as long as we feel our place is safe and our interests are not jeopardised."[40] Besides, he also felt that membership of the Commonwealth would give Ceylon an international stature equal to that of India despite its being 'an artificial but useful equality', which would give a dignity and stability in its diplomatic negotiations. Moreover, as Ceylon was not admitted to the UNO immediately after independence like her other Asian neighbours (India, Pakistan and Burma), the Commonwealth served as the only international forum where she could have had the opportunity to participate in international conferences and discussions and be a partner in a large comity of nations on an equal footing. Throughout the period of his premiership, D. S. Senanayake's view of the Commonwealth connection was always emphasised in the Throne speeches. In one of the speeches he reiterated that "My Government is keenly aware of significance and unity of purpose of the Commonwealth in the effort to preserve peace in the post-war world and will use its utmost endeavour to cherish and safeguard those valuable associations."[41] Expressing his faith in the Commonwealth, Sir Oliver Goonetilleke, the then Minister of Home Affairs and Rural Development, declared that

> never once has there been an attempt at interference. On the contrary, there had been a studied attempt on the part of Ministers and officials of all grades to make sure that the smallest and newest of the Commonwealth countries has a full share in the decisions of the Commonwealth.[42]

Emphasising this point D. S. Senanayake, during his official visit to New Zealand, declared : "Ceylon appreciated the need for closer relationship within the Commonwealth and had increased her understanding with the other Commonwealth countries, since she achieved Dominion Status."[43]

Faith in fundamental principles of the Commonwealth was cherished by the later two UNP Prime Ministers. In his first public statement on foreign policy after becoming the Prime Minister Kotelawala declared, "Ceylon believed in the British Commonwealth. We are members of a club which believes in mutual assistance like the Colombo Plan."[44] On another occasion he said, "I am a firm believer in the British Commonwealth of Nations as an influence for peace and the safeguarding of democratic liberties of free countries."[45] His faith in the Commonwealth was reiterated in his statement of policy in the Ceylon House of Representatives : "We value our membership of the Commonwealth of Nations based as it is on the free association of independent countries for mutual assistance. We shall extend a hearty welcome to the Head of the Commonwealth, the Queen of Ceylon, when she visits us a few months hence."[46] It was reaffirmed again when he enumerated the advantages of being in the Commonwealth :

> So far as we in Ceylon are concerned, the right of a small island... to live in peace, to govern itself according to laws and the wishes of its people and to fortify its economy to meet its needs are fundamentals. We believe that the goodwill of the members of the Commonwealth who share those ideals is the best guarantee we can have of our own security in a troubled world.[47]

Like the older Dominions, Ceylon accepted the full membership of the Commonwealth adopting British conventions. This decision of Ceylon was quite a deliberate one. In Senanayake's opinion acceptance of the Commonwealth relationship involved acceptance of monarchy. Having remained in the Commonwealth, he attached deep value and significance to the retention of the Crown as the link which binds together the Commonwealth of Nations. He, therefore, was very critical of India's decision to remain within the Commonwealth as a republic.[48]

The decision of the Ceylon Government to remain in the Commonwealth was supported by the Ceylon newspapers. One of the papers stated :

> Ceylon rejoices with the rest of the Commonwealth.... As long as Ceylon chooses to remain within the family of free nations linked by allegiance to democratic ideals and as long as constitutional monarchy remains consistent with those ideals Britain's king is Ceylon's king.[49]

It is remarkable that in Ceylon care was taken to see that both the Sovereign and the Governor-General are required to observe the constitutional conventions in the exercise of their functions, as the conventions are usually observed in the UK.[50] As in Canada, Australia, New Zealand and South Africa, in Ceylon also the formal relationship with the Crown remains unchanged even after 1948. It became closer both as a matter of fact and of law because, the Government of the UK having been removed as an intermediary, the Crown appeared directly in the Constitution of Ceylon. Since 1948, the Governor-General represents the Crown while the Government of the UK, like other Governments in the Commonwealth, is represented diplomatically by a High Commissioner. In matters affecting Ceylon, the Queen is advised by the Government of Ceylon either directly or through the Governor-General.

For preserving monarchy D. S. Senanayake had his own sentimental reasons when he stated that Ceylon has a monarchical tradition derived through the Kandyan kingdom from the ancient Sinhalese kingdom, that the first Prime Minister could claim to be the representative of the oldest monarchy in the Commonwealth, and that the Queen on whom the Kandyan convention was binding could sit on the Kandyan throne in the Assembly Hall of the Kandyan Kings when she visited Ceylon.[51]

Ceylon was the only Asian member of the Commonwealth which acknowledged the Queen as the Head of the State. Not only did Ceylon retain monarchy but changed the title of the Queen according to the declaration taken up at a Commonwealth conference in 1952. Separate titles containing a common element were then agreed upon. It then became necessary for each of the Commonwealth countries (except

India) to pass legislation to authorize a form of title for the Queen. This was done in Ceylon by the Royal Title Act I of 1953, by which Ceylon adopted the titles "Elizabeth II, Queen of Ceylon and of Her other Realms and Territories", "Head of the Commonwealth".[52] Whilst Her Majesty assumed separate titles as Queen of the UK, Canada, Australia, New Zealand, South Africa and Ceylon, in Pakistan her title was that of "Queen of the UK and of Her other Realms and Territories" with no specific reference as Queen of Pakistan.[53] For Pakistan, it was yet to be decided whether she would adopt a republican form of government or continue to be a monarchy, whereas in the case of Ceylon no question of making Ceylon a republic came up until 1955 when it was raised by the Government Parliamentary Group consisting of UNP's group of Senators and members of Parliament.[54]

Explaining the title in the House of Representatives, Dudley Senanayake said that Queen Elizabeth II "is not Queen because she is Queen of the United Kingdom but because she is Queen of Ceylon under our Constitution and we have the power to alter that Constitution if we like".[55] So the Queen remains as integral part of the Ceylon Constitution, which is essentially British in its context and texture and a creation in particular of the British Parliament. Commenting on the Ceylonese attitude towards the Crown, *The Times* (London) in its editorial wrote : "The Ceylonese understands the place of the Crown at the apex of the parliamentary structure and honours its wearer as the Head of a free society."[56] This was repeatedly demonstrated during royal visits to Ceylon on various occasions. The spontaneous welcome given to the Duke of Gloucester, a member of the Royal family, when he opened the first session of Parliament to be held since the coming into operation of the Ceylon Independence Act, and the cordiality of the reception given to the Queen, when she visited the island on Sir John Kotelawala's persistent efforts[57] in 1954, were instances of eloquent demonstrations of the emotional links of Ceylon with British institutions. It needs to be mentioned that of all the Asian Dominions, Ceylon alone welcomed Her Majesty the Queen to her shores. This gesture was given recognition by the UK when Ceylon's High Commissioner, Sir Claude Corea, was given precedence over the representatives of both India and Pakistan at a Royal luncheon accorded by the Corporation of London to the Queen and the Duke of Edinborough on their return from the Royal tour.[58]

Besides the retention of monarchy Ceylon has also persisted with the same judicial structure as was existing in the pre-independence period.[59] Ceylon, unlike India and Pakistan, has retained (though she could remove it whenever she wishes) the practice of sending appeals from her courts to the judicial Committee of the Privy Council[60] which as a UK institution, usually consisted of British judges and had its sittings in London.[61] The Union Jack and the British national anthem continued to be used at official ceremonies till the end of October 1953 when the practice was stopped by an official directive issued by Sir John Kotelawala on the ground that as the Queen had been proclaimed Queen of Ceylon there was no need for a second flag or anthem.[62]

The policy of the UNP Governments towards the Communist countries

In view of the UNP leaders' long association with the UK, it was not unnatural that in their foreign policy they had developed an attitude which was one of sympathy for the UK and antipathy towards the Communist bloc countries. All the three UNP Prime Ministers had personal prejudice against and intense dislike of Communism and the Communist countries even in the colonial period. In the pre-independence years it was the Leftist parties which always opposed the reforms for constitutional development of Ceylon which were acceptable to the Senanayakes and their associates who were active members of the Ceylon National Congress. D. S. Senanayake's dislike of Communism was demonstrated when, after the Nazi German attack on the Soviet Union, the Communist Party, then following a People's Front policy, sought entry into the national movement led by the Ceylon National Congress, and was refused by D. S. Senanayake who resigned on this issue.[63]

After independence, D. S. Senanayake's attitude towards Communist countries, particularly Russia, was made known to the public in one of his speeches immediately after his assumption of premiership when he said that though they had attained independence the greatest fear that he had was that "they would fall victims to the plague that was spreading all over the world from Russia...." "He continued in politics", he added, "only to fight communists at home and abroad as well".⁶⁴ Clarifying the difference in his attitudes towards Britain and Russia, he stated in the House of Representatives during the debate on the Motion on Independence :

> I do not want to go into whatever policies the British people may have pursued in the past or whatever good or bad they may have done but I can say this, that it is they who are helping us to become a free nation once again, and it is they, who can, I feel, keep us free, even from the intrusion of this Russian menace.⁶⁵

Though shortly after the attainment of independence, Senanayake defined the basic principles of Ceylon's foreign policy as that of the "middle-way"—the way of peace free from involvement in the conflict of rival ideologies and power blocs—he maintained throughout the same attitude towards communist countries. This attitude was aggravated by the Soviet Union's behaviour in the Security Council on the issue of her admission to the UN. In the Security Council, the Soviet delegate, Jacob Malik vetoed the admission of Ceylon to the UN on the ground that Ceylon was still a 'puppet' of Britain and therefore not genuinely a sovereign state. The Soviet delegate specifically pointed to the powers vested in the Governor-General as the highest executive officer, of the Queen, to certain rights which Ceylon had given Britain for her air and naval bases, and to the fact that Ceylon's diplomatic interests in some cases were sometimes looked after by the British diplomatic representatives.⁶⁶ It is this allegation of the Soviet delegate that Senanayake had in mind when he stated in the House of Representatives, "When we obtained our independence after a number of years, we obtained it not for the purpose of becoming a puppet of any other nation."⁶⁷ At the same time he made unmistakably clear his admiration for the British when he said, "I, for one, can assure you that if we are to be the puppets of any nation or to be associated with any nation, there is no greater nation than the British nation for which I have a great admiration."[68] Till Ceylon was able to protect herself, he felt it safe "to depend on the people who have not got a sort of madness to upset this world and who are not anxious to bring about revolution".[69]

Even though Ceylon was one of the first Asian countries to recognise Communist China, D. S. Senanayake and his two successors consistently refused to establish diplomatic relations with China because of their suspicion that the Communist countries would utilise every opportunity to make contact with leftist parties inside the country and if necessary would even use normal diplomatic privileges. Senanayake's government not only refused applications for visas by Communist delegates from Russia and China to enter Ceylon,[70] but also denied permission to the British Science writer J. G. Growther, who was the President of the Communist-led British Peace Committee, on the plea that "the enemies of democracy would not be permitted to take advantage of democratic liberties to campaign for the extinction af democratic institutions".[71] A confirmed opponent of Communism, Senanayake's eagerness to support any policy of "containment" of communism was made clear when he granted harbour facilities to an American flotilla on its way to the Korean War on the ground that the UN was opposing aggression by international communism.[72]

Sir John Kotelawala toed the same line of policy laid down by his predecessor towards Communist countries. If Dudley Senanayake kept up the same tempo set up by his father, Sir John went a step further. Being the 'Hammer of the Hammer and Sickle' and an arch adversary of Communism, he stated, "I have all my life been opposed to this lamentable creed. And if there is anything that I can do, whether in my country or anywhere else to stop the further advance of Communism, I shall certainly do it."[73] Thus he took steps to deny Henry Politt, Secretary General of the British Communist Party, to land in Ceylon.[74] He refused a request from Red China to send a goodwill mission to Ceylon.[75] He maintained that Ceylon's relationship with China was only for business, the reason being that in his view visiting communists were liable to disseminate more harm than goodwill.[76] He made charges against the local Communist Party that it received large sums of money from Russia through Switzerland.[77] He took steps to prevent Dr. Cheddi Jagan, a Communist (the deposed Prime Minister of British Guiana) from entering the country. He warned the Soviet delegate to ECAFE Conference in Colombo for holding hotel room discussions with local communists.[78] His Government deported two foreign women, Mrs. Joe de Silva, an American, and Mrs. D. Henry, a British citizen, who were the wives of prominent Ceylon communists, for their subversive activities against the State.[79] He dissuaded the Russian football team from coming to Ceylon as the Government desired "to keep to the last as far as possible contact between Ceylon and Communist countries."[80] He also refused to let Russian astronomers observe the 1955 solar eclipse from Ceylon on the ground that the Russian team was "too big", whereas permission had been granted to scientists from America, Britain, Canada, Japan and India.[81] In December 1954 at the Bogor Conference, although Sir John did not object to the decision to invite China to the Afro-Asian Conference at Bandung, he reiterated his convictions on Communism that he could not be blind to the international nature of Communist doctrines, nor could it be assumed that the aims and objectives of Communism had undergone any radical change.[82] While addressing the Political Committee of the Afro-Asian Conference at Bandung Sir John made a frontal attack on Communist Colonialism by asking them whether the satellite countries of Eastern Europe like Albania, Bulgaria, Czechoslovakia, Esthonia, Hungary, Latvia, Lithuania, Poland and Rumania were not colonies of Soviet Russia.[83] The Ceylonese leader provoked sharp reaction from Chou-En-lai when he asked, "If we are united in our opposition to colonialism, should it not be our duty openly to declare our opposition to Soviet colonialism as much as to Western imperialism." He even demanded that Russia and Red China dissolve the Cominform as proof of their good intentions in proposing a peaceful co-existence programme.[84]

Immediately after the conference, Sir John had to defend himself in the House of Representatives against the Opposition charges contained in a no-confidence motion condemning his attitude at Bandung Conference as one calculated to vitiate the unity achieved at the Colombo Powers Conference and to disrupt the unity of the participating countries at the Bandung Conference, besides damaging the interests of Ceylon.[85] But in the western circles he was hailed for his outspokenness against Communism.

Though the UNP's policy was to keep the Communist countries at an arm's length, it had to establish trade relations with them, in view of the economic interest of the country. In 1951, Ceylon sold rubber to China "not so much from economic motives as from economic compulsions."[86] This is evident from the pronouncement of R.S.S. Gunawardene (the then Ambassador to the USA) that "Ceylon's trade agreement with Communist China was a desperate expedient it reached after a breakdown of economic negotiations with the United States."[87] The circumstances that led to the trade relations with China need special examination particularly in view of the fact that all the UNP Prime Ministers were uncompromising opponents of communism.

Ceylon's economy, being essentially an export economy based on three products—rubber, tea and coconut—existed and could exist only as part of an international economy that provided suitable markets for her products. Hence, whenever the price for her products in the world market declined she suffered serious economic dislocations. This she experienced when the price she obtained for her rubber during the Korean boom rapidly declined and the cost of her principal import price rose sharply in the world market. At this critical juncture, when Ceylon's traditional Western trade partners failed to help her out of her economic crisis, she was compelled to explore new avenues in the field of trade relations.

After the entry of China in the Korean War in 1950, the UNO imposed, on a resolution sponsored by the USA, a ban on the export of strategic materials including rubber to China and Northern Korea.[88] Meanwhile China had been buying small amounts of rubber from Ceylon as a purely private commercial arrangement between Chinese buyers and Ceylonese sellers. In order to strengthen the effectiveness of the embargo, the USA passed in June 1950 Kem Amendment legislation which provided for the withdrawal of the USA economic aid from the countries contravening the UNO resolution; but in October 1951, the Battle Act replaced the Kem Amendments and down-graded rubber to the level a strategic material over which there was no embargo but which was to be the subject of specially negotiated arrangements with the USA.[89] At the same time negotiations, going on between the USA and the Ceylon Government for the bulk purchase of Ceylon rubber, failed as the USA Government offered the Singapore price which was significantly lower than the Colombo price. Meanwhile, the Ceylonese traders were already selling rubber to Chinese buyers at prices above the world market. To the USA's continued representation against Ceylon's sale of rubber to China, Senanayake was reported to have replied that "the Ceylon market is open and if the USA wants to buy she is at liberty to buy even the whole of it."[90] Having failed to ban rubber shipments to China, the USA Government suspended all the Point Four Aid to Ceylon.[91]

Meanwhile Ceylon was facing great financial difficulties due to the decline in the price of tea and rubber and the difficulty in getting rice at reasonable price. A ministerial mission was sent to the USA to negotiate the urgently-needed rice supplies, economic aid for development programmes, and an agreement to sell rubber at the Singapore price level.[92] But the negotiations failed again on the question of price.

By this time the food crisis had taken a critical turn in Ceylon. Taking advantage of the situation the Opposition in Parliament took every opportunity to urge the government to increase trade with China. Dudley Senanayake had already hinted in Parliament about the Chinese government's invitation to Ceylon to send a delegation to Peking to negotiate a bulk purchase of rice.[93] Having failed in the negotiation with the USA, a mission led by R. G. Senanayake, the Ceylon Minister of Commerce and Trade, was sent to China. By a short-term trade agreement China agreed to supply Ceylon with 8,000 metric tons o rice "within a short period" in exchange for rubber and other products.[94] This was followed by a long-term trade agreement in December by which China agreed to sell annually 270,000 metric tons of rice to Ceylon in exchange of 50,000 metric tons of rubber. The terms of price were also stated but subject to negotiations every year by the two governments.[95]

The agreement assumed importance in the Ceylon-UK relations soon after its conclusion. The UK was a party with the USA in the imposition of the ban on the export of strategic materials to Communist China. The Ceylon Government's firm stand on this issue was that if the USA and the UK found USSR, China and other Communist countries going against their interests and policies, they should rather settle matters straight with the Communist countries instead of "trying to starve us into obedience for our sale of rubber to that country."[96] In order to tighten the embargo on supply of strategic materials to "aggressor nations", the UK's pledge to the USA to secure the co-operation of other countries to exclude shipping of strategic materials to China "received the first shock when Ceylon rejected a British request to stop her rubber exports to Communist China."[97] By this refusal Ceylon put Britain in an embarrassing position and raised a Commonwealth problem : on the one hand, if British ships continued to bring Chinese rice from Chinese ports to Colombo,[98] the UK would be a party to helping China take rubber from Ceylon; on the other hand, as Britain was more aware of Ceylon's needs, any step amounting to coercion would be repugnant to Britain, concerned as she was with the food and general economic difficulties of a Commonwealth country. This incongruous position was cleared soon after a talk between the Prime Minister Dudley Senanayake and the British High Commissioner Sir Cecil Sayers when the Ceylon External Affairs Ministry forthrightly announced "no change in China's trade agreements."[99] This showed Ceylon's assertion of her stand on the issue.

As far as Ceylon's relations with the Communist China were concerned, this trade agreement did not effect any departure in Ceylon's foreign policy towards China during the UNP regime. Though Ceylon Government agreed to let Communist China open an agency in Colombo to ship rubber under the trade pact, the agency was to have no diplomatic status but only to look after sheet rubber shipments to China under trade agreements ratified by the two Governments.[100] Sir John Kotelawala maintained that his country would wait until China allowed herself to be better known by Ceylon for the establishment of diplomatic relations. Meanwhile Ceylon's relations with China were confined only to trade.[101] But, after the Bandung Conference Kotelawala's attitude towards

Communist countries seemed to have softened, when his Government established trade relations with some Socialist countries—with Poland[102] and Czechoslovakia[103] in December 1955, and with Rumania in March 1956.[104]

Ceylon's Foreign Policy under the UNP Government

The main lines of Ceylon's foreign policy were laid down by her first Prime Minister D. S. Senanayake, in an address delivered over the BBC in London on January 1951. In his address he defined Ceylon's position in international affairs as that of "the middle way"—the way of peace free from involvement in the conflicts of rival ideologies and power blocs. He said :

> We in the East... are convinced that only through clearer knowledge of the fundamental spiritual values of existence can international understanding be reached. We believed in a way of life which it may be permitted to call the middle way and in which the rule of moral law founded on a firm faith in the oneness of human life would hold sway, where 'power politics' or 'power economics' would not find place in the conduct of international affairs, where there will be no armament race as a direct result of a fear of insecurity and where instead of force as arbiter in international disputes, there would arise mutual confidence and co-operation as a pre-requisite of lasting peace.[105]

Senanayake's enunciation of this doctrine, shortly after the achievement of independence, demonstrated the continuity of Ceylon's foreign policy after independence. It was a policy which was in keeping with the most deep-rooted national traditions of Ceylon.

The tone set by D. S. Senanayake in Ceylon's foreign policy followed by Dudley Senanayake when he stated in the House of Representatives : "Our foreign policy... is not to align ourselves with one bloc or other blindly and regardless of the interests of our people. When there are two contending blocs our foreign policy will be primarily guided by the interests of the people of this country."[106]

It was Sir John Kotelawala who tried to evolve the theoretical conception of the 'middle-way' into a practical policy in international relations. He took an active part by looking beyond the shores of the little island. Moreover, when Sir John took up the job of putting Ceylon on the world's political map, the Asian and international situation had changed considerably from what it was during the time of his predecessors. In the intervening period, the hostilities of the two rival blocs had grown sharper.

It is by keeping in mind this climate in international politics, that Sir John Kotelawala declared the policy of his government :

> Of policy she (Ceylon) avoids joining any power bloc or participating in ideological warfare.... We have chosen this course—it has sometimes been called the Middle Path—after every careful deliberation, and we are convinced that it is the only means of preventing a permanent division of the world into two camps, as well as keeping ourselves from being drawn into a war which is not of our seeking.[107]

The "policy of neutrality" was defended by R.S.S. Gunawardene, Ceylon's Ambassador in the USA, when he said : "We also feel that in a world which is already split between two violently hostile factions, the only hope for reconciliation lies in the presence of a third element committed to neither and for that reason capable of winning the confidence and respect of both."[108] Speaking to a reporter in London Sir John Kotelawala emphasised,

> We do not believe in power blocs and do not propose to join any.... Power blocs defeat what our aim should be—unity. We have no intention of standing by or keeping aloof, but we want to be in a position where we can bring everyone together and prevent conflict.[109]

Against this background of the UNP's foreign policy, an attempt will be made to assess the stand that Ceylon took in relation to some specific international issues—the Indonesian question, the Korean War, the Indo-China War and the South East Asian Treaty Organisation (SEATO).

Ceylon's stand on the Indonesian Question

The Netherlands Government's "police action" against the Indonesian Republic on 19 December 1948 evoked widespread resentment in the countries of the Middle East and South East Asia. In India, the Prime Minister Nehru declared on the same day that the reactions of the Dutch military action would soon be heard over all Asiatic countries. On 23 December the Netherlands Ambassadors in Delhi and Karachi were informed by the Indian and Pakistan Governments that the Royal Dutch Air Lines (KLM) would be banned from landing in, or crossing the territories of those countries. The Ceylon Prime Minister D. S. Senanayake also lost no time in issuing a statement on the Indonesian situation that it would not be possible for Ceylon to allow the use of harbour and airfield facilities for ships and aircrafts carrying troops, arms and warlike materials of any kind which might be against the Indonesian Republic.[110] This decision of the Government of Ceylon was formally intimated in categorical terms by the Ceylon High Commissioner to the Netherlands Ambassador in London :

> We expect all nations including the Dutch to help us to observe the strictest neutrality. No harbour or aerodrome in Ceylon is owned by any other government other than the Government of Ceylon. We have, as is known, given certain user rights to Britain for a definitely specified object—namely defence against aggression in the mutual interest of Ceylon and the UK. It follows that the decision of Ceylon to deny entry to ships and aircrafts or any nation, not only the Dutch which may be carrying personnel or material for the purpose of fighting the Indonesian Republic will be automatically observed by the armed forces now in Ceylon.[111]

Sir Oliver Goonetilleke, the Ceylon High Commissioner, speaking at a Press Conference emphasised Ceylon's stand when he said, "Ceylon had taken the action regarding Indonesia entirely on her own initiative and without prior consultation with any one, though the UK and the Dominions had been informed."[112] The Ceylon Government's action met with approval from all ranks of Ceylonese.

Ceylon's quick and firm stand on the Indonesian question aroused a mixed reaction from the British press and people. If in Ceylon, opinion was unanimous in condemning the Dutch, in Britain there was a whole spectrum of views varying in accordance with political creeds and interests. But the majority note was undoubtedly one of criticism of the Dutch and of concern with the UN's efforts in maintaining peace and relations between the East and the West. The USA was reported to have decided to ask her representative Philip Jessup, to press the Council to get the Dutch troops to cease-fire.[113]

Having realised the failure of the Security Council—a body which was then dominated by Western Powers—to take any firm action against the Netherlands, Nehru convened an Asian Conference in New Delhi consisting of representatives of the Government of Afghanistan, Australia, Burma, Ceylon, Egypt, Ethiopia, India, Iran, Iraq, Lebanon, Pakistan, the Philippines, Saudi Arabia, Syria and Yemen, and observers from China, Nepal, New Zealand and Siam[114] from January 20 to 23 to consider the Indonesian situation created by 'the most naked and unabashed aggression' of the Dutch. The purpose of the conference was to mobilise world public opinion against the effort made by the Dutch Government in Indonesia to revive, in the words of Nehru, "a dying imperialism and colonialism" and also to bring the solid weight of unified Asian opinion to bear on the Security Council.[115]

The initial hesitancy of the Government of Ceylon when the invitation for the conference was received from the Government of India created the impression in some quarters that Ceylon's sympathies for the Indonesian cause were luke-warm. But the Prime Minister's assurance to the contrary in the House of Representatives was definite enough though, unfortunately, he somewhat confused the issue by discussing it in relation to Ceylon's membership of the UNO. He stated that

> so far as we are concerned, we are not members of the Security Council. We cannot be heard as we have no authority to appeal to them.... But merely because we

are not members of the Security Council, that is no reason why we should not assert ourselves and try to find out from others what action they are going to take.[116]

As Ceylon, even without any standing as a member of the UNO, was anxious to demonstrate her sympathy with the Indonesian Republic and explore ways and means of making her own contribution in support of the Indonesian struggle, she was represented in the Conference at Delhi by a delegation which did not have any plenipotentiary powers. On the first day of the Conference Nehru's condemnation of the Dutch action in Indonesia was reinforced by speeches from a number of delegates. Ceylon's attitude towards the Indonesian issue was expressed by S. W. R. D. Bandaranaike, the Ceylon delegate, when he spoke in forceful terms : "We have not met here to decide whether or not a wrong has been done. We have met here as those who are convinced that a wrong has been done, and wish to discuss it."[117] He felt that those believing in a democratic way of life and those who wished to establish close and friendly collaboration with other democratic countries, particularly in the West, had suffered grievously and were shocked by the Netherlands Government's action. The Indonesian incident, he emphasized, "could not be characterised by any other term than as an attempt to reintroduce the principle of Imperialism and Colonialism—an evil which they all thought was dead."[118]

The resolution on Indonesia prepared by the drafting committee (which consisted of the Commonwealth members— India, Australia, Ceylon and Pakistan) and passed by the Conference was not first a compromise, but a forceful one as it retained the substance of all the principal demands of the Indonesian Republic. The unanimity of the Asian opinion on the Indonesian question was too strong to be ignored. It was incumbent on the Security Council to devise immediate and effective means to secure complete independence of the Indonesian Republic as the West could not afford to ignore the emergence of an Asian bloc in a world already divided into two power blocs. Nor could the Western democracies ignore the strong possibility of communist influence spreading further in Asia as a reaction to the resurgence of old colonialism.[119]

Ceylon's stand on the Indonesian question could be interpreted in terms of anti-colonialism and Asian solidarity.

Ceylon's attitude towards the Korean War

On 25 June, 1950 a serious international crisis broke out as a result of the invasion of South Korea (a zone of occupation by the USA) by the forces of North Korea (a zone of occupation by the Soviet Union). Immediately the Security Council passed a resolution in an emergency meeting convened at the request of the USA and boycotted by the Soviet Union, to the effect that the action of the North Korean forces constituted a breach of peace.[120] In another resolution passed on 27 June 1950 the Security Council called for help from Members of the UN to repel aggression.[121] The UK was one of the first countries which responded immediately to the call of the Security Council. Making a statement in the House of Commons, Attlee announced that steps had already been taken to support the US action in Korea by immediately placing their naval forces in Japanese waters at the disposal of the US Authorities to operate on behalf of the Security Council in support of South Korea.[122] All the other members of the Commonwealth—Australia, New Zealand, Canada, India and Pakistan (who were also members of the UN)—also pledged their full support for the Security Council.

The Ceylon Government's immediate reaction to the Korean War was expressed in an unofficial statement made by D. S. Senanayake when he said,

> Ceylon is not involved at the moment because the latest directive to the member-nations of the UN organisation to assist South Korea does not concern us as Ceylon is not a member of the UN.... In the circumstances, the use of Ceylon bases by either party in the dispute does not arise.[123]

Commenting on the Government of Ceylon's failure to make any official declaration of her attitude on the Korean War, the *Times of Ceylon* wrote: "It is not suggested that Ceylon is in a position to offer active aid to South Korea. But it is suggested that we can offer at least moral support to the UN only to show that Ceylon means to play a real part in curbing Soviet-inspired expansion in the East."[124] On the same day J. R. Jayawardene, the Finance Minister announced in the House that "Ceylon has joined the nations backing the UN military action against Communist-led North Korea." "This Government," he added, "intends, so long as we are in power, to follow the USA."[125] Referring to the Finance Minister's statement D. S. Senanayake told the House :

> "As far as the United States is concerned, there is not the slightest doubt that she holds the view that we hold.... As long as they are for democracy, and as long as it becomes necessary for us to associate ourselves with either the United States or with any one else, we will join that said; .."[126]

The Ceylon Government's attitude towards the Korean war became more pronounced when it granted facilities to an American Flotilla in Colombo harbour on its way to Korean waters. This action of the Government provoked vehement criticism especially from the ranks of the Left Wing Opposition. Dr. N. M. Perera, the leader of the Opposition, protesting in the House of Representatives stated :

> Just as much as on the Indonesian question we refused to grant any facilities to the belligerents, I do not see any reason why we should not follow the same procedure and not grant any facilities to any of these ships. If they are really adopting an attitude of neutrality, then they might as well refuse to grant any facilities to these American ships which are obviously going across to help one particular side.[127]

The Communist member Pieter Keuneman referred to Truman's announcement regarding the defence of Formosa and pointed out that the grant of facilities to American or any other vessels to be used in the defence of Formosa and the blockade of the Chinese mainland might involve the Ceylon Government in hostility against the new Chinese Government which Ceylon had recognised.[128] Replying to the critics D. S. Senanayake told the House that he saw no reason why facilities granted to the Americans in the past should not be granted now.[129]

Ceylon's attitude towards the Korean war, in which both the Western and Communist countries were involved, is thus a clear indication of her orientation towards the Anglo-Americans.

Ceylon and the Indo-China War

In March 1954 a grave situation in French Indo-China was created by the siege of the French fortress of Dien Bien Phu by the Communist-dominated Viet-Minh. The war had reached a stage when it was imperative to stop it unless the Powers involved were prepared to run the risk of precipitating a third world war.

In conformity with the resolution, adopted by the British, the French, the USA and the Soviet Foreign Ministers at the Berlin Four-Power Conference from 28 January to 18 February 1954, representatives of nineteen countries[130] met at Geneva to discuss the problem of restoring peace in Indo-China. This conference coincided with the Colombo conference of South East Asian Prime Ministers which was to meet from 28 April to 2 May to discuss problems of common interest and which acquired immediate significance in the light of developments in Indo-China. Though the USA and France tried to have the Indo-China problems discussed as early as possible, the UK succeeded in delaying it till the outcome of the Colombo Conference on the subject was known to them,[131] because the UK realised the importance of the conference of the Colombo Powers, out of whom three—India, Pakistan and Ceylon—have been members of the Commonwealth. Though the UK was not bound to accept the opinion of the Asian members of the Commonwealth, she could not ignore it either,[132] she was afraid that the Commonwealth idea might be weakened by such a regional gathering.

But a few days before the Asian Prime Ministers' Conference was to start a certain lack of common objectives was felt among the members. An apparent divergence in the attitude of the members towards the Indo-China War could be discerned. After India and Burma refused permission for American military aircraft carrying French troops to Indo-China to fly over India, Ceylon allowed American globe masters carrying French troops to Indo-China to make use of Ceylon airports.[133]

Making an official statement clarifying the British view in the matter, in view of the right of usage granted to her by the Defence Agreement, the UK High Commissioner's office in Colombo announced that the landing of the planes in Ceylon was a matter entirely between the Ceylon and American Governments.[134] This statement clarified essentially the assertion of Ceylon's independence.

The view taken by the Ceylon authorities was that it saw no distinction between foreign air transport and troop ships which frequently used Colombo harbour. There was no question of assisting in a colonial war but Ceylon was definitely against Communist aggression and infiltration.[135]

As the Asian Prime Ministers' Conference took place simultaneously with the Geneva Conference, they helped to influence the course of events on Indo-China as the Delhi Conference did in the case of the Indonesian question in 1949. Throughout the conference, Anthony Eden, the British Foreign Secretary kept the Asian Prime Ministers informed of the British stand on Indo-China at the Geneva Conference. On 29th April, Eden was reported to have given an assurance to the three Commonwealth Prime Ministers of Ceylon, India and Pakistan that the British Government did not wish to be a party to any decision likely to be taken at Geneva which would conflict with the legitimate aims of the Asian countries and to have asked the Prime Ministers whether they were prepared to participate on a guarantee to assure the future of Indo-China if the Geneva Conference arrived at an acceptable decision.[136] In reply to Eden's letter Sir John Kotelawala expressed his agreement with the UK that any settlement reached at Geneva on the Indo-China question should be acceptable to Asian opinion, and also stressed that whatever settlement was arrived at should be acceptable to all the parties concerned.[137] Though Eden expressed 'appreciation' of Sir John's view-point on Indo-China, it is significant that Ceylon's name was deliberately omitted, without giving any reason, the British proposal of a possible armistice supervising commission for Indo-China.[138] Nevertheless, the Colombo Conference could claim to have helped, to some extent, in bringing the Geneva Agreement on Indo-China.

Immediately after the conference the Opposition called

upon the Ceylon Government to state its stand in view of the appeal made by the Conference of Asian Premiers for a cease-fire in Vietnam, and to clarify whether the Ceylon Prime Minister would prohibit the use of any part of the territory of Ceylon for the passage of troops and ammunition to Viet Nam. The Ceylon Prime Minister immediately retorted that he did not anticipate the parties behind Viet-Minh approaching him for that purpose. There was no purpose in asking him to stand neutral for the benefit of the wrong side. He added, "even if the devil wants my help to fight communism I am on his side."[139]

In the whole question of the Indo-China War, Ceylon's attitude which differed from that of India and Burma, highlighted her policy orientation towards the West, as it did in the case of the Korean problem.

Ceylon's reaction towards the South East Asia Treaty Organisation (SEATO)

During the preliminary diplomatic exchanges for setting up a collective defence for South East Asia, the British Foreign Secretary, Anthony Eden, had also sounded the Five Colombo Powers about their views with regard to the setting up of SEATO. As a result, on 2 August 1954, the Prime Minister of Ceylon, Sir John Kotelawala, proposed to the Premiers of four other countries that a conference of the Colombo Powers should be held before September, either in Rangoon or Colombo, to discuss their joint attitude to the SEATO proposals and thereby to strengthen the unity achieved at the Colombo Conference.

Defining Ceylon's attitude towards the SEATO, the Prime Minister told the House:

> There are these two blocs—Russia and China on the one side, America and England on the other—trying to prevent each other from upsetting the *status quo*. Therefore, small countries like Ceylon, are in a position to say that they will continue to follow the democratic way of life.[140]

He had in his mind the Opposition (who labelled the SEATO as "a dirty and dangerous proposal to sabotage the Geneva and Colombo Conference decisions"[141]) when he continued: "Once such countries decide to follow the democratic path quite naturally they would wish to resist by force, if necessary, any interference with their way of life. I will align myself with the devil if necessary to fight against loss of freedom of action of speech and of democracy."[142] Justifying his decision to have called a meeting of Five Colombo Powers before September in Rangoon or Colombo to discuss the proposed SEATO, the Prime Minister said that his aim was to make Ceylon the "Switzerland of Asia", in the matter of neutrality, and Colombo the "Geneva of the Orient."[143]

Sir John's invitation did not get a favourable response from India and this led the Ceylon Prime Minister Kotelawala to harbour a misunderstanding that the Indian Prime Minister had an alternative to the SEATO, which was later denied by Nehru.[144] Like India, Burma and Indonesia had expressed their opposition to the SEATO; only Pakistan was prepared to participate in the discussions.[145]

In view of the fact that all the Colombo Powers had expressed opposition to any SEATO scheme, an official statement was issued in Colombo on 12 August announcing :

> Ceylon will not be represented at the conference on forming a SEATO to be held at Boguio in the Philippines on 6 September. But Ceylon was prepared to maintain an open mind on the subject. The nature of machinery for maintaining peace was the important question and it was mainly for the purpose of discussing such machinery that Ceylon had proposed an early meeting with the other four Colombo Powers.[146]

Thus the abortive efforts of Sir John Kotelawala to have Asia speak with one voice of the SEATO, as it had done on Indo-China, was brought to an end.

But doubts still persisted in the ranks of the Opposition about Ceylon's attitude towards the SEATO. They called upon the Government on 7 September to make a statement on the "fact-finding mission" of Dodds-Parker (the Parliamentary Under-Secretary to the British Minister of Commonwealth Relations) through whom the British Government, in concurrence with the USA Government, tried to persuade the Asian members of the Commonwealth to join the SEATO. They also demanded an assurance from the Government that "the territory of Ceylon will not be used for purposes of implementation of any arrangements under the SEATO if the Government of Ceylon stays out of it." Assuring the House the Prime Minister pointed out how the West went "the wrong way" in their proposal for a SEATO.[147]

When the SEATO treaty was signed at Manila on 9 September 1954, the Ceylon Prime Minister issued a statemen saying that it was too early to say what the attitude of Ceylon towards the organisation should be. He must have the time to think, observe and review the entire situation in consultation with his colleagues and the Prime Ministers of other Colombo Conference countries. He found that SEATO left it open to other non-signatory nations such as Ceylon to join if they liked and that the signatory nations were prepared to come to their aid in case they need it. Those were not gratuitous or meddlesome offers and could not be criticised on such grounds.[148] On the next day, he told a correspondent of the *Observer* that Ceylon did not propose even to be made use of any power bloc for any purpose with which it could not agree. Ceylon continued to keep "an open mind" on SEATO, but he added, "we have no reason to consider Red China a growing menace to peace in South East Asia and so long as it keeps its Redness to itself and does not seek to impose it on others, there would be little justification to consider it a menace.[149] This change in the attitude of Sir John Kotelawala towards Communist China might be attributed to the Chinese Premier's declaration of the 'Five Principles' of Peaceful Co-existence along with Nehru and U Nu, the Prime Ministers of the two Colombo Powers, during Chou En-lai's visit to their countries in June 1954.

Sir John Kotelawala suggested to the Colombo Powers the idea of second conference to review the situation created in Asia by the formation of SEATO and to assess whether SEATO helps or hinders the cause of peace in Asia.[150] But Sir John's suggestion was immediately ruled out by "the firm and ungratified refusal of India, Burma and Indonesia to have anything to do with SEATO"—a refusal which sprang from their basic policy of not entering into entangling alliances and their contention that SEATO could but lead to increasing tension.[151] It was this prolonged indecision which made the *Hindustan Times*, one of the leading newspapers of India, call into question for Ceylon's attitude to SEATO in its editorial "Time for Decision": "It is time Sir John Kotelawala made up his mind about SEATO in the interests of Ceylon and a hundred years of development he is so concerned about and of the Colombo Powers who should know where he stands."[152]

This non-committal attitude of Sir John towards SEATO leads one to describe him as having been favourably inclined towards SEATO. That SEATO was essentially a pact against Communism could account for his leaning towards that organisation. But he was caught between contending forces— both international and internal—and prevented from declaring himself clearly. Internationally, one of the Colombo Powers— Pakistan—had signed the pact while the other three—India, Burma and Indonesia—had boycotted it. If Ceylon came out either for or against at this stage, the Unity of South East Asia for which Sir John had worked hard, would have been lost, creating two opposing camps in the region.

Internally, public opinion had reacted unexpectedly against SEATO. Even the influential pro-Government *Ceylon Daily News* which consistently alerted the nations of South East Asia against international communism, commented that the SEATO treaty might be used by the West for intervening in the internal affairs of countries of the region. While pointing out this danger of SEATO, it reminded the Government that

> Ceylon must naturally regard the creation of SEATO from the standpoint of her own interests and integrity and in the context of her existing international obligations. The sheet anchor of Ceylon's security remained her defence treaty with Britain and her partnership in the Commonwealth. This relationship offers, as a small country, security in a troubled world, and her free and equal standing in the Commonwealth gives her a guarantee this defence arrangement will not affect her political sovereignty. This relationship has worked harmoniously in the past.[153]

The Ceylon *Observer*, in its article "SEATO is not for Ceylon", warned the Government that although SEATO provided an eastern dam against any spill-over of communism into South Asia, it was not necessary for Ceylon to become part of it to benefit by the shelter it provided. The establishment of the SEATO in the face of opposition from the countries of the region made it imperative for these countries to reiterate their desire not to involve themselves in power blocs, but to prevent subtler forms of active aid from reaching local 'Quislings'.[154] The *Times of Ceylon* called SEATO a "billion dollar fallacy" and accused the USA and Britain of having failed to understand the situation :

> Here in the East the real danger of Communist expansion lies not in the threat of a Chinese invasion, but in the frustration and misery of ordinary decent-minded people who have been badly treated by their so-called democratic governments and in fact they are ready to seek salvation at the hands of anybody who opposes the existing regimes.[155]

Inside the UNP itself, the powerful Senanayake cousins— Dudley Senanayake, the ex-Prime Minister and R. G. Senanayake, the ex-Cabinet Minister—started a movement to oppose international entanglements of any kind. On 16 September R. G. Senanayake told a Moslem audience : "Those Asian countries that join the Pact will be compelled to allow their economy to be developed by the Western Powers."[156] A. E. Goonasinha, Envoy Extraordinary and Minister Plenipotentiary-designate to Burma, emphatically said, "Ceylon should not be in SEATO. No South East Asian country had asked for SEATO. The British Government was trying to retain colonialism. There was no doubt that it was only because of strong public opinion against colonialism that England was going slow on SEATO."[157]

With all these cross currents working against SEATO Sir John had difficulty in defending himself against charges of ambiguity and wavering. Still he continued maintaining his indecisive attitude towards SEATO when he said in Colombo in February 1955 :

> The door is open and will continue to be open. We might join SEADO [sic] if we thought it advantageous

or be away from it if we decided to observe neutrality in the event of a war. SEADO [sic] is nothing but a defence agreement and we may or we may not avail ourselves of the benefits of that arrangement as the case may be. We shall keep an open mind.[158]

Nevertheless, he justified his stand in his Autobiography *"An Asian Prime Minister's Story"* and explained why he did not find it possible to agree with SEATO but still kept an 'open mind', and that what SEATO failed to take into account was the fact that the defence of Asia was first and foremost to be on economic front while the stress was wrongly on the military aspect.[159] Sir John's reaction towards another defence agreement is justifiable on the ground that as far as the defence of Ceylon was concerned, Ceylon did not need to enter the SEATO agreement because it was already linked to it through a military understanding with Britain.

To sum up, an assessment of Ceylon-UK relations during the UNP period reveals four aspects : (a) alliance with Britain for defence, (b) close association with the Commonwealth of Nations, (c) ideological affinity with the West, and (d) common opposition to Communism.

Ceylon's defence agreement with Britain and her retention of British bases were motivated to serve the national interest of safeguarding the independence of the country from any threat from ny power, particularly India.

All the UNP Prime Ministers were staunch advocates of the Commonwealth of Nations and hence they retained monarchy for sentimental reasons, and also permitted British bases to continue. For Ceylon, membership in the Commonwealth served a variety of purposes; politically it secured for her an international status by making her a partner in a large comity of nations on an equal footing and also brought her into the system of intra-Commonwealth consultation on all important world problems; economically she secured the benefit of economic and technical assistance through the Colombo Plan.

All the UNP Prime Ministers, being western-oriented, adopted the political system of the West. Ideologically, the UNP policy was pro-West though the UNP Prime Ministers professed a policy of neutralism. The only deviation from this policy was made when Dudley Senanayake signed a trade pact with China. But he emphasised the fact that, as far as Ceylon was concerned, the trade pact had only economic and not political significance.

The UNP Prime Ministers' pro-western orientation, reinforced by the Leftist opposition they experienced in their efforts to get constitutional reforms passed during the pre-independence years, resulted in their personal antipathy towards Communism. Their anti-communist feeling was aggravated by the Soviet Union's behaviour in the Security Council objecting to Ceylon's admission to the UNO. On any issue in which the Communist bloc was involved as in the case of Korean War they always favoured the other party. Even after the trade pacts were signed with China, Poland, Czechoslovakia and Rumania, they consistently refused to establish any diplomatic relations with these countries. The UNP Prime Ministers' leaning towards the West continued as long as the UNP was in power. But the general election of 1956 which returned the MEP to power brought about a new phase in Ceylon's foreign policy, in general, and in Ceylon-UK relations in particular.

NOTES

1. *Ceylon Daily News*, (Colombo), 4 July, 1947.
2. UK, *H. C. Deb.*, series 5, vol. 444, 1947, col. 1522.
3. *Ceylon Daily News*, 25 November 1947.
4. *Ibid*. 5 February 1948. Also see *The Times* (London), 5 February 1948.
5. Ceylon, *H. R. Deb.*, vol. 1, 1947, col. 444.
6. *Ibid*.
7. *Ibid*., col. 445.
8. *Ibid*.
9. Proposals for conferring on Ceylon fully responsible status within the British Commonwealth of Nations : *Cmd.*, 7257 (London, 1947), p. 2. See Appendix I.
10. *Ibid.*, pp. 2-3.
11. *Ceylon Daily News*, 15 November 1947.
12. *Ibid*.

13. Nicholas Mansergh, *The Commonwealth and the Nations* (London, 1948), p. 23.
14. Sir Ivor Jennings, *The Constitution of Ceylon* (London, 3rd edition, 1949), p. 140.
15. *Ceylon Daily News*, 19 November 1947.
16. Ceylon. *H. R. Deb.*, vol. 1, 1947, col. 445 and cols. 732-3.
17. *Ibid.*, col. 731.
18. *Ceylon Daily News*, 15 November 1947.
19. Quoted in *The Times* (London), 11 February 1955.
20. *The Hindu* (Madras), 17 February 1955.
21. *Times of Ceylon* (Colombo), 20 February 1955.
22. *Ibid*, 24 February 1955.
23. *Ibid.*, 19 May 1955.
24. *Ibid.*, 25 May 1955. Also see *The Times* (London), 25 May 1955.
25. Cmd., 7257, p. 3. See Appendix II.
26. *The Times* (London), 11 January 1950.
27. The High Commissioners, though having an equal status with the Ambassadors, have still some advantages over them. "Whereas the Ambassador must do all his business through the Department of External Affairs, the High Commissioner is entitled to deal with other deparments of Government. The result is that the High Commissioner and his staff at appropriate levels have contacts of an informal sort throughout the machinery of government." K. C. Wheare, *The Constitutional Structure of the Commonwealth* (London, 1960), pp. 137-8.
28. Nicholas Mansergh, *Survey of British Commonwealth Affairs* (London, 1958), p. 401.
29. S. U. Kodikara, "Ceylon's Relations with Communist Countries", *South Asian Studies*, (Jaipur), vol. 2, p. 108.
30. Cmd., 7257, p. 3.
31. Sir Ivor Jennings, *The Approach to Self-government* (Cambridge, 1956), p. 48.
32. *Administration Report of the Controller of Immigration and Emigration for 1953* (Colombo), pcc. 5.
33. *Ceylon Daily News*, 29 June 1948.
34. *The Times* (London), 7 January 1950.
35. *Ceylon Daily News*, 2 May 1950.
36. S. Namasivayam, *Legislatures of Ceylon* (London, 1950), p. 158.
37. Jennings, *n.* 14, p. 25.

38. The preamble of the two Agreements runs as : "Whereas Ceylon has reached the stage in constitutional development at which she is ready to assume the status of a fully responsible member of the British Commonwealth of Nations, in no way subordinate in any aspect of domestic or external affairs, freely associated and united by common allegiance to the Crown." Cmd., 7257, pp. 2-3.

39. Sir Ivor Jennings, "The Commonwealth in Asia", *International Affairs* (London), vol. 32, p. 138.

40. *The Times* (London), 5 November 1948.

41. Ceylon, *H. R. Deb.*, vol.8, 1950, col. 486.

42. *The Hindu*, 21 January 1950.

43. *Ceylon Daily News*, 24 October 1951.

44. *The Times* (London), 26 October 1953.

45. *Ceylon Daily News*, 19 November 1953.

46. Ceylon, *H. R. Deb.*, vol.16, 1953, col. 709.

47. *The Times* (London), April 1954.

48. Senanayake regarded India's decision to remain a republic within the Commonwealth as very discourteous on the part of India, and compared it to accepting an invitation to dinner but refusing to wear the appropriate costumes. Jennings, *n.* 39, p. 138.

49. *The Times* (London), 16 November 1948.

50. Sir Ivor Jennings and H. W. Tambiah, *The Dominion of Ceylon* (London), 1952, p. 72.

51. Jennings, *n.* 39, p. 137.

52. K. C. Wheare, "The Nature and Structure of the Commonwealth", *The American Political Science Review* (Wisconsin), vol. 47, pp. 1021-22.

53. United Kingdom : "Elizabeth the Second, by the Grace of God, of the UK of Great Britain and Northern Ireland, of Her other Realms and Territories, Queen Head of the Commonwealth, Defender of the Faith". Canada : "Elizabeth the Second, by the Grace of God, of the UK, Canada and Her other Realms and Territories, Queen, Head of the Commonwealth, Defender of the Faith". Australia : "Elizabeth the Second, by the Grace of God of the UK, Australia and Her other Realms and Territories, Queen, Head of the Commonwealth, Defender of the Faith". New Zealand : "Elizabeth the Second, by the Grace of God, of the UK, New Zealand, and Her other Realms and Territories, Queen, Head of the Commonwealth, Defender of the Faith". South Africa : "Elizabeth the Second, Queen of South Africa and of Her other Realms and Territories, Head of the Commonwealth". Pakistan : "Elizabeth the Second, Queen of the

UK and of Her other Realms and Territories, Head of the Commonwealth". *Ibid.*, pp. 1021-22.

54. *The Times* (London), 11 January 1955.
55. Ceylon, *H. R. Deb.*, vol. 13, 1953, cols. 2781-82.
56. *The Times* (London), 17 October 1951.
57. There was considerable opposition to the Queen's visit on grounds of economic austerity as was evident from a petition signed by 60,000 Ceylonese and submitted by two M.Ps. to the Governor-General to call off the Queen's visit. It, however, goes to Sir John Kotelawala's credit that he went through the schedule of the visit in spite of the opposition at home. *Ceylon Daily News*, 17 October 1953.
58. *Ibid.*, 20 May 1954.
59. For details of judicial structure of Ceylon, see Sir Kenneth Robert Wray, *Commonwealth and Colonial Law* (London, 1966), p. 695.
60. Though this jurisdiction of the Privy Council in hearing appeals in criminal cases was challenged in 1964 in *Ibralebbe* V. *R.* (1964 AC 900), the Judicial Committee disagreed with the decision of the Ceylon Court of Criminal Appeal that Privy Council's jurisdiction in criminal matters had been terminated by the grant of independence. *Ibid.*, pp. 695-96.
61. Wheare, *n.* 52, p.1024.
62. *The Times* (London), 30 October 1953.
63. W. Howard Wriggins, *Ceylon : Dilemmas of a New Nation* (Princeton, 1960), p.106.
64. *Ceylon Daily News*, 24 November 1947.
65. Ceylon, *H. R. Deb.*, vol. 1, 1947, cols. 731-32.
66. *Ceylon Daily News*, 19 August 1948.
67. Ceylon, *H. R. Deb.*, vol. 6, 1949, col. 197.
68. *Ibid.*, cols. 197-8.
69. *Ibid.*, vol. 10, 1951, col. 261.
70. *The Times* (London), 6 September 1950.
71. *Ceylon Daily News*, 18 June 1951.
72. J. R. Jayawardene, "D. S. Senanayake's Foreign Policy", *Ceylon Historical Journal* (Dehiwala), vol. 5, p. 55.
73. *Between Two Worlds* (Ceylon, 1954), p. 30.
74. *Ceylon Daily News*, 25 November 1953.
75. *Ibid.*, 14 December 1953.

76. Sir John Kotelawala, *An Asian Prime Minister's Story* (London, 1956), p. 115.
77. *Ceylon Daily News*, 21 December 1953.
78. *Ibid.*, 10 February 1954.
79. *Ibid.*, 18 March 1954.
80. Ceylon, *H. R. Deb.*, vol. 20, 1954, cols. 1887-88.
81. *Times of Ceylon*, 31 March 1955.
82. *Ceylon Daily News*, 29 December 1954.
83. *Bandung 1955* (Ceylon), p. 18.
84. *Ibid.*
85. Ceylon, *H. R. Deb.*, vol. 20, 1955, col. 4309.
86. John Cardew, "Ceylon's Trade with China : The Economic Background", *New Commonwealth* (London), vol. 25, p. 377.
87. *New York Times* (New York), 22 September 1954.
88. Cardew, *n.* 86, p. 377.
89. Ceylon, *H. R. Deb.*, vol. 14, 1953, col. 446.
90. *The Times* (London), 4 October 1951.
91. *Ibid.*, 5 October 1951.
92. Cardew, *n.* 86, p. 378.
93. Ceylon, *H. R. Deb.*, vol. 13, 1953, col. 1473.
94. *The Times* (London), 7 October 1952.
95. *Ibid.*, 22 December 1952.
96. *Ibid.*, 10 March 1953.
97. *The Hindu*, 21 March 1953.
98. Rubber was carried from the island by non-British ships, mainly Polish. *The Times* (London), 10 March 1953.
99. *The Hindu*, 21 March 1953.
100. *New York Times*, 6 January 1953.
101. *Times of Ceylon*, 20 January 1955.
102. Trade and Payments Agreements Between the Government of Ceylon and the Government of the Polish People's Republic. *Ceylon Treaty Series, No. 2 of 1956* (Colombo).
103. Trade Agreement Between the Government of Ceylon and the Government of the Czechoslovak Republic. *Ceylon, Treaty Series No. 3 of 1966* (Colombo).
104. Trade and Payments Agreement Between the Government of Ceylon and the Government of the People's Republic of Rumania. *Ceylon, Treaty Series No. 8 of 1956* (Colombo).

105. D. S. Senanayake, "Speech delivered over the B. B. C. on 'the Middle Way' of moderation as a path of Peace", *The Ceylon Historical Journal*, vol. 5, p. 114.
106. Ceylon, *H. R. Deb.*, vol. 14, 1953, cols. 554-5.
107. Sir John Kotelawala, "Ceylon as Switzerland-in-Asia", *New Commonwealth*, vol. 29, p. 316.
108. *Ceylon Daily News*, 23 September 1954.
109. *The Times* (London), 20 November 1954.
110. *Ibid.*, 23 December 1948. Also see *Ceylon Daily News*, 23 December 1948.
111. *Ceylon Daily News*, 24 December 1948. Also see *The Times* (London), 24 December 1948.
112. *Ibid.*
113. *Ibid.*
114. R.I.I.A., *Documents 1949-1950* (London, 1953), p. 567.
115. *Ceylon Daily News*, 19 January 1949.
116. Ceylon, *H. R. Deb.*, vol. 5, 1949, col. 799.
117. G. H. Jansen, *Afro-Asia and Non-Alignment* (London, 1966), p. 89.
118. *Ceylon Daily News*, 22 January 1949.
119. *Ibid.*, 25 January 1949.
120. R.I.I.A., Documents, pp. 630-1.
121. *Ibid.*, pp. 631-2.
122. U.K., *H. C. Deb.*, vol. 476, 1950, col. 2319.
123. *The Hindu*, 1 July 1950.
124. *Times of Ceylon*, 5 July 1950.
125. *New York Herald Tribune*, 6 July 1950.
126. Ceylon, *H. R. Deb.*, vol. 8, 1950, col. 487.
127. *Ibid.*, cols. 1856-57.
128. *Ibid.*, col. 1857.
129. *Ibid.*, col. 1860.
130. The countries participating were France, Great Britain, the USSR, the USA, the People's Republic of China, the Korean Democratic Republic (North Korea), the Republic of Korea (South Korea), Australia, Belgium, Canada, Colombia, Ethiopia, Greece, Luxemberg, the Netherlands, New Zealand, the Philippines, Siam and Turkey.
131. Kotelawala, *n.* 76, p. 119.

132. Sir Ivor Jennings, "Politics in Ceylon since 1952", *Pacific Affairs* (New York), vol. 27, p. 350.
133. *Ceylon Daily News*, 24 April 1954.
134. *Ibid.*
135. *The Times* (London), 24 April 1954.
136. *Ibid.*, 30 April 1954.
137. *Ceylon Daily News*, 8 May 1954.
138. The British proposal was that the commission should consist of three Colombo Powers and two continental neutrals. One of the two continental neutrals should be Communist, possibly Czechoslovakia, and one of the Colombo Powers should be India. It also suggested that the choice of the two Colombo Powers be from Indonesia, Burma and Pakistan. *Ibid.*, 15 June 1954.
139. Ceylon, *H. R. Deb.*, vol. 17, 1954, col. 369.
140. *Ibid.*, vol. 19, 1954, cols. 411-12.
141. *Ibid.*, cols. 393-94.
142. *Ibid.*, col. 412.
143. *Manchester Guardian*, 5 August 1954.
144. Jennings, *n.* 132, p. 350.
145. Ceylon, *H. R. Deb.*, vol. 19, 1954, col. 424.
146. *The Times* (London), 14 August 1954.
147. Ceylon, *H.R. Deb.*, vol. 20, 1954, cols. 35-36 and 49.
148. *Ceylon Daily News*, 10 September 1954. Also see *The Times* (London), 10 September 1954.
149. *Observer* (Colombo), 12 September 1954.
150. *The Times* (London), 13 September 1954.
151. *Ceylon Daily News*, 15 September 1954.
152. *The Hindustan Times* (Delhi), 16 September 1954.
153. *Ceylon Daily News*, 10 September 1954.
154. *The Hindu*, 12 September 1954.
155. *Manchester Guardian*, 18 October 1954.
156. *Ceylon Daily News*, 18 October 1954.
157. *Ibid.*, 5 October 1954.
158. *Times of Ceylon* (Colombo), 23 February 1955.
159. Kotelawala, *n.* 78, p. 140.

3
NON-ALIGNED CEYLON AND THE UNITED KINGDOM

In the general election of 1956 the UNP (heir to the legacy of D.S. Senanayake through the first decade of independence) suffered a jolting reversal in the sweeping victory of the People's United Front (Mahajana Eksath Peramuna—MEP) led by S.W.R.D. Bandaranaike, the former leader of the Opposition in Parliament. The MEP, a joint front of various Opposition political parties and groups—the SLFP of S.W.R.D. Bandaranaike, the Viplavakari Lanka Sama Samaja Party, (VLSSP) a left wing group led by Philip Gunawardene and the Bhasa Peramuna, a Sinhalese communal onganisation associated with W. Dahanayake and some Independents—was formed on the eve of the general election of 1956 with the purpose of defeating the UNP, then in power.

As in the case of the Indian National Congress in India the UNP was not a politically homogeneous party but a conglomeration of groups. The intra-wranglings within the groups due to personal ambitions led to defections. For instance, in July 1951, S.W.R.D. Bandaranaike (the Minister of Health and Local Government, and the leader of the House of Representatives and who it was generally understood would succeed D. S. Senanayake as the leader of the second largest component of the UNP) crossed the floor with a few colleagues on the Budget day under the assumption that D. S. Senanayake was grooming his nephew, Major John Kotelawala to succeed him.[1] Another event occurred in March 1952 on the sudden death of D. S. Senanayake, when Dudley Senanayake, a less ambitious person, was induced to inherit[2] the post of Premiership against the claims of the then leader of the House of Representatives, Sir John Kotelawala, who used to preside over the Cabinet meetings and officiate as the chairman of the UNP in D. S. Senanayake's absence. Instead he was deprived of the post on the ground that he was unacceptable to several groups among the ruling party's Members of Parliament.[3] With this incident Ceylon set up a unique record, as there is no instance in history of a father being immediately succeeded by his son as Prime Minister. Deep resentment, disappointment and bitterness created by this incident in Sir John Kotelawala, were reflected in August when a weekly entitled *Trine* published the contents of a document known as "Prime Minister's Stakes 1952" in which was related the story of intrigue within the Government Party[4] immediately after the death of D. S. Senanayake. Dudley was not destined to continue long as Premier since he was forced to resign from the Premiership by circumstances. Though ostensibly Dudley Senanayake's resignation was based on ill-health, other factors forces—the crisis which led to a state of emergency,[5] lack of genuine support in his own Cabinet throughout his Premiership,[6] and his disagreement with the Governor-General about the Queen's visit to Ceylon[7]— precipitated the resignation of the Prime Minister. Dudley's successor Sir John had neither very many supporters within the Party nor was very popular among the masses, particularly the villagers who considered him a 'brown sahib'. But his accession to the Premiership was an overdue tribute to his forceful statesmanship because in March 1952 he had nearly become Prime Minister but was squeezed into a minor position because of cabinet jealousies. The defection of R. G. Senanayake from Kotelawala's cabinet, and the withdrawal of the Ex-Premier Dudley from active politics and participation in the general election of 1956, added to the unpopularity of the UNP leadership in general and Sir John Kotelawala in particular. During the Kotelawala regime which lasted till 1956, these rifts persisted.

Besides these intricacies of intra-party manoeuvres at the top of the UNP, the party had grown out of touch with the country. Hence, unlike the other nationalist parties in Asian countries, like the Indian National Congress in India, the UNP could not give expression to the tides of nationalist feeling which began to agitate the country during the Premiership of Sir John Kotelawala. The national feeling which was aroused by the revival of Buddhism,[8] linguistic nationalism[9] and resurgence of traditional culture[10] and certain 'progressive' measures in the election manifesto of the Mahajana Eksath Peramuna,[11] supported by certain other factors[12] voted the MEP coalition to power in 1956. This election, fought on domestic and cultural issues rather than on the foreign policy issues was a reflection of a common resistance of the rural middle class to the encroachment of Western values which were identified with the UNP in 1956.

The MEP, a heterogeneous complex of political parties, did not have a common programme for the implementation of its manifesto and as a result, difficulties arose immediately after it came to power. Between the Right wing (S.W.R.D. Bandaranaike's SLFP which was the strongest component of the MEP) and the Left wing (under Philip Gunawardane) of the cabinet, Bandaranaike was, however, able to maintain a precarious balance until his assassination in September 1959.

After an interval of ten months during which there was first an uneasy caretaker Government under W. Dahanayake (from September 1959 to March 1960) and a short-lived UNP Government under Dudley Senanayake (from April 1960 to July 1960), Mrs. Sirimavo Bandaranaike, S.W.R.D. Bandaranaike's widow, who pledged to continue the policy of her late husband, was voted to power with majority in July 1960 general election. In December 1964, with the crossing of the floor by C. P. de Silva, the then leader of the House, Mrs. Bandaranaike's Government was defeated and the dissolution of the Parliament became inevitable. Thus, ended, what may be called 'the Bandaranaike era' during which period emerged a 'New Ceylon' with a 'changed look' in foreign affairs observing a 'neutralist policy' as enunciated by S.W.R.D. Bandaranaike.

Neutralist policy as enunciated by S.W.R.D. Bandaranaike and followed up by Mrs. Bandaranaike till 1965

With Bandaranaike's assumption of power in 1956, Ceylon's foreign policy underwent a re-orientation. On 12 April, in a Press interview outlining his policy in foreign affairs, he said, "he was in general agreement with the policy pursued by Mr. Nehru".[13] While in opposition, Bandaranaike had emphasised that in foreign relations the proper position for a country like Ceylon was that of a country like Switzerland in Europe. For an Asian country in the context of world affairs, Ceylon's position must be one of not only friendliness with all nations but a certain aloofness from any of those blocs.[14] Even after he became the Prime Minister, he maintained the same attitude when he said, "What we would like to be is the Switzerland of Asia, that means following a neutralist policy."[15] Pursuing that policy, Ceylon was able to retain old friends and make new ones.

There were two essential facets of Bandaranaike's policy : (1) Co-existence and (2) Neutralism. In the course of an interview with the Editor of the *Eastern World*, he explained the philosophy of co-existence : "The peoples of the world cannot afford to hate each other so much that there is any chance of it flaring up into war. We must also realise that man is more important than 'issues'. Just as it was said 'Sabbath was made for man and not man for the Sabbath'."[16] Explaining the second facet—the philosophy of neutralism—he observed that Ceylon, like some other Asian countries which have re-emerged from colonial status into freedom, was faced with a dual problem of converting a colonial society—politically, socially and economically—into a free society and of achieving that change in the context of a world of peace which itself had changed.[17]

> In the search of such a solution in the dual problem, we naturally do not wish to bind ourselves to any particular power bloc or ideology. We wish to look about us in building a society for our country most suited to our own genius and the needs of the modern world. There may be things we like from the West or the Communist East.[18]

Politically, he said, the Western idea of democratic freedom was something he thought valuable : but economically, he believed in socialism. While subscribing to his own programme of "democratic socialism" he did not make the distinction that Western Socialists make between their brand of parliamentary socialism and the totalitarian Soviet brand. Continuing his argument for Ceylon's 'middle-way' he believed that, given twenty-five years of peace, the experiment he launched in democratic socialism for Ceylon would surely succeed.[19]

On assumption of power, in 1960 Mrs. Bandaranaike was content to follow the same line of policy when she emphasized in a statement to the Press on 21 July that "her party would follow the neutralist policy pursued by her late husband".[20] The same attitude was maintained in the Governor-General's Throne speech at the opening of the Parliament : "In external affairs My Government will maintain its policy of non-alignment with power-blocs and of neutralism and co-existence".[21] But she deviated from her husband's 'Centre party policy'[22] towards the Left and that accentuated the downfall of her Government in 1964.[23]

Reaction of the UK towards the neutralist policy in the Bandaranaike era

From Bandaranaike's election to power in 1956 to the fall of Mrs. Bandaranaike's Government in 1964, the UK, especially with a conservative Government in power, was apprehensive about the neutralist policy in international affairs advocated by the Socialist Bandaranaike Governments. On 6 April 1956 in a statement to British Press correspondent, Bandaranaike suggested that Ceylon should play the role of an "Asian Switzerland" and serve as "a bridge between East and West". He favoured "a form of dynamic neutralism" in foreign policy which did not imply any kind of hostility towards the Western Powers. He wished to maintain the friendliest relation with Britain which he regarded as "providing a sane balance between the extreme American and Russian views". He also assured the British that there was no cause to fear abrupt upheavals or changes if he became the Prime Minister.[24] Despite all his assurances, his earlier statements about the withdrawal of British bases from Ceylon and the nationalisation of plantations had already dismayed the UK. *The Daily Mail* (London) even suggested that Lord Home, the Secretary of State for Commonwealth Relations, "should fly to Ceylon to see the new Premier to explain the perils of the solution to Bandaranaike" and also added "if the election promises were carried out it would be a disaster for Britain".[25]

British reaction to the growth of neutralism in Ceylon was significant in the sense that the British who seemed to consider Nehru's "neutralism" as an influential factor in international affairs, did not welcome Ceylon becoming 'neutralist'. This paradox in the British attitude *vis-a-vis* the Ceylonese and Indian neutralist policies can be explained by the fact that Ceylon's neutralist policy would lead to quite a different consequence for Britain, *i.e.* the undermining of Britain's strategic position in the Indian Ocean area.

According to the pronounced policy of Bandarnaike, Ceylon was to follow India and Pakistan in becoming a republic. In tune with India's neutralist policy and from the strategic point of view there was to be the withdrawal of British naval and air bases from Ceylon. On 14 April 1956, the new Ceylon Cabinet, at its first meeting decided to request Her Majesty that "she should graciously refrain from conferring honours on citizens of Ceylon" in future. It also decided not to recommend any names in future for the conferment of Imperial Honours on the Queen's birthday which was one of the last links with colonial tradition. Not to serve any intoxicating liquor at state and official functions not only in Ceylon but also in all Ceylon diplomatic missions abroad and also to close the bars in the Houses of Representatives were some of the other decisions taken by the Cabinet.[26] Bandaranaike also welcomed the renunciation of Imperial Honours already conferred when he announced at his weekly Press conference about Sir Senarath Gunawardane's, the then Ceylon's Ambassador in Washington, renouncement of his Knighthood.[27] On 4 May, C.A.S. Marikkar, the Minister of Posts, Broadcasting and Information, declared in Parliament the Government's decision to censor the contents of the broadcasts from the "Voice of America".[28] This policy of the Government was not to rupture the agreement between Ceylon and the USA, but was meant to ensure that the contents of the broadcast did not offend China or the Soviet

Union with whom Bandaranaike was courting friendship. The Colombo Plan Exhibition which was to have been opened by Queen Elizabeth, the Queen Mother in February 1957, was postponed by the Government on the plea that the UNP Government had organised it as a propaganda stunt without giving thought to many aspects of national interest.[29] Commenting on these actions of the Bandaranaike Government under the heading "Unnecessary gestures", *The Times* (London) stated that although independence was accorded to Ceylon eight years ago, "the leaders of the UNP evidently did not purvey the sensation of independence in sufficient force" and that seemed to have contributed to Bandaranaike's success in the general election followed by his eagerness to make immediate changes in the policy hitherto followed by the previous Government.[30]

On 9 October 1957, following the show of a film "Bloodless Arena" on the BBC television and the refusal of the BBC to allow the Ceylon High Commissioner in London to examine the film which was alleged to have depicted Ceylon as "uncivilized and possibly anti-British", the Government of Ceylon decided to introduce legislation to prevent foreign organizations from taking out of Ceylon films shot in the country without the approval of the Ceylon Government.[31] On the eve of the tenth year of Independence of Ceylon, *The Times* (London), commenting on Ceylon's foreign policy, described Bandaranaike as

> an avowed disciple of Mr. Nehru's non-alignment, but lacking the carefully balanced attitude of the Indian Prime Minister appears almost simultaneously to profess opposite points of view—at one moment a eulogy of Britain and the Commonwealth, at the next, an endorsement of the International policies of Russia and the Communist bloc.[32]

In the economic field, the official policy since 1956 had given rise to fellings of economic insecurity in some quarters due to (a) vague threats to nationalise free enterprise assets as tea and rubber estates (most of them British-owned), and (b) the appearance of China and Russia on the economic scene.[33]

When Mrs. Bandaranaike came to power, the British Press which was fascinated by Ceylon's choice of a woman as Prime Minister, for the first time in the history of any country in the world, extended a 'tempered welcome'. But it also expressed its anxiety over the probable attitude of Mrs. Bandaranaike's Government to British interests in the island by virtue of the fact that her party's national aspirations tended highly towards the left.[34] In this context an attempt is made to assess how the implementation of some issues—the withdrawal of British bases from Ceylon, the establishment of a democratic republic and the nationalisation of essential industries including foreign-owned plantations, transport, banking and insurance was carried out and in what direction it tended to lead Ceylon in her relations with the UK.

Withdrawal of bases

To carry through the policy of 'strategic non-involvement for Ceylon' which S.W.R.D. Bandaranaike so strongly advocated in the past, he took steps to effect the withdrawal of all the 'so called foreign bases' from Ceylon which had been granted to Britain under the Defence Agreement of 1947. While in opposition, Bandaranaike had pointed out in the House that Ceylon was the only country to obtain Dominion Status "subject to certain agreements" and did not possess so much freedom in foreign affairs as India and Pakistan.[35] Immediately after his assumption of power, he made his position clear in an interview with the *US News and World Report*, and claimed that "British forces based in Ceylon would have to go".[36] But he wished to do it in a friendly way "without causing dislocation, inconvenience or embarassment to the British Government or indeed to ourselves".[37] In the Governor-General's address to both the Houses at the opening of Parliament, Bandaranaike's Government's policy on bases was stated as : "In its foreign policy, My Government will not align with any power blocs. The position of the bases at Katunayake and Trincomalee will be reviewed."[38] He assured at his first weekly conference that he did not foresee any difficulty in getting rid of British bases as there were no secret clauses to the defence agreement between Britain and Ceylon.[39] The doubts, created by the news that the *New York Times* had advised the Commonwealth Prime Ministers at their forthcoming meeting in London 'to put all reasonable pressure' on S.W.R.D. Bandaranaike to modify his stand in regard to the removal of bases from Ceylon, as it would be unsound both economically and strategically for Britain to withdraw her bases from the Island,[40] were cleared when Bandaranaike reiterated his view :

> The continuance of bases in this country by Britain fundamentally conflicts with my entire conception both of my philosophy on foreign affairs and the position I visualize for my country in world affairs or in the trend of foreign events. That is why I cannot change my views even under pressure.[41]

This act of withdrawal, he added, "is in no way an act of hostility to any country, whether in the Commonwealth or outside it, and I would like to have the most cordial, happy and friendly relations between my country and other countries, especially those in the Commonwealth and in particular England". To counterbalance the loss of security which would be brought about by the withdrawal of British bases from Ceylon, he stated his proposal to negotiate non-aggression pacts not only with Asian countries but with many other countries.[42] When his attention was drawn to the British Press Reports which advocated that the bases should be placed in individual Commonwealth countries or some sort of combined Commonwealth control and specifically expressed that bases in Ceylon and Singapore should be regarded as Commonwealth bases and not British bases, Bandaranaike categorically countered that he did not agree to any Commonwealth Plan which bound Ceylon to any mutual defence scheme. To him, the Commonwealth scheme was "not a defence scheme of Commonwealth and other Western countries as such, but as a scheme of defence aimed against the Soviet bloc".[43] Commenting on Singapore's demand for freedom *vis-a-vis* Ceylon's demand for the withdrawal of British bases at his weekly conference, he admitted that his own attitude with regard to British bases in Ceylon had something to do with the stiffening of the British attitude to Singapore, and asserted that "Ceylon, as a Dominion had the absolute right in these matters to have her views respected and accepted as much as India and Pakistan".[44]

When questioned at a Press interview about any specific document in evidence about bases, he confirmed the fact that there was "not even a scrap of paper available" relating to the use of any bases in Ceylon by the British "unless the previous Government was playing a type of double game" in saying that there was no such agreement while, all the while, they had secretly come to some agreement granting some concessions.[45] In making a statement in the House of Representatives about the bases, the Prime Minister said that whenever the question of 'bases' was raised with the previous Government it always denied that it had conceded any rights to the British to utilise Trincomalee or Katunayake as bases.[46] Explaining his unflinching position for the withdrawal of British bases, he said he was not opposed to continuing the defence agreement with Britain after ther position about the bases had been adjusted; what he was opposed to, was to range on the said of a particular bloc and that situation must cease.[47] Bandaranaike neither agreed with D. S. Senanayake's agreement of 1947 that the British alone could be trusted to protect Ceylon's independence nor did he refrain from accusing Sir John Kotelawala of having played a double game of protesting all over the world that he was not for aligning Ceylon with SEATO, while he permitted Britain, one of the important SEATO powers, to have bases in Ceylon.

On arrival at London for the Conference, referring to his Government's attitude to the British bases in Ceylon he declared : "Our desire not to have bases stems from our basic foreign policy, indeed accepted by the previous Government, that we should keep clear of power blocs."[48] He defended Ceylon's demand for the withdrawal of British bases from Ceylon on the basis that there was strong feeling among political parties in Ceylon over the bases because firstly, they represented a 'dimunition of our sovereignty', secondly, 'they ranged Ceylon on the side of the Power blocs', and thirdly, 'they tied Ceylon's defence to British forces'. The settlement question, he added, would 'certainly help' to strengthen friendly relations between Britain and Ceylon.[49] On various occasions he had contemplated the possibility of a regional pact between Asian countries—India, Pakistan, Ceylon, Burma, Malaya and Indonesia—bordering on the Indian Ocean. But when questioned at a meeting of Ceylon students in London about how he intended to fill the vacuum which would be caused by the evacuation of British troops from the Island, he said he did not agree that the present world position required any very big defence of Ceylon because he did not contemplate anybody invading his country except in the event of a general cataclysm of a world war. Moreover, he was doubtful if only the presence of the British at Trincomalee and Katunayake would save them.[50] Meanwhile it was understood that Britain was anxious to recognise Ceylon's sovereignty over her bases but at the same time hoped for a solution of bases along the lines of that reached with South Africa for the Simonston base in June 1955.[51] When questioned at a Press Conference at London, if Russia made a request to grant similar facilities to the Soviet Union, he said, "I consider our relations with Britain are much closer than that of a country such as Russia or for that matter the United States. We have very close and friendly relations with Britain as a member of the Commonwealth."[52]

The Anglo-Ceylonese agreement, reached on 6 July at the end of the Commonwealth Prime Ministers' Conference, recognised the principle of removal of British control of bases, declared the intention of the Ceylon Government to grant UK certain facilities for communications, movements and storage. The agreement needed further elaboration for which negotiations were arranged to be held at London and Colombo.[53]

The Opposition circles in Ceylon expressed 'disappointment' at the Ceylon-UK agreement of July. Colvin R. de Silva, representing the Trotskyite Party, told the PTI that "since Britain is to have rights of use of these bases for her purposes and Ceylon is a weak little country in relation to imperial Britain, the position really is that Ceylon is to manage and administer her bases for the use and purposes of Britain". He also suggested that "the only road left to Ceylon to maintain her neutrality would be to develop her moral strength on the basis of complete disarmament and friendship with her immediate neighbours".[54] J. R. Jayawardane, a senior member of the UNP, said that the agreement represented a pyrrhic victory for Bandaranaike. On the contrary, Dr. E.M.V. Naganathan, Propaganda Secretary to the Federal Party, was of the opinion that "the existence of foreign institutions such as the bases in

Ceylon would, in the present context of the Island's politics, act as a moral check on Sinhalese Imperialism".⁵⁵

Making a statement in the House of Representatives on the 'bases', the Prime Minister assured that "whatever facilities are agreed upon will be subject to the overriding decision that we and we alone are in control of the bases at Trincomalee and Katunayake". He further added that it had not occurred to him to refuse such facilities when dealing with a friendly people. He had not wished to be churlish by refusing them such facilities, but he assured the House that whatever facilities were accorded would be made in such a way as not to derogate from the fundamental position of Ceylon regarding the bases. It was 'fallacious', it was stated, to suggest that the granting of these facilities was equivalent to the granting of bases. It gave him satisfaction that even the UK did not consider the facilities as a "substitute for bases" and that the British Government was even considering making alternative arrangement for the Headquarters of the East Indies Squadron, which only meant Ceylon's stand had been upheld.⁵⁶ All along, Bandaranaike's argument was that the two bases in Ceylon were owned by the UK and such a situation was inconsistent with the independence of Ceylon. But with the UK's withdrawal, the bases belonged to Ceylon and she could do with them as she pleased—"she can even hand them over to a Power hostile to Britain if she chooses and that being the case", he argued, "there is nothing wrong now in allowing Britain a friendly Power, facilities at Trincomalee and Katunayake".⁵⁷ When negotiations for the withdrawal of naval bases were continuing between Ceylon and the UK, the Suez Canal dispute started. Bandaranaike declared in the House that at the outset of the Suez crisis he had sought for and received an assurance from the British Government that "our bases at Trincomalee and Katunayake would not be used by them for any purpose connected with any military action in the event of the outbreak of hostilities".⁵⁸

After the final Anglo-Ceylonese agreement was concluded on 7 June 1957 which 'tied up the loose ends' regarding the final date of withdrawal and the nature of facilities granted to Britain during and after the withdrawal of bases, it was agreed that the British Government would formally transfer the naval base at Trincomalee on 15 October and the Air Force Station at

Katunayake on 1 November to the Ceylon Government.[59] The United Kingdom was to continue to use certain facilities for a limited time (here after referred to as "the rundown"). The use of some of the facilities was to cease within two to three years and of all the facilities by 1 March 1962, provided that, if the process of rundown was interrupted by causes outside the control of the UK Government, the period of "rundown" might be increased as mutually agreed on.[60] It was provided that during the "rundown" the use of facilities would be subject to the general control of the Ceylon Government and even might be denied to the UK Government, if any situation arose. Subject to this condition, the Ceylon Government would grant the UK Government free and uninterrupted use and operation of these facilities and right to administer their establishment as existed. Another important provision in the sub-para 9 of the agreement was that during the period of "rundown" and even after it the Ceylon Government would, in accordance with the normal Commonwealth practice but subject to the general policy of the Ceylon Government, continue to allow, (a) the UK naval vessels to refuel at Colombo; and (b) the aircraft of the UK forces and those on charter to overfly and stage through Ceylon. By the agreement Ceylon also agreed to pay Rs. 22 million over a period of 5 years, 1957—1962, for the installations to be transferred and for the final settlement of certain other claims arising out of the occupation or disposal of the bases by the UK forces.[61]

Making a statement in the debate on the Appropriation Bill Bandaranaike told the House that, with the removal of bases, "the last remnants of colonialism in this country have been removed".[62] Declaring on the historic ceremony on 1 November, 1957 that "our independence is complete", he paid a tribute to the British Government which handed back control of Ceylon's affairs to the people of Ceylon with "dignity, cordiality, friendship and good grace".[63]

Despite the withdrawal of bases, certain sections of people both at home and abroad held some doubts about the legal status of the Defence Agreement. Some scholars like B. H. Farmer held the view that Bandaranaike "soon after his electoral victory in April 1956 abrogated the defence agreement".[64] Others like Sir Charles Collins were of the

opinion that the Defence Agreement was a dead letter and it
could be invoked at any time as and when Ceylon found it
necessary.[65] But most of the Ceylonese held the view
that the Defence Agreement still stood.[66] There was neither
any documentary nor legal evidence abrogating the Defence
Agreement, nor had Bandaranaike any intention of abrogating
it, which was evident from his categorical statement to the
special correspondent of the *Daily Telegraph* : "There is no
question of the abrogation of the Defence Agreement since it
is merely a friendly agreement such as might be concluded
between any two countries."[67] Hence one is led to conclude
that there are basically two agreements which could be
operated at any time; one is the Defence Agreement of 1947
which is not abrogated, though one of its important provisions
became ineffective after the removal of bases, and which can
be invoked at any time; the second is the Exchange of Letters
between the Government of Ceylon and the Government of the
UK regarding UK service establishments in Ceylon (Treaty
Series No. 4 of 1957) of which sub-para 9 is significant.
According to sub-para 9, the Ceylon Government, even after
the completion of "rundown" period will continue to allow
(a) naval vessels to refuel at Colombo, and (b) the aircraft of
the UK forces and those on Charter to overfly and stage
through Ceylon.[68]

The India-China border dispute became a test of the
efficacy of clause 9 of 1957 agreement. In an article published
in *Ceylon Daily News* titled "Former UK bases an issue", the
Defence and External Affairs Ministry Officials were reported
to have drawn the attention of the Prime Minister to the fact
that a worsening of the Sino-Indian situation was likely to
involve Ceylon in the dispute. The decision of Britain to align
herself with India and offer aid against the Chinese aggression
might necessitate Britain's asking for the use of Trincomalee
and Katunayake for service movements, applying the sub-para
9 of the Treaty Series No. 4 of 1957. In the event of Britain
furnishing aid to India and wanting to use Trincomalee and
Katunayake, they added, "Ceylon's position should be
clarified".[69] Though the report was denied by a Press
communique issued by the Ministry of Defence and External
Affairs,[70] it is significant that on similar occasions Britain

could apply clause 9 of the new agreement of 1957.

By removing British naval and air bases from Ceylon, Bandaranaike asserted the sovereignty of Ceylon and kept Ceylon outside the range of power blocs. The last vestiges of the British bases were removed when 800 acres of land, which continued to be owned by the Admiralty for storage tanks even after the post was handed over in 1957, were sold to the Ceylon Government for about £250,000.[71]

Establishment of a democratic republic

After his assumption of power, Bandaranaike took steps for the implementation of another plank of his party's election manifesto—the establishment of a democratic republic. Soon after becoming the Premier, Bandaranaike emphasised in an interview with the *US News and World Report*, that "Ceylon would become a Republic" and would probably stay in the Commonwealth, quite contrary to his party's original policy to remain out of the commonwealth; because the example of India had shown that it was possible to remain within the Commonwealth without impairing one's sovereignty.[72] But he still had certain reservations about the Commonwealth as, in his opinion, there were many advantages 'in staying out' :

> If we wanted to enter into certain regional agreement with other countries, with the United States for example, it might be easier if we were not members of another grouping like the Commonwealth. With the growth of international organisations, the practical advantages of Asian countries remaining in the Commonwealth are greatly reduced since there are other groupings we can become members of. Regional relationships are more important than the Commonwealth relationship these days. We have to look further into this matter of remaining in the Commonwealth.[73]

His final decision about remaining in the Commonwealth was disclosed for the first time when he stated to the correspondents in London that "remaining in the Commonwealth will not in any way derogate from the sovereignty and a number of advantages will accrue. These included membership of the Sterling Area, Colombo Plan for South East Asia development, and the fact that the countries concerned had a common tradition for democratic parliamentary government".[74] Making a statement in London, he developed the theme that the Commonwealth could make a positive contribution to the world's progress as a "third force" between Russia and the USA, and this would not be in the 'aggressive sense' of a third bloc and could be a tremendous power for the preservation of world peace. Bandaranaike believed that, despite all the advantages of the Commonwealth like the membership of the sterling area and a way of life which united the members together in spite of their differences, "the far-flung Commonwealth must think in terms of either dissolution at some distant date or else of getting more compact and closer together on certain moral principles".[75] To overcome some of the difficulties that he foresaw in developing this 'third force' because of "the commitments of some Commonwealth countries to regional defence pacts", he asked "why they could not even as member of such pacts support the theory of 'third force' and so assist in the preservation of peace". He also felt that unless the Commonwealth developed along such lines it would disintegrate and in the end might consist only of those countries whose people were predominantly of British stock.[76]

Bandaranaike's announcement to the Commonwealth Prime Ministers of his Government's decision to make Ceylon a republic within the Commonwealth, at least in a year or two, received the wholehearted acceptance from the other members of the Commonwealth, and was only a matter of formality : but its significance was the emergence of another republic within the Commonwealth. Talking to the Commonwealth Correspondents Association in London, he disclosed his feelings towards Britain and the Commonwealth when he said : "We consider your Queen to be a gracious leader. We understand your feelings towards her, but, we do not share them. We are not hostile to her or Britain. But we prefer a Republican form of Government and we want to remain within the Commonwealth."[77] In the House of Representatives, the Prime Minister stated : "As India herself has decided, I think the wise course would be for us to be a republic within the Commonwealth."[78] But in December 1956, the Opposition party called for severing ties with the Commonwealth in retaliation against the British policy towards

Egypt over the issue of Egypt's nationalization of the Suez Canal. Leslie Goonewardane, a Leftist Member of Parliament, pointed out that foreign policies of the Asian members of the Commonwealth seemed to be fundamentally different from the foreign policies of the other members of the Commonwealth and that "our continued membership of the Commonwealth is becoming an unreality".[79] Replying to the critics, Bandaranaike told the House that the question of remaining in the Commonwealth or quitting it, should not be dealt with "impulsively", because of the Egyptian incident.[80] But he was more explicit in advocating that the Suez affair was not an adequate reason for quitting the Commonwealth when he told the Indian Council of World Affairs in India :

> The people of Great Britain could not be judged by some aberration of their government however unfortunate that aberration may be. More than 50 per cent of the British people have expressed their resentment over Britain's involvement in the Suez crisis. If we are to leave the Commonwealth, he added, we must leave for much better reasons than the part played by Britain Egypt.[81]

The desire to institute a Ceylonese republic was not realised in the Bandaranaike era. This issue involved the question of amendment of the constitution which required a two-thirds majority in the Parliament—a Herculean task to be carried out under the political set up that obtained in Ceylon. Nevertheless, the first step to deal with this problem was taken by Bandaranaike when a Joint Select Committee of both the Houses was appointed by the House to go into various matters pertaining to the amendment of the constitution.[82] This Joint Committee did not complete its work during the life-time of Bandaranaike.

During Mrs. Bandaranaike's Premiership (1960-1965), though the Select Committee of both Houses of Parliament was re-appointed to consider Constitutional Reforms to establish a Republican form of Government,[83] nothing substantial was done in this direction.

Nationalisation of essential industries vis-a-vis Ceylon UK relations

"All essential industries including foreign-owned plantation, transport, banking and insurance will be progressively nationalised"[84]—was one of the promises in the MEP election manifesto. Having come to power, Bandaranaike realised that on the question of the nationalisation of the foreign-owned plantations there was little to be gained by experimenting with the country's best source of revenue. Meanwhile, foreign investors had already begun to have doubts about the government's nationalisation programme. Moreover, Philip Gunawardane, the Food and Agriculture Minister, had talked in strong terms at a public meeting that all Ceylon plantations would be nationalised within 5 to 10 years and "White companies must pack up and get out without trying to dictate terms to us".[85] Hence, to encourage foreign private investment in Ceylon, Bandaranaike had to give continued assurances on several occasions that his Government had no immediate programme for nationalisation of plantations, particularly tea-estates.[86] Reassuring the planters that his Government would not nationalise plantations for at least another 10 years, he described the talk of nationalisation of estates as "a bogey of which plantation interests seemed to be dreaming. Any Government with a socialist outlook", he added, "like his government, must necessarily consider schemes of nationalisation, and it was sure that nationalisation was no magic word which could solve all the economic ills of the country".[87] So, Bandaranaike's Government postponed this part of the nationalisation plan despite pressure from his left allies in his coalition cabinet. But all these measures failed to encourage the foreign private investment and also to reduce the outflow of money in annual dividends.

But the MEP Government of Bandaranaike carried out some schemes of nationalisation. On 28 October 1957, the Cabinet decided to partially nationalise the commercial sector of the Colombo port by setting up a public corporation for it.[88] Despite the protest by the British Government against the modalities of compensation in respect of the dock-side properties of British-owned landing companies which were to be requisitioned by the Ceylon Port Cargo Corporation,[89] the port of Colombo was nationalised by the Ceylon Government. The House of Representatives approved the Bill on 11 April 1958 on the basis that nationalisation would do away with the multiplicity of private operators and improve the efficiency of the port. The Bill also authorised the Government to acquire the properties of the private operators and stipulated that compensation for properties so acquired had to be determined by a Board to be appointed by the Government.[90]

The policy of nationalisation started by Bandaranaike was continued by Mrs. Bandaranaike's Government. On the question of nationalisation of foreign-owned plantations she followed the same policy of Bandaranaike, as is evident from the Governor-General's speech at the opening of the Parliament on 12 August : "My Government does not consider it advantageous to undertake the nationalisation of estates and plantations."[91] Though occasional threats were publicly made by Government officials[92] they never materialised during the SLFP Government's regime.

Preliminary steps which had been taken to nationalise life insurance companies by Bandaranaike were followed up by Mrs. Bandaranaike. Outlining Mrs. Bandaranaike Government's economic policy, the Governor-General in the Throne speech emphasised that "in pursuance of Government's policy of progressive nationalisation, life insurance business will be nationalised and legislation will be introduced to regulate and control insurance business generally in order to prevent abuses".[93] The bulk of Ceylon's insurance companies were British and according to the *Financial Times* (London), the assets of the UK companies were estimated at about £15 million sterling.[94] The Government's take-over of life insurance meant that foreign companies operating in Ceylon had to confine themselves to general insurance. Nevertheless, the Government permitted the practice of marine insurance abroad to be continued and consequently tea for the London auctions and other exports could be so covered; but it was specifically mentioned that any marine insurance transacted in Ceylon had to be with the Corporation.[95] Following the Ceylon Government's take-over of all insurance business of the island through the Ceylon Insurance Corporation from 1 January 1964, the British Insurance Companies, through their Government, represented their case for compensation under four main headings (a) loss of goodwill; (b) obligations to staff; (c) expenses incurred in serving existing contracts; and (d) loss on fixed assets.⁹⁶ Speaking at a ceremony marking the take-over of all insurance business, T. B. Illangaratne, the Ceylon Minister of Finance, declared in categorical terms that the Government did not intend to pay compensation for loss of business and goodwill.⁹⁷

Though Mrs. Bandaranaike's Government had decided not to nationalise foreign banks immediately, it enforced restrictions on the Ceylonese doing business with foreign banks. Thereby all accounts opened by the Ceylonese individuals and their establishments were restricted by law to the two indigenous banks—the state-owned Bank of Ceylon and the People's Bank.⁹⁸ By June 1963, the Government, in order to tighten the banking transactions of all Ceylonese individuals and establishments, proposed to give all the Ceylonese who still maintained accounts in foreign commercial banks a deadline before which they should transfer their existing accounts to one of the two Ceylonese banks.⁹⁹ In November 1964, Dr. N. M. Perera, the Ceylon Finance Minister threatened five British banks in Ceylon with nationalisation if they did not join the Government Banking Corporation.¹⁰⁰

Three oil companies—the British Shell, the American Standard Vacuum Oil, and Caltex—had the monopoly of the oil market in Ceylon. But, by a legislation enacted in May 1961 the Government was empowered to acquire with compensation the installations of private oil companies and to fix maximum and minimum prices at which petroleum products should be sold. The act also provided to set up a Ceylon Petroleum Corporation, a state-owned organisation for the import and distribution of oil within Ceylon.¹⁰¹ The unsettled argument over compensation over the assets of the oil companies led America to suspend aid payments after repeated warnings to the Ceylon Government. But the British Government was not in a position to follow the American line of policy though the British controlled Shell Petroleum Company was the biggest oil importer in the island. The Shell had 60 per cent of the island's oil trade while Caltex and Standard Vacuum Oil Companies had 20 per cent of the trade.¹⁰² While the American investment in the island was insignificant, apart from the comparatively unimportant remaining assets of the two American oil companies, the British 'hostages' in the form of tea and rubber plantations were extensive though the British aid to Ceylon was trivial. Under these circumstances even after discounting the Commonwealth connections, Britain was disinclined to overbid her hand in the hope of recouping the Shell Company's losses. Though the Shell Company itself had duly filed a compensation claim, no settlement was reached between Mrs. Bandaranaike's Government and the oil companies on the question of compensation.

After the take-over of the insurance and petroleum enterprises, Mrs. Bandaranaike, in a New Year message to the nation, asserted the fact that the policy of nationalisation which she carried out was "in keeping with her late husband's desire to free the people from the strangle-hold of vested interests".[103]

The policy of the Bandaranaikes' Governments towards Communist countries

Striving to follow a neutralist policy by steering clear of involvement with power blocs, Bandaranaike wanted to establish friendly relations with all countries. Immediately after his assumption of power, the Prime Minister said in an interview with the *US News and World Report*, that there was no danger of communist subversion in Ceylon and that the country should exchange diplomatic missions with China, the Soviet Union and the East European countries as she had no such relations with them.[104] Though Ceylon had trade relations with a few socialist countries—with China since 1952, Poland and Czechoslovakia since December 1955, and Rumania since March 1956—which were negotiated and operated by *ad hoc* arrangements, no attempt had been made by the UNP Governments to establish even trade missions in the countries.

In a policy statement, Bandaranaike indicated that the trade policy of his Government was to open its doors to all nations, irrespective of their political creeds, if it was to the benefit of Ceylon.[105] In early May, he announced his intention of sending missions to the Soviet Union and Communist China to discuss the establishment of diplomatic relations as well as to examine the question of expansion of trade with those countries.[106] His decision to establish diplomatic relations with both the Soviet Union and Communist China was a sign of his desire to strengthen Ceylon's links with the Communist countries, marking a definite break with the policy of the previous Governments which frowned on close association with the Communist countries. Speaking at Oxford, Bandaranaike said that although many people saw the world as divided into two great power blocs, he preferred to adopt a "middle-way". There are many things in Communism, he continued, that "I do not personally like, but I have no particular fanatical hatred of it".[107]

At the Commonwealth Prime Ministers' Conference in July 1956, Bandaranaike pleaded emphatically for a more sympathetic attitude towards Communist China by the Commonwealth of Nations. He argued that as 'China was virtually the heart of the East', there could be no relaxation of the tension in the Far East unless the Western Powers, particularly America, called off the cold war against China. And China should be admitted to the UN and the recurrent vetoing of its admission into the world forum was a major stumbling bloc in the world's quest for peace.[108] In September 1956, a Government delegation under Sir Claude Corea concluded agreements with the official representatives of the Communist China regarding the establishment of diplomatic relations between the two countries.[109] The Chinese Premier Chou En-lai's six day visit in early 1957 strengthened the Sino-Ceylonese relations. Chou En-lai took the opportunity to impress upon Ceylon's predominantly Buddhist population, who had hitherto shunned communist doctrine because of the UNP Government's effort to represent Communism as the enemy of Buddhism, that Communists do not restrict religious freedom. In a joint statement issued by the Prime Ministers of Ceylon and China at the conclusion of Chou En-lai's visit to Ceylon, they called for another Asian-African Conference at the earliest opportunity "to implement the five principles of co-existence enunciated at the Bandung Conference of 1955. Asian countries were engaged in peaceful construction. They needed help, but the help must be genuine, with no strings attached".[110] The question of diplomatic representation between Ceylon and China was finalised during Chou En-lai's visit, and on 8 February 1957, Ceylon Government announced the appointment of Wilmot A. Perera as Ceylon's first

Ambassador to China.[111]

When the existing trade agreement expired at the end of 1957, Ceylon signed a new five-year Trade and Payments agreement with China for the exchange of rubber, rice and other commodities. A new departure in Sino-Ceylonese relations occurred when an agreement on Economic Aid was also signed between Ceylon and China on the basis of "the Resolution on Economic Co-operation and Mutual Assistance adopted at the Bandung Conference and the five principles of *Panch Sila*". By this agreement China granted economic assistance for Ceylon's Rubber Replanting Programme to the extent of Rs. 75 million spread over a period of five years.[112] Besides these economic and diplomatic relations between Ceylon and Communist China, educational and cultural co-operation was also developed between the two countries. Ceylonese teachers were allowed to go on educational and goodwill tours.[113] A Ceylon-China Friendship Association was opened in Ceylon.[114] Ceylon Communist leaders were allowed to go to Peking to represent Ceylon at the Congress of the China Communist Party.[115] Though arrangements were made by Mrs. Vimla Wijewardane, the then Ceylon Minister of Health, to secure the services of Chinese doctors to train Ceylon doctors in the methods of ancient Chinese diagnosis and treatment, it could not materialise as doctors practising Western system of medicine were debarred from professionally associating with the medical personnel who were not recognised by the British Medical Association.[116] Also an air-transport agreement based on the principle of equality and mutual benefit was signed between Ceylon and Communist China Governments.[117]

Bandaranaike's Government established diplomatic, economic, educational and cultural relations with other Socialist countries also. In September 1956, an agreement was concluded between the official representatives of Ceylon and the Soviet Union regarding the establishment of relations between the two countries.[118] In 1957, a Ceylon Parliamentary delegation visited the Soviet Union.[119] Russian experts were sent to Ceylon to start work on an iron and steel project which was being financed by the Soviet Union.[120] Ceylon accepted two five-year scholarships for Ceylonese students at Moscow University.[121] A cultural agreement was signed between

Ceylon and the Soviet Union to strengthen and develop cultural co-operation between the two countries in the fields of literature, science, education, health, sports, tourism, etc. In furtherance of the agreement on cultural co-operation, a Soviet delegation of experts in arts arrived in Colombo to assist Ceylon in the setting up of a fully-equipped national theatre.[122] On 17 April 1957, an official announcement was made in Warsaw to establish diplomatic relations between Ceylon and Poland.[123]

Friendship and close co-operation that had developed since 1956 between Ceylon and the Socialist countries, particularly Communist China and the Soviet Union, were expanded constantly during Mrs. Sirimavo Bandaranaike's regime. Regarding the admission of Communist China into the United Nations Mrs. Bandaranaike took the same firm stand as that of her husband. At the opening of the Commonwealth Prime Ministers' Conference in 1961, she described the Western strategy of keeping the People's Republic of China out of the UNO as not only "unrealistic but also dangerous". No settlement of world problems could be made without taking China into account. This attitude, she reiterated, was "a very real threat to the possibility of peaceful co-existence between nations".[124] Under the Economic Aid Agreement between Ceylon and China, an agreement was signed on 7 August, 1961 between the two countries for the establishment of a Cotton Spinning and Weaving Mill.[125] On the invitation of the Health Minister of China, a medical team from Ceylon left for China for the purpose of "exchanging experiences between medical workers of the two countries".[126] An Economic Aid Agreement under which China undertook to give Ceylon a grant of Rs. 50,000,000 spread over a period of 5 years was signed between the two countries. The five-year Trade Agreement which expired in 1962 was renewed for another five years.[127] When on a peace mission to Communist China, to try to solve the border dispute between India and China, Mrs. Bandaranaike warned the Asian countries against running "the risk of succumbing once more to the rapacious designs of the West, unless the nations that have newly emerged in Asia and Africa stood together in their struggle". She added : "We in Asia must turn to Asia again and re-establish the close contacts with our neighbours which were denied to us when we were colonies of foreign powers."[128]

In July 1963, a "Maritime Transport Agreement" with the People's Republic of China was signed by Mrs. Bandaranaike.[129] The Government was questioned in Parliament by the Opposition about the necessity of the agreement when Ceylon had already had a "barter agreement and friendship [sic] with China from about 1951" and, after twelve years, was seeking to give China "the most favoured nation treatment".[130] Replying to the critics, Felix Reginald Dias Bandaranaike, the then Minister of Agriculture, Food and Co-operatives and Parliamentary Secretary to the Minister of Defence and External Affairs, justified the agreement on the basis of its being a purely commercial one, dealing with commercial vessels engaged in cargo and passenger services between the two countries or with a third country. 'The most favoured nation treatment' granted to China meant nothing more nor less than what Ceylon would grant to other nations in respect of taxes, dues, and charges on vessels and other customs and quarantine formalities. In the event of war, he assured the House, the terms of the agreement like those of any other would be subject to review depending on the circumstances then prevailing. He also added that a similar agreement was signed with the Government of the USSR on 22 February 1962.[131]

Cultural relationship with Russia was continued by Mrs. Bandaranaike's Government, which sent twelve delegates to the Soviet Union to participate in the Moscow World Youth Festival.[132] With the Soviet Union Ceylon, signed a contract for setting up a State Tyre and Tube Factory in Ceylon with the Soviet Assistance.[133] In October 1963, Mrs. Bandaranaike visited the Soviet Union, Czechoslovakia and Poland, and she agreed to promote further economic and cultural co-operation with these countries.[134]

The new trend in Ceylon's policy towards the Communist countries won for her new friends who could provide economic and technical assistance.

Ceylon's stand on some of the international issues—Suez Dispute, Hungarian Uprising, and Jordan Crisis

SUEZ DISPUTE

While negotiations for the withdrawal of British bases from Ceylon were in progress, the Suez Canal dispute started on 26 July 1956 with the nationalisation of the Suez Canal Company by Egypt. Bandaranaike expressed his concern about the Suez crisis when he described the situation as

> the most serious one single thing that has happened to jeopardize the rather uneasy peace which we are enjoying at the moment in the world, since the end of the last war, in many ways. We are personally concerned because most of our trade, our exports of goods, pass through the Suez Canal, and so do most of the imports we receive from Europe.[135]

From the very outset the Ceylon Government held the view that the question of nationalisation of the Suez Canal was a matter that was within the sovereign jurisdiction of Egypt. This stand of the Government was endorsed by many political parties in Ceylon when they affirmed at a public meeting Egypt's right to claim control over her own territory in the same way that Ceylon was claiming control over foreign bases in the island.[136]

At the London Conference in August 1956, the Ceylonese delegate Sir Claude Corea defended Egyptian action in nationalizing the Suez Canal Company. However, he pointed out that the 1888 Convention guaranteed to the whole world for all time the free use of the waterway—a position which had been accepted and reaffirmed by the Egyptian Government itself. Hence, he supported a compromise solution of the problem that the Suez Canal should be operated by Egypt with the assistance of a consultative international body which Egypt would consult on matters of importance relating to the operation of the canal. If any dispute arose between Egypt and the consultative body, provision could be made for suitable arbitration by the UN.[137]

Meanwhile, a grave situation was created in the Middle East by the invasion of Egypt by Israel followed by the landing of British and French troops in the Egyptian territory. Within the Commonwealth itself, the Prime Ministers of Ceylon, India, and Pakistan and, in the UN, the Afro-Asian Group forthrightly denounced this "recrudescence of imperialism in its most objectionable form".[138] For Ceylon, the new situation posed the question of her bases being used by Britain in a war which was not in Ceylon's interests and was bound to incur the detestations of national sentiment in the island. At a Press Conference the Prime Minister of Ceylon gave the assurance that nothing would be done by his Government to infringe Ceylon's neutrality and added that he had received an assurance in writing from the British Government that bases in Ceylon would not be used in any hostilities connected with the Suez Canal crisis.[139] Both in the Parliament[140] as well as in the UN,[141] Bandaranaike took a clear stand that the invasion of the Egyptian territory by Israeli troops, followed by the Anglo-French action, was unjustified and demanded the immediate withdrawal of military forces as they had no legal or moral right to remain in the territory of Egypt. The Ceylon Government served on the Advisory Committee to help the Secretary-General to form the UN Emergency Force and also contributed to the UNEF.[142] In January 1957, the Ceylon Parliament passed unanimously a sum of Rs. 70,140 as Ceylon's contribution for the clearance of the Suez Canal and the maintenance of UNEF in Egypt.[143]

HUNGARIAN UPRISING

The Ceylon Government was as much upright in the beginning in denouncing the action of Soviet military forces in Hungary as it did in the Suez crisis. At a Press Conference, Bandaranaike declared : "I feel that the steps taken by the Soviet Union in Hungary are to be deplored. Violence whether it be in the Middle East or in Hungary could not solve international problems."[144] All the political parties in Ceylon, with the exception of the Communist Party, expressed similar sentiments on the Hungarian situation. In November 1956 at the Colombo Powers meeting in New Delhi, Ceylon, Burma, Indonesia and India in a joint statement demanded that "the Soviet forces should be withdrawn from Hungary speedily and that the Hungarian people should be left free to decide their own future without any external intervention".[145] At a Press Conference in London, Bandaranaike pointed out the importance of the Asian powers in finding a solution to the Hungarian problem as they could put their views across to Russia without meeting the automatic hostility that greeted the Western Powers' proposals.[146] To Bandaranaike the happenings in Egypt and in Hungary were of great significance for Asians, as they were a manifestation once again of a certain resurgence of the spirit of colonialism, the desire of a strong power to achieve its purposes and to impose its will, even by force, on a weaker power.[147] On his way back from the United Nations, Bandaranaike in London asserted his belief that there was a definite connection between violence in Hungary and the Anglo-French aggression in Egypt. "Had Britain and France not already prepared the climate in which such aggression could be launched against world opinion, Hugary would have been spared the horrors of those tragic weeks."[148]

Although Ceylon deplored and condemned the Hungarian incident throughout, she abstained from all resolutions sponsored by the West on Hungary in the UN. Explaining the reason for absention R. S. S. Gunawardane, Ceylon Ambassador to the USA and Permanent Delegate to the UN, said that his delegation was not prepared to be a party to any campaign of recrimination.[149] The only resolution amongst those sponsored by the West which was supported by Ceylon was the one to support the idea of an investigating committee to collect information by observation in Hungary.[150] Ceylon along with Australia, Denmark, Tunisia and Uruguay served on the Special Investigation Committee set up by the General Assembly resolution (1132 XI) on 10 January 1957 to collect evidence on the situation in Hungary. On 20 February 1957, the Committee submitted an unanimous report spotlighting Russia's intervention in Hungary. But strangely enough, when the report was put to vote in the Assembly, R. S. S. Gunawardane, Ceylon's representative in the UN, abstained from voting on the basis that the Ceylon Government considered the report incomplete owing to lack of assistance from the USSR and Hungarian Governments.[151] Recalling that Ceylon had voted for the earlier General Assembly resolution (1131 XI) of 12 December 1956 condemning the USSR for its actions in Hungary,

Gunawardane stated his Government considered that "no useful purpose will be served by attempting to repeat such a resolution which may not improve the situation but rather tend to aggravate it".[152]

The sudden shift in Ceylon's attitude towards Hungary could be attributed to three factors : (a) Gunawardane, the Ceylon Permanent Representative to the UN became a target of criticism at home both for having accepted the membership of the Special Investigation Committee as well as for signing the report. In early July 1957, a no-confidence motion against Gunawardane was moved by S. D. Bandaranaike at a Government parliamentary group meeting but was withdrawn at the Prime Minister's request.[153] In Parliament on 17 July 1957, Dr. Colvin R. de Silva, a Leftist member, criticised Gunawardane for having made a statement in the course of a talk at the YMCA, Colombo, about the feasibility of Ceylon recognising the leadership of the US in the Free World which went directly against the announced policy of the Government.[154] Pieter Keuneman, another Leftist member, insisted in the Parliament that a person of Ministerial rank should be sent to the UN to speak as the representative of Ceylon Government, as Gunawardane had shown, in theory and in practice, that he was violently opposed to or in disagreement with the fundamentals of the policy adopted by the Government.[155] Gunawardane was also charged with carrying out the policy of the previous Government during whose time he was appointed.[156] (b) The second factor which might have influenced the decision of the Ceylon Government was the effort of the Communist Government's Three-Man Political Mission from Hungary which visited Ceylon in August 1957 and made a strong case to the Ceylon Prime Minister not to vote for the report on Hungary.[157] (c) Lastly, Bandaranaike's personal desire not to prejudice but to maintain friendship with the Soviet Union—a friendship of recent origin—could be considered to be a third factor which influenced him in his decision.

JORDAN CRISIS

In the interests of peace through a general policy of anti-colonialism, anti-imperialism and adherence to the Bandung resolution—an important aspect of which resolution was the non-intervention of one country in the internal affairs of another—Ceylon felt that the UK forces which had entered Jordan, must be withdrawn without delay.[158] The justification of the British Government's action in Jordan on the grounds of Art. 51 of the Charter in conjunction with the two resolutions—"The Essentials of Peace Resolution" and "The Peace through Deeds Resolution"—passed by the UN General Assembly in 1949 and 1950, was not acceptable to the Ceylon Government because, in the name of a right to intervene conferred by the two resolutions "any foreign country might move into another country to bloster up in their interests an unpopular Government against the wishes of the majority of the people of that country."[159] In the UN, Sir Claude Corea, the Permanent Representative of Ceylon in the UN, demanded the complete withdrawal of British forces from Jordan at an early date. Though the withdrawal of those forces in Jordan "could leave an immediate vacuum and create some degree of political instability", the presence of these troops, he added, in Jordan was a potential danger to peace.[160]

In the Jordan crisis where the UK was directly involved, Ceylon took a clear stand in the interest of peace through her general policy of anti-imperialism.

To sum up, a noticeable change in Ceylon-UK relations may be perceived during the period 1956-1965. Strategic 'non-involvement' of Ceylon after the withdrawal of British bases from Ceylon, maintenance of the Commonwealth link, and ideological neutrality were the main features which determined the Ceylon-UK relations during this period.

S. W. R. D. Bandaranaike exercised the right of Ceylon to get the removal of British bases from Ceylon, as their continued occupation was doubly irksome to his Government, on grounds both of nationalist sentiment and of neutralist policy. The elimination of British control of bases not only provided for the affirmation of the declared policy of neutralism but also for the avoidance of all entanglements in foreign alliances of an undesirable kind. With the withdrawal of British bases, Ceylon stood to gain doubly in the sense, that not only did she assert her sovereignty, but she also enjoyed the same advantage as before in the matter of defence as Bandaranaike did not abrogate the defence agreement, still had the option to invoke the agreement as and when she found it necessary. Neither to the UK did the withdrawal of bases prove a loss because (1) the UK secured the right to refuel at Colombo, and also for her aircraft of her forces to overfly and stage through Ceylon according to sub-para 9 of the Treaty Series No. 4 of 1957; (2) the air-staging point in Maldives provided nearly all the services Britain required at a fraction of the cost of the Ceylon bases; and (3) in view of new developments in the evolution of weapons of mass destruction, it was doubtful whether Trincomalee could have the earlier importance as a naval post against the changing background of the strategic picture.

Bandaranaike continued to maintain the Commonwealth link, like his predecessors. But the nature of this link underwent a substantial change. From the constitutional point of view Bandaranaike desired Ceylon to be a republic. Within the Commonwealth, in both political as well as economic matters Ceylon moved away from the UK and closer to the Asian countries. On international issues Ceylon's political alignment with the Commonwealth remained no longer the same. In the Suez dispute Ceylon strongly opposed the policy of her senior Commonwealth partner.

The Suez crisis assumed importance in Ceylon-UK relation for three reasons : (a) Since the new government took over, it was the first international issue in which both Ceylon and the UK were directly involved and in which the new Ceylon Government *vis-a-vis* its positive non-alignment policy was put to test. To Ceylon, support to Egypt was not only a matter of principle but also a defence of her own legitimate national interest. The Ceylon Government's fear should have been that if the precedent was once established that nationalisation even with compensation could be opposed by military force, there was nothing to prevent Britain resorting to the same methods if Ceylon found it necessary to nationalise British estates and other economic assets. (b) The Anglo-French action in Suez led to a serious rift in the Commonwealth. Britain embarked on a policy of provoking war flinging aside the counsels of her fellow Commonwealth members, Ceylon and India. For Ceylon, the membership in the Commonwealth became less meaningful. (c) It also resulted in the consolidation of the Afro-Asian group in the UN.

To Bandaranaike neither the Western capitalist nor the Eastern Communist systems were acceptable or rejectable *in toto*. Politically, he valued the Western idea of democratic freedom while economically he valued the Eastern idea of socialism, and this enabled him to put forward his own programme of democratic socialism. This was his conception of ideological neutrality.

Striving to follow a neutralist policy, Bandaranaike established diplomatic, economic and cultural relations with the communist countries. Differences of ideology need not rule out friendly relations, for mutual benefit was the conviction of Bandaranaike. On some of the international issues in which Britain was directly involved, like the Suez dispute and Jordan crisis, Ceylon was always upright in denouncing British imperialist policy.

During Mrs. Bandaranaike's Premiership, the balance seemed to have consistently tilted against the Western countries, particularly the UK. Much of the legislation passed by Mrs. Bandaranaike Government, for example nationalisation of Life Insurance, and establishment of a State Petroleum Corporation which made the position of the foreign companies virtually untenable, indicated some strain in Ceylon's relationship with the UK as these policies discriminated sharply against foreigners including the British. Mrs. Bandaranaike also tended to be more friendly with China in view of the emergence of that country as an important power in Asia, in spite of its ideology, and also other political developments in the continent. The leftist leanings of Mrs. Bandaranaike, boosted by her left-wing allies in the coalition, moved Ceylon still farther away from the neutralist position as enunciated by S. W. R. D. Bandaranaike to an anti-West policy.

NOTES

1. W. Howard Wriggins, *Ceylon : Dilemmas of a New Nation* (Princeton, 1960), p. 110.

2. A story goes that D. S. Senanayake in the course of a conversation, with the Governor-General Lord Soulbury, in the hospital where he had gone for a medical check up, had expressed his desire that his son Dudley should succeed him in the event of his

death. But it seemed to be 'a great campaign of political mischief' organised by Lord Soulbury who was on leave in England with the connivance of Sir Alan Rose, then Acting Governor-General because D. S. Senanayake was too much of a gentleman to suggest his son as his successor. Moreover, in a statement made in reference to S.W.R.D. Bandaranaike's crossing the floor, he had clearly pointed out that the question of his successor was not a matter for him to decide. Kotelawala, Sir John, *An Asian Prime Minister's Story* (London, 1956), p. 79. This version was confirmed in interviews the author had with ex-officials who expressed a desire to remain anonymous.

3. J. L. Fernando, *Three Prime Ministers of Ceylon* (Colombo, 1963), p. 47.

4. For details see *ibid.*, pp. 39-50.

5. In August 1953, the Prime Minister became worried when in a state of emergency several persons were killed following violent demonstrations during riots against the increase in the subsidized price of rationed rice. Wriggins, *n.* 1, p. 112.

6. Sir John Kotelawala, the Minister of Transport and Works nursed his bitterness being sulky at the cabinet meetings while R. G. Senanayake also a cabinet member constantly embarrassed his cousin Dudley by his political antagonism towards J. R. Jayawardane, the Minister of Finance, on whom Dudley heavily depended. Fernando, *n.* 3, pp. 52-53.

7. Dudley Senanayake, afraid of possible Marxist demonstrations against the Queen during her visit to the island, particularly after the 1953 hartal incident, sent a message to London requesting her to postpone the visit. The message was so timed that Lord Soulbury had already left London for Ceylon. On his return to the island, Lord Soulbury (who was keen on the Queen's visit) found Dudley disagreeing with him on the issue of withdrawal of the message sent to the Queen and hence requested him to resign. He invited Sir John Kotelawala to be the Prime Minister (in spite of his earlier prejudices against him) who agreed to cancel all the messages against the visit. (Revealed in the author's interviews with ex-officials who wished to remain anonymous.)

8. Since the Buddhist revival of 1880s the main grievance of the Buddhists was that the privileged positions that Buddhism had enjoyed under the Sinhalese kings were now denied though they were a majority in the country. An important event which contributed to the growing self-awareness among the Buddhists was the Buddha Jayanti, the celebration of the 2500th anniversary of the Buddha. Buddha Jayanti year had a peculiar Sinhalese significance as the landing of Vijaya the founder of

22. Immediately after her assumption of power, Mrs. Bandaranaike, announcing that her Government would follow the 'definite Centre Party Policies' of her late husband, defined those policies as representing the interests of the rural population of the country. She added : "No Government serving the interests which we do, can be extreme Left or Marxist. Nor are we a Left-Wing Government serving vested interests. It would be correct to describe us a 'Central Party Government'." *The Hindu* (Madras), 30 July 1960.

23. C. P. de Silva, the Leader of the House during Mrs. Bandaranaike's Government and one of the founder-members of the SLFP, first threatened to walk out of the Government if Mrs. Bandaranaike had an alliance with the Left; he eventually crossed the floor with some of his supporters in early December, which resulted in the defeat of Mrs. Bandaranaikes' Left coalition Government. E.F.C. Ludowyk, *The Modern History of Ceylon*, (London, 1966) pp. 264-65.

24. *The Times* (London), 7 April 1956.

25. *Ceylon Daily News*, 10 April 1956.

26. *The Times* (London), 16 April 1956.

27. *Ibid.*, 3 May 1956.

28. Ceylon, *H. R. Deb.*, vol. 24, 1956, cols. 281-2.

29. *The Times* (London), 7 May 1956.

30. *Ibid.*

31. *Ibid.*, 10 October 1957. See also *Ceylon Daily News*, 12 October 1957.

32. *The Times* (London), 4 February 1958.

33. *Daily Telegraph* (London), 23 June 1958.

34. *Ceylon Daily News*, 25 July 1960.

35. Ceylon, *H. R. Deb.*, vol. 19, 1954, col. 437.

36. *Times of Ceylon*, 19 April 1956.

37. S.W.R.D. Bandaranaike, "Ceylon and the Commonwealth", *Asian Review* (London), vol. 52, p. 219.

38. Ceylon, *H. R. Deb.*, vol. 24, 1956, col. 25.

39. *The Times* (London), 26 April 1956.

40. *Ceylon Daily News*, 7 May 1956.

41. *The Times* (London), 10 May 1956.

42. *Ibid.*

43. Ceylon High Commission *Press Release* (London), 18 May 1956.

the race coincided with the death of the Buddha. Wriggins, n. 1, p. 173.

9. The rural middle classes like the Ayurvedic physicians, the Sinhalese school teachers, the Buddhist priests and businessmen in the coastal areas, who resented the privileged role of the English speaking classes, advocated 'Sinhalese only'. *Ibid.*, pp. 337-42.

10. This was marked by a plea for national dress and customs in place of western dress and customs. For details, refer to B.M. "A 'People's Government': Social And Political Trends in Ceylon." *The World Today*, (London), Vol. 12, pp. 285-87.

11. The measures which were declared in the MEP Manifesto were : (a) amendment of the Constitution to establish a Republic, (b) complete withdrawal of British bases to 'steer clear of involvement with power blocs', (c) introduction of Sinhalese as the official language, (d) nationalization of key industries, and (e) removal of the economic discontent created by the withdrawal of rice subsidy. I.D.S. Weerawardane, *Ceylon General Election 1956* (Colombo, 1960), pp. 66-9.

12. The factors were (a) The desire of the electorate for a change in Government as the UNP were to long in power; (b) the no-contest agreement between the SLFP and the Left Wing parties which prevented the splitting of votes against UNP; (c) the influence used by the younger *bhikkhus* in the rural areas against the UNP. Wriggins, *n.* 1, pp. 331-48.

13. *Times of Ceylon* (Colombo), 13 April 1956.

14. Ceylon, *H. R. Deb.*, vol. 14, 1953, col. 509 and 511.

15. *Ceylon Daily News*, (Colombo), 25 May 1956.

16. H. C. Taussig, "Ceylon in the New World," *Eastern World* (London), vol. 11, March 1957, p. 18.

17. Ceylon, *H. R. Deb.*, vol. 28, 1957, col. 1777.

18. Taussig, *n.* 16, p. 18.

19. *Manchester Guardian* (Manchester), 9 January 1958.

20. *Times of Ceylon*, 22 July 1960.

21. Ceylon, *H. R. Deb.*, vol. 39, 1960, col. 51.
It is significant to note that in the statements of Ceylonese official spokesmen, there appears to be a conceptual synonymity in the use of the phrases, 'Neutrality', 'Neutralism' and 'Non-alignment'. For the convenience of the argument and exposition, the interchangable manner in which these words are used, has been retained although the author may not be in agreement with it.

44. *Ceylon Daily News*, 18 May 1956.
45. *Ibid.*, 14 June 1956. Also see *The Times* (London), 14 June 1956.
46. Ceylon, *H. R. Deb.*, vol. 25, 1956, cols. 226-7.
47. *The Times* (London), 14 June 1956.
48. *Ibid.*, 25 June 1956.
49. *Ceylon Daily News*, 29 June 1956.
50. *The Times* (London), 4 July 1956.
51. Britain handed back the Simonston base to South Africa and recognised South African sovereignty over the base while South Africa agreed that Britain could continue to use the base facilities in peace and war. *Ceylon Daily News*, 4 July 1956.
52. *Ibid.*, 8 July 1956.
53. *The Times* (London), 7 July 1956.
54. *Times of Ceylon*, 8 July 1956.
55. *Ibid.*
56. Ceylon, *H. R. Deb.*, vol. 25, 1956, col. 228-9.
57. *The Times* (London), 16 July 1956.
58. Ceylon, *H. R. Deb.*, vol. 27, 1956, col. 426.
59. Exchange of Letters between the Government of Ceylon and the Government of the United Kingdom regarding United Kingdom Service Establishments in Ceylon. Ceylon, *Treaty Series No. 4 of 1957* (Colombo). For the full text see Appendix III.
60. *Ibid.*, p. 1.
61. *Ibid.*
62. Ceylon, *H. R. Deb.*, vol. 28, 1957, col. 1778.
63. S.W.R.D. Bandaranaike, *The Foreign Policy of Ceylon* : Extracts from statements, 3rd edn. (Colombo, 1961), p. 21.
64. B. H. Farmer, "Nine Years of Political and Economic Change in Ceylon", *The World Today*, vol. 21, p. 194.
65. Revealed in an interview with the author.
66. The author interviewed many Ceylonese, both official and non-official.
67. *Ceylon Daily News*, 12 June 1956.
68. Ceylon, *Treaty Series No. 4 of 1957*, p. 2.
69. *Ceylon Daily News*, 16 November 1962.
70. *Ibid.*, 20 November 1962.
71. *Daily Telegraph*, 3 April 1964.

72. *Times of Ceylon*, 19 April 1956.
73. *Ibid.*
74. *Ceylon Daily News*, 19 June 1956.
75. *Ibid.*, 3 July 1956.
76. *Ibid.*
77. *Times of Ceylon*, 12 July 1956.
78. Ceylon, *H. R. Deb.*, vol. 26, 1956, col. 147.
79. *Ibid.*, vol. 27, col. 1061.
80. *Ibid.*, col. 1153.
81. *Ceylon Daily News*, 12 November 1956.
82. Ceylon, *H. R. Deb.*, vol. 33, 1958, col. 198.
83. *Ibid.*
84. Weerawardane, *n.* 11, p. 69.
85. *The Times* (London), 22 July 1958.
86. "Some 593 estates in Ceylon are exclusively foreign-owned and they cover an area of nearly 257,000 acres, little less than half of the total acreage in the island. Nearly four-fifths of the foreign-owned tea in Ceylon belonged to Sterling companies." *Ibid.*, 3 October 1958.
87. *Ibid.*, 19 September 1959.
88. *Times of Ceylon*, 8 November 1957.
89. *The Times* (London), 14 April 1958.
90. Ceylon, *H. R. Deb.*, vol. 30, 1958, col. 4957.
91. *Ibid.*, vol. 39, 1960, col. 56.
92. Illangaratne, the then Finance Minister, was quoted in *Ceylon Observer* to have said that if any Western country was unsympathetic and tried to estrange trade relations because of his 1 August Budget proposals to nationalise all insurance, "I will not hesitate to take swift measures to nationalise all foreign-owned tea-estates." *The Financial Times* (London), 7 August 1963.
93. Ceylon, *H. R. Deb.*, vol. 39, 1960, col. 56.
94. *Ceylon Daily News*, 27 August 1960.
95. Chamber of Commerce of Ceylon, *Annual Report and Accounts* (Colombo), 1964, p. 12.
96. *Ceylon Daily News*, 1 January 1964.
97. *The Times* (London), 2 January 1964.
98. *Ceylon Daily News*, 6 June 1961.

99. *Ibid.*, 19 June 1963.
100. *Daily Telegraph*, 23 November 1964.
101. Ceylon, *H. R. Deb.*, vol. 42, 1961, col. 5135.
102. *The Times* (London), 30 June 1961.
103. *The Times* (London), 2 January 1964.
104. *Times of Ceylon*, 19 April 1956.
105. *Ceylon Daily News*, 28 April 1956.
106. *Ibid.*, 3 May 1956.
107. *The Times* (London), 5 July 1956.
108. *Ceylon Daily News*, 5 July 1956.
109. *The Times* (London), 20 September 1956.
110. *Ibid*, 6 February 1957.
111. *Ceylon Daily News*, 8 February 1957.
112. *Ceylon Today*, vol. 6, October 1957, p. 26.
113. *Ceylon Daily News*, 1 June 1956.
114. *Ibid.*, 3 July 1956.
115. *The Times* (London), 7 September 1956.
116. *Ceylon Daily News*, 14 October 1958.
117. *Ibid.*, 28 March 1959.
118. *The Times* (London), 20 September 1956.
119. *Ceylon Daily News*, 27 April 1957.
120. *The Times* (London), 7 August 1957.
121. *Ceylon Daily News*, 24 September 1957.
122. *Ceylon Today*, vol. 7, September 1958, p. 32.
123. *Times of Ceylon*, 19 April 1957.
124. *Ceylon Daily News*, 10 March 1961.
125. *Ceylon Today*, vol. 10, September 1961, pp. 27-28.
126. *Ibid.*, p. 30.
127. *Ibid.*, vol. 11, November 1962, pp. 28-29.
128. *Ceylon Daily News*, 3 January 1963.
129. According to the Agreement, the contracting parties agreed to permit the vessels flying the national flag of the People's Republic of China and the vessels under Charter to any Ceylonese or Chinese organisations to sail to and from between the ports of Ceylon and the ports of the People's Republic of China and to engage in cargo and passenger services with a third

country. Article 2 provided that Ceylon as one of the contracting parties should give "the most favoured nation treatment" to the vessels of People's China along with their crew in sailing in the territorial waters or in entering, leaving or berthing in the harbours. Article 4 stated that these facilities should be provided irrespective of whether these were state or private properties. Article 9 stated that this Agreement should continue to be effective indefinitely...unless six months notice for termination was given in advance. *Ibid.*, 6 and 16 March 1965.

130. Ceylon, *H. R. Deb.*, vol. 53, 1963, cols. 709 and 880.
131. *Ibid.*, col. 986.
132. *Ceylon Daily News*, 20 July 1961.
133. *Ceylon Today*, vol. 10, October 1961, pp. 29-31.
134. *Ibid.*, vol. 11, November 1963, pp. 4-5.
135. Ceylon, *H. R. Deb.*, vol. 25, 1956, col. 1104.
136. *Ceylon Daily News*, 8 August 1956.
137. James Eayrs, (ed.), *The Commonwealth and Suez* (London, 1964) p. 279.
138. *Ibid.*, p. 195.
139. *The Times* (London), 2 November 1956.
140. Ceylon, *H. R. Deb.*, vol. 27, 1956, col. 794.
141. *Official Records of the General Assembly of the United Nations* (New York) First Emergency Special Session 561st Plenary meeting, 1 November 1956, pp. 4-5.
142. Eayrs, *n.* 137, p. 282.
143. *Ceylon High Commission Press Release* (London), 23 January 1957.
144. *Ceylon Daily News*, 8 November 1956.
145. Ceylon, *H. R. Deb.*, vol. 27, 1956, col. 794.
146. *The Times* (London), 20 November 1956.
147. GAOR, Eleventh Session, 590th Plenary meeting, 22 November 1956, p. 234.
148. *Ceylon Daily News*, 5 December 1956.
149. GAOR, Second Emergency Special Session, 571st Plenary meeting, 9 November, 1956, pp. 70-71.
150. *Ibid.*, Eleventh Session, 663rd Plenary meeting, 9 January 1957.
151. *Ibid.*, 677th Plenary meeting, 13 September 1957, p. 1459.
152. *Ibid.*

153. *The Times* (London), 3 July 1957.
154. Ceylon, *H. R. Deb.*, vol. 29, 1957, col. 1082.
155. *Ibid.*, 1957, col. 161.
156. *Ceylon Daily News*, 31 July 1957.
157. *Ibid.*, 19 August 1957.
158. Ceylon, *H. R. Deb.*, vol. 32, 1958, col. 315.
159. *Ibid.*, col. 314.
160. GAOR, Third Emergency Special Session, 742nd Plenary meeting, 20 August 1958, p. 116.

4
ECONOMIC RELATIONS

The priorities of Ceylon's economic development since independence were largely influenced by her economic history and the economic circumstances obtaining on the eve of independence. These circumstances were basically the product of centuries of foreign domination. The main feature of this domination was the subservient position of Ceylon as the supplier of raw-materials to the advanced industrial nations of the West. This specialisation in the production of primary commodities, though it undoubtedly resulted in some degree of growth of her economy, was not able to generate a process of self-sustained growth. The UNP Government of independent Ceylon was fully aware of her economic problems and her economic dependence on the world in general and the UK in particular. It was this economic dependence on the UK which was expressed by S.W.R.D. Bandaranaike, the then Minister of Health and Local Administration, when he declared immediately after independence that,

> those countries in Asia who had attained political freedom

ECONOMIC RELATIONS

had found that they were called upon to deal with a very difficult task.. it was economic advancement and economic emancipation. Political emancipation, could be obtained overnight. But it was not so easy to secure the economic emancipation of a country. The countries in South East Asia would have to move on from a rudimentary economy...That was not a task, that they could deal with alone. They would have to have the co-operation of other nations—particularly the co-operation of Great Britain. Let not Great Britain think that they had done with this part of the world. The responsibility of Great Britain was greater than ever now.[1]

The colonial economy of Ceylon had been based on plantation agriculture, mainly tea, rubber and coconut. As already mentioned in the first chapter, most of the tea and rubber plantations were mainly owned and managed by British nationals. When Ceylon became independent, the British ceased to make legislative decisions but continued to make significant business decisions as managers, directors and shareholders of plantations, and commercial and financial enterprises. They also continued to derive income from salaries, profits and dividends.[2] Hence, it was natural that Ceylon nationalists, who were eager to achieve national economic independence and control over the island's economy, should seek ways and means for transfer of the ownership of estates from British nationals to the Ceylonese. All these proposals led to Ceylonization of employment, ownership of estates, and commerce and trade.

Ceylonization

Even before the independence of Ceylon, Ceylonization had been introduced as a measure to give exclusive benefits to the Ceylonese in some spheres of economic activity. It was first applied in public services. As early as 1831, the Colebrooke Commission had recommended that,

the public service should be freely open to all classes of persons according to their qualifications; the exclusive principle of the civil service should be relaxed, and means of education held out to the natives whereby they may in time qualify themselves for holding some of the higher appointments.[3]

By 1928, the British Government had agreed to the recruitment of an equal number of Ceylonese and Europeans into the Civil Service.[4] The Donoughmore Commission further elaborated the policy of Ceylonization when it stated :

> The ideal aimed at, is the ultimate staffing of the Ceylon Services by Ceylonese...that with this object in view there should be a progressive increase in the number of posts assigned to Ceylonese candidates, and a corresponding decrease in the number of posts filled by the appointment of candidates from outside Ceylon.[5]

Shortly after the inauguration of the Donoughmore Constitution, as a result of the agitation of the elected representatives of the people that no non-Ceylonese should be appointed to any post in the Government service unless there was no Ceylonese capable of filling it, the Secretary of State accepted the principle in 1932.[6] Thus, a series of resolutions relating to the Ceylonization of public service and the terms and conditions on which non-Ceylonese were thereafter to be appointed were passed in the State Council on 1 March 1933.[7] Ceylonization was further extended to local government service through some ordinances, such as the Land Development Ordinance of 1935, the Fisheries Ordinance of 1940, and the Omnibus Service Licensing Ordinance of 1942.[8] Though, by virtue of the definition of the term 'Ceylonese' in those Ordinances "as a person domiciled in Ceylon and possessing a Ceylon domicile or origin", it was to exclude all non- nationals, it was principally aimed at excluding only Indians and not any other non-nationals including the British.[9] However, there was no question of Ceylonization of employment, ownership of estates, and of trade and commerce during the pre-independence era. These issues assumed importance only after independence in the light of Ceylon's increasing population, growing unemployment and declining standard of living.

With a view to controlling immigration for residence and employment in Ceylon, the Immigrants and Emigrants Act was passed by the Ceylon Parliament in 1948.[10] Prior to 1949 and the enforcement of the Immigrants and Emirgrants Act, there was no effective control over the entry of non-nationals, for residence or employment, into Ceylon. According to the Act, those who were present in Ceylon on the stipulated date *viz.*, 1 November 1949, were permitted to remain in Ceylon for periods in excess of six months. Nevertheless, British subjects who had been ordinarily residents for five years immediately preceding 1 November 1949, were entitled to the issue of Temporary Resident Permits while others received them under the discretionary powers vested in competent authorities.[11] So in the case of British nationals the control could be effective only in respect of new immigrants after the stipulated date, 1 November 1949. Any substantial progress in the advancement of Ceylonization was possible only by refusing residence facilities to those persons whose immigration into Ceylon would have been prejudicial to the interests of Ceylon nationals. As a rule, permission was not given for the recruitment of a new non-national, if such recruitment resulted in an increase in the number of non-nationals in the service of the firm concerned on the stipulated date. Even in the case of replacements, a new recruit from overseas was permitted entry only if he possessed qualifications and experience which were not available in the island for the post. Sometimes a condition was also imposed that a Ceylon national should concurrently be selected and trained for appointment to the post after a given period.

In implementing the measures for Ceylonizing employment a further step was taken in 1954 by the establishment of a close liaison with the Ministry of Labour which advised the Immigration and Emigration Department on individual applications for issue or renewal of permits. Restrictions imposed in this respect on new immigrants took into account the natural desire of foreign investors to entrust the management and control of their investment to their own nationals.[12] It was this policy which was stated in the Senate on 16 February 1954 by Sir Oliver Goonatilleke, the then Finance Minister of Ceylon:

> Our immigration policy will be so shaped as to enable foreign investors to secure residence permits for such of the personnel as would allow them to have a proper

control and management over their investments. We do hope, however, that they will take active steps to train Ceylonese personnel from the very beginning and, eventually, employ the largest possible complement of our nationals consistent, of course, with foreign investors need to retain control over the management of their investments.[13]

Till March 1954, permits issued on the ground of residence were renewed automatically; however, after 1954 automatic renewal of permits was discontinued and all applications were considered on discretionary grounds. Under this system it was possible to plan for the progressive Ceylonization of employment, by permitting the residence of persons whose investments or services were beneficial to the country and by denying residence to those whose activities were prejudicial to the interests of Ceylonization.[14]

The issue of Permanent Residence Permits came more or less to a standstill in 1955.[15] The immigration policy of the Government was tightened by statutory changes brought about by Act No. 16 of 1955 which replaced both the Permanent Residence Permit and Temporary Residence Permit issued by the Department under the provisions of the Immigrants and Emigrants Act of 1948, by Residence Visas.[16]

For further Ceylonization of employment, another step was taken in 1961 when the Temporary Residence Tax Act was enforced from 8 July 1961.[17] From 1962 onwards, new immigrants were not issued residence visas for employment in Ceylon, unless they were technicians or, were replacements of executives or directors in large firms.[18] Businessmen were granted residence visas or permitted renewal of their visas if they had a capital invesment of Rs. 25,000 in Ceylon on March 1958, or a minimum capital of Rs. 10,000 in a partnership with a total capital of Rs. 25,000.[19]

Government's Ceylonization policy had an effect on the ownership of plantations in Ceylon. The uneasiness created by that policy resulted in a steady transfer of ownership of the estates from European to Ceylonese hands, impeded only by restrictions on transfer of funds. In 1947, it was estimated that approximately 80 per cent of the tea estates were either in the hands of European proprietary planters, Sterling companies or Rupee companies operating in Ceylon.[20] But in due course the European proprietary planters slowly disappeared and, in many cases, the companies sold their estates whenever they were uneconomical. In 1953-54, 47 per cent of the acreage under tea was owned by Sterling companies and Europeans, 4 per cent by Indians, 26 per cent by Ceylonese and 12 per cent were in small holdings mostly owned by Ceylonese.[21] Over the years ownership steadily passed hands and, by 1964, 31.40 per cent of the acreage only was owned by Sterling companies, 26.15 per cent by Rupee companies, 2.98 per cent by non-Ceylonese individuals, 22.09 per cent by Ceylonese individuals, 0.19 per cent by the State, 16.17 per cent in small holdings and 1.02 per cent by others.[22] In rubber, the Ceylonese shares were more than they were in the case of tea. As for the acreage under rubber in 1949, 39 per cent was owned by Sterling companies, 3 per cent by the Rupee companies and 58 per cent by the Ceylonese.[23] But in 1964, only 12 per cent was owned by Sterling companies, 13.2 per cent by the Rupee companies, and 74.8 per cent by the Ceylonese.[24]

The Ceylonization policy not only affected the ownership of estates but also the European staff employed in the estates by placing restrictions on the recruitment of Europeans to certain positions. In 1954, an agreement was reached between the then Ceylon Government and the British interests in Ceylon to the effect that the number of Britons occupying managerial and executive posts (between 3000 and 5000 then) be reduced to 500 by 1964. Accordingly, it was estimated that the number of Britons employed in 1962 in the estates came down to less than 500.[25] In pursuance of its policy of Ceylonization, the Ceylon Government decided in 1962 that visas should not be issued to foreigners to hold managerial posts in plantations.[26]

Another important aspect of Ceylonization was the control over commerce and trade of the island. For many years, the import trade of the island had been handled by European, Indian and Ceylonese firms either holding agencies on behalf of overseas manufacturers or importing directly on their account. But the trade in capital goods and chemicals had mostly been in the hands of European firms. The proportion of import trade in "foreign hands" was about 90 per cent of the total.[27] It was in 1949 that the Government took the first step towards a new policy of Ceylonization of trade, aimed at channelling more of the island trade into the hands of the local people. In March 1949, citizen traders were invited to register as 'new comers'. About 2,000 traders responded to this and licenses were issued to them to import certain consumer goods. Imports of numerous consumer items from certain countries like Japan, Germany etc. were reserved for Ceylonese 'new comers'.[28] By the end of 1950, about 60 per cent of the licensed trade within non-dollar sources was reserved for Ceylonese traders. Towards the end of 1951, the policy of Ceylonization was extended further when all imports from Germany and Japan were allocated to Ceylonese traders. This policy of the Government granting only Ceylonese firms or Ceylonese-controlled companies the right to import goods into the island; was criticised by R. C. Bonstead, the then President of the Ceylon Association in London, as 'discriminatory', and 'morally indefensible' and that it was hardly in accordance with "the declaration of the late Prime Minister or present Prime Minister who on his appointment had said that everyone among you, whatever language he speaks, whatever religion he professes, whatever race he belongs to, may live and move on terms of absolute equality".[29] In spite of this criticism the Government made further efforts to increase the share of foreign trade in the hands of Ceylonese nationals and Ceylon registered companies when trade operations with a number of countries were confined almost entirely to the Ceylonese nationals, and trade under an agreement with Yugoslavia signed in July 1953 was done through Ceylonese firms.[30]

From 1957 onwards, more steps were taken to increase Ceylonization of import trade as well as export trade. Following the policy of Ceylonization of the import trade the Government allowed only registered Ceylonese traders to import goods produced or manufactured in Austria, China, Czechoslovakia, Germany, Japan, Poland, USSR and Yugoslavia on General Import Licenses issued by the Import and Export Control Department. Individual Import Licenses were issued to registered Ceylonese traders for the importation of goods produced or manufactured in Albania, Bulgaria, Formosa,

Hungary, Rumania and Spain. Registered Ceylonese traders enjoyed the concession of importing from all sources. The total value of the import trade handled by registered Ceylonese traders increased from 12.7 per cent in 1957 to 16.5 per cent in 1958.[31]

The export trade with Bulgaria, China, Czechoslovakia, Formosa, Poland and Rumania was Ceylonized when export licenses were issued only to registered Ceylonese traders. Exports of Ceylon produce to Albania, Austria, Hungary and the USSR, through the Commissioner of Commodity Purchase who was the sole exporter till then, was discontinued and licenses were issued by the Department of Imports and Exports control to registered Ceylonese traders to export Ceylonese produce to these countries. But the issue of licenses for the exportation of rubber to these countries continued to be made by the Commissioner of Commodity Purchase.[32]

In pursuance of the policy of Ceylonization of trade, even leading British firms in Ceylon, doing import and export business, like Messrs. A. F. Jones & Co. Ltd., were Ceylonised when a change was brought about in the Company's shareholdings and in the appointment of three new Ceylonese directors [33] With a majority of directors and shareholders as Ceylonese in the Company, the firm was entitled to import and export goods which under law were exclusively reserved for Ceylonese firms. Many other big business firms and stores also became more or less Ceylonese owned.

Though only a little change had been effected by the Ceylonization of the trade and commerce of the island, there were difficulties a non-Ceylonese trader had to face in carrying on business in Ceylon. For instance, a pre-requisite apart from shareholding, which needed to be fulfilled by a Ceylonese firm was that 50 per cent of those drawing salaries of over Rs. 500 and 75 per cent of those drawing less, should be Ceylonese.[34]

The UK Investments and Remittances

The progressive Ceylonization policy of the Ceylon Government and the uncertainty which it created in the minds of those who had invested, or were contemplating investing, capital in the island as well as of the British nationals in plantations, firms and business companies led not only to repatriation of significant amounts of British capital from Ceylon but also discouraged further investment in the island. Consequently in 1950, many UK-owned estates were sold at a time when very remunerative prices were being realised for their crops with high profits.[35] Added significance was attached to the sales of the plantations in view of the Double Taxation Agreement between Ceylon and the UK which substantially added to the net profits of British concerns operating in the island.[36] Another factor which impeded foreign investment was the existence of restrictions on the outflow of money from Ceylon. During the first six months of 1951, a sum of Rs. 65,500,000 was remitted to the UK from Ceylon by way of incomes on investment profits on various commercial undertakings, interests and dividends on British capital, and payments for shipping and other forms of transportation as well as insurance.[37] During the same period the island received from the UK only Rs. 8,700,000 as income on the same items.[38] This indicated a clear trend towards the withdrawal of the British capital which formed bulk of the foreign capital invested in the island.

Recognizing fully the important role that foreign capital could and should play in the economic development of the island, and in order to create a suitable climate for the investment of such foreign capital in Ceylon, the Government from time to time publicly reiterated its favourable attitude towards foreign investment. It also assured that remittances abroad of all profits and dividends earned on such capital would be freely permitted and that the Government would not place any impediments on the repatriation of either the capital or the income earned from it. It also assured foreign investors that the proposed Imports and Exports (Control) Bill would not be administered to cause any setback to its avowed policy in regard to foreign investments.[39]

Despite these assurances, the UK capital as interests, dividends, profits and other investment incomes that went out in 1954 was greater by Rs. 7.6 million than it was in 1953.[40] Though greater facilities were promised for foreign investments by the Government in its budget proposals by a relaxation of the restrictions on investors taking profits back to their own countries, the investors' contention was that these new concessions were extended only to new investments and that immovable capital already invested in the island did not enjoy the same advantages as it was subject to exchange control regulations which permitted the remittances of only dividends, taxation charges, and certain administrative expenses [41] In addition to these, uncertainty regarding the policy of investment, employment of foreign personnel etc. undermined the confidence of foreign investors. As the policy bristled with irksome regulations which were "prohibitive" rather than "attractive," a number of foreign investors called off their negotiations with the Ceylon Government after initially offering to invest in the island.[42]

In 1956, the emergence of a socialist government and its pronounced nationalisation programme strengthened the British concern for their already invested capital in Ceylon. Further British investment in Ceylon was hampered by the various economic controls imposed by the Government in response to the pressure exerted by Ceylonese interests to limit the scope of foreign industrial expansion in Ceylon in fields where local capital and technical skills were available.[43] Consequently, the British plantation owners had been more willing to sell their holdings than before. The private remittances and migrants' transfers in 1956 were Rs.7.9 million more than in the previous year. The repatriation of capital by the British investors who had sold out the plantations to the Ceylonese and the transfer of Sterling to London by the Ceylonese who bought shares in London companies with plantations in Ceylon, drained the country's reserves of foreign exchange. Hence to halt the drain on the foreign reserves the Government imposed exchange restrictions on the movement out of Ceylon of the capital of companies incorporated outside Ceylon and the individuals resident outside Ceylon.[44] Moreover, banks in Ceylon were directed not to give loans to the Ceylonese for the purchase of foreign-owned estates.[45] Though British investors who wanted to pull out from Ceylon were not debarred from doing so, they found it more difficult to find buyers for their holdings in Ceylon. This new policy was in sharp contrast to that followed earlier when even agencies set up by the Government actively helped in the replacement of the British by local capital by advancing money for plantation purchases. With this policy Ceylon was faced with a situation in which foreign funds, concurrently invested, tended to be drawn out while new capital was very shy to come in.

The withdrawal of private remittances and migrants' transfers was most marked in the years 1956-58 when the average amount was Rs. 25 million as compared to the average of 18.8 million in 1953-55. With a view to attract more foreign capital investment "in fields which will strengthen the country's economy," the Government not only gave a wide range of concessions to foreign investors by permitting eventual repatriation of capital, including appreciation thereof, and of the remittances of dividends, but also gave assurance that they would not for the next ten years consider the question of nationalizing new private foreign investment in the country.[46] It was not surprising that these assurances did not prove effective, especially in the face of the report issued by Philip Gunawardena, the Minister of Food and Agriculture, outlining in detail his plan to nationalize foreign-owned tea and rubber estates. This atmosphere of uncertainty was enough to depress tea shares in London and to dissuade other potential investors from taking the plunge in Ceylon at that time. It also tended to overemphasize many other minor irritants, such as some of the restrictions on the export of capital and the effects of ill-conceived new tax proposals introduced in that year's budget. With capital then flowing from the UK to the Commonwealth at the rate of some £ 200 million a year,[47] it was noticeable, how little of it did find its way to Ceylon in the past two years. An official estimate put the net inflow of the British capital in 1957 at no more than Rs. 3,400,000 (about £250,000).[48] When British investments alone in Ceylon were worth well over £200 million,[49] this was a remarkably small addition in the course of a full 12 months. The major problems which a potential investor had to consider were lack of confidence, in which was included the security of the employees who naturally wished to be free from anxiety in regard to remittances to his family and dependents outside Ceylon and to provident funds in the UK.

In 1960, following the tightening of exchange control regulations with a view to conserve foreign exchange, non-nationals were permitted to repatriate only a maximum of Rs. 25,000 in a year, and the rest of the assets had to be invested in the island itself.⁵⁰ In 1961, private remittances and migrants' transfers to the UK which amounted to Rs. 17.8 million were the largest amount sent to any country on that account.⁵¹

The exchange control measures which were adopted by the Government in the course of 1961, stopped completely capital remittances of profits, dividends and income belonging to non-residents which were accounted after deductions were made to meet local liabilities. In the case of non-residents, transfers of sale proceeds of assets, whether movable or immovable, were not permitted, but in exceptional cases, on grounds of hardship, remittances up to a maximum of Rs. 10,000 were allowed⁵². While exchange for the maintenance of dependents of non-nationals were allowed upto definite ceilings not exceeding one-third of the gross monthly income, remittances of two-thirds of the gross monthly income were allowed, in the case of temporary residents on short term contracts. Emigrants were not permitted remittances of capital but were allowed their holiday ration if it was available.⁵³

After the formation of a new coalition Government in June 1964, Dr. N. M. Perera, the new Finance Minister in his budget for 1964, for balance of payments reasons, imposed a moratorium on the remittances of dividends, of interest and profits and introduced a series of proposals which were expected to bear heavily on the predominantly British-owned tea industry.⁵⁴ Apart from the uncertainty affecting British investment in Ceylon, these budgetary measures were particularly damaging to the British interests as it brought immediate and severe hardships to those who were living in Britain on pensions or other remittances from Ceylon after many years of service in the island. The particular discriminatory taxation measures included an additional 2nd. per pound export duty on teas shipped for sale in the London tea auctions (mostly teas from estates owned by Sterling companies) and an additional and retrospective tax on 10 per cent of profit of the Sterling companies.⁵⁵ Hardship to British nationals in Ceylon was caused not only by further increases in personal taxation but also by suspension of exchange for leave and by the severe reduction in the overall limit of savings and retirement benefits which a repatriate could take out of Ceylon. Despite many representations from British nationals through the Government, the measures were implemented which resulted in the departure of many British nationals who were employed in tea estates and in commercial firms in Ceylon.

Ceylon and the Sterling Area

The Sterling Area membership in the period before World War II was a 'natural policy' for many countries, who took for granted the advantages of membership and considered the disadvantages as negligible. They had every reason to hold bulk of their foreign exchange reserves in London and use them for international transactions and for maintaining a fixed exchange parity with the Pound Sterling. But in the post-war period, for some countries, especially those which achieved independence, both advantages and disadvantages became significant in the continuance of Sterling Area membership.[56]

Emphasising one of these advantages J. R. Jayawardene, the then Finance Minister, stated that "60 per cent to 70 per cent of our trade, import and export, goes through London, and that this trade, is with the Sterling Area.... The only area we can be in, on the basis of our trade, is the Sterling Area."[57]

Another reason for Ceylon's continuance in the Sterling Area was the fact that her withdrawal from or the further contraction of the currency area would have made it necessary for her to conclude a series of bilateral payments agreements, balancing her trade with all her principal suppliers; there would always have been the restricting factor of having to ensure in advance that payments were received in a currency generally acceptable in world commerce. Moreover, if the world prices of Ceylon's primary products had fallen, and she was without Sterling Area membership, she would have faced economic strangulation. Hence, she had better trading prospects if she remained in the Sterling Area. The Sterling she earned, being one of the two key currencies widely used in international transactions, could be used to buy goods from any country. Moreover, she could enjoy the benefits of the payments agreements existing between the Sterling Area and various other countries. Her immediate future, therefore, was bound up with that of the Sterling Area, and it was clearly not in her interest to disown the monetary system at that time.

To opt out of the Sterling Area would have meant much more than losing the chances of sizeable releases from the blocked balances in the immediate future to wipe out her adverse trade balances.[58] In the event of a withdrawal from the Sterling Area, the UK would have tried to begin with a clean slate by dividing the old balances from any new Sterling that Ceylon would have earned and by guaranteeing only those future earnings in terms of gold or goods.[59] Hence, it was certainly better for Ceylon to stay for a longer period in the Sterling Area so as to derive the advantages of having contributed to its growth in the pre-war years, than to stay only for some years.

Even in the post-independence years, in conformity with the convention of the major monetary areas, the Sterling Area remained as the predominant partner in her trade accounting for over half of the aggregate external trade of Ceylon. Its share of the island's exports and imports in 1964 was 54 per cent and 48 per cent against 26.74 per cent and 26.85 per cent respectively in 1948.[60] Thus it was evident that the traditional markets were yet the best markets for Ceylonese marchandise.

For Ceylon, therefore, remaining in the Sterling Area became an economic and financial compulsion.

Devaluation of 1949 and its implications on Ceylon

In the financial sphere, unlike India which had an independent currency, Ceylon was an 'advanced monetarily-dependent' Sterling Area member which had no Central Bank till September 1950.[61] Therefore, the working of her currency was affected by foreign exchange regulations. Her currency had ties with Sterling as well as the Indian rupee.[62] Hence any change in the fortune of Pound Sterling affected Ceylon and the pattern of her trade because of her membership of the Sterling Area. In September 1949, when the UK devalued the Sterling due to the Sterling-dollar problems, she had to follow suit. A decision not to devalue the Ceylon rupee would have required an amendment of the Ceylon Currency Ordinance making it equivalent to about Rs. 1.20 in Indian money and about 1s. 9d. in Sterling if those currencies were devalued by 20 per cent.[63] But such a course of action could not be justified because her export products—tea, rubber, coconut and its products—would have been handicapped owing to a rise in the prices in her chief markets—the UK and the Sterling Area countries.[64] If Ceylon had kept the parity of her currency unchanged, Ceylonese exports would have become costlier relatively to Indian and other Sterling Area countries' exports, and Ceylon's exports to these countries would have been adversely affected. On the other hand, on the import side she would not have gained because if the sale of the commodities had been on a long-term contract (as in the case of coconuts), the buyers would have made a deduction on account of the high cost of rupee exchange from the price they would have offered to Ceylon. Ceylon's import commodities like food being scarce all the world over, the increased world demand for them would have driven the prices up. As for other commodities, a high exchange value of the rupee would have increased the total value of imports and also decreased the competitive power of whatever industries were being fostered within the country. Thus, on balance the losses sustained by export industries were likely to outweigh the favourable terms on which she obtained her exports. Hence, following the UK and some other Sterling Area countries[65], Ceylon also devalued her rupee by 30.52 per cent in terms of the dollar. The Ceylon rupee for the first time was defined in terms of gold with 2.88 fine grams to the rupee and continued to maintain the Sterling parity of 1s. 6d.[66]

Although devalution resulted in a depreciation of Ceylon's assets accumulated during the war, she could not draw on these assets before devaluation owing to the Sterling Balance Agreement concluded between the Governments of Ceylon and the UK in May 1948. Thus, while Ceylon's assets were mainly in dollar earnings added to the Sterling Area's dollar pool,[67] Ceylon suffered an exchange loss as a result of devaluation, because she was not permitted to keep her surplus earnings in dollar or gold reserves.[68] With the establishment of the Central Bank of Ceylon in 1950, the responsibility of providing dollars for authorised dealers in Ceylon was taken over by the Bank from the Bank of England. Arrangements were also made, after discussions between the two governments, under which Ceylon did not have to surrender to the dollar pool the entire surpluses of dollars earned by her on current account.⁶⁹

Sterling Balance Agreements

The problem of Sterling balances was one of the most outstanding issues to be settled between Ceylon and the UK on the eve of her independence. In fact, the future relationship between the two countries depended a great deal on a fair and satisfactory settlement of this problem.

Underlying the basic framework of the Sterling Area financial network according to which the bulk of foreign exchange reserves of member regions were held in London, Ceylon had accumulated her reserves in London. To these reserve funds were added, during the World War II, surpluses from favourable trade, resulting from Ceylon's increasing trade activities and the enormous expenditure of money with which England financed her war efforts in Ceylon. And thus at the end of the war her sterling balances amounted to Rs. 900 million.⁷⁰ But as Ceylon had an unfavourable balance of trade in the post-war years, Ceylon's Sterling balances came down to Rs. 772 million at the end of 1947.⁷¹ As World War II had left Britain a debtor nation, she found it difficult to pay all her creditors who had the Sterling balances in London. Hence the UK had to enter into agreements regarding the scaling down of the rate of withdrawal with those countries. In comparison to other countries, Ceylon was in a different category altogether for various reasons. First, even in the post-war years Ceylon collaborated in saving dollar and other hard currency exchange in order to assist British Government. This was expressed by Sir Oliver Goonatilleke, the then Minister for Home Affairs, when he said that "in recent times we have made every effort in saving Sterling exchange in our joint interests."⁷² Secondly, British assets in Ceylon belonging to British nationals far exceeded the assets which Ceylon held in London. In spite of this exceptionally strong position of Ceylon in the matter of withdrawal of her Sterling balances, a sense of appreciation of the UK's problems underlined the official statements in Ceylon. Sir Oliver Goonatilleke, before his departure for London for talks on Sterling balances, declared that we shall approach the problem with a full realization of the difficulties of the British Government and Ceylon's short term and immediate Sterling and dollar requirements would be confined to her most essential needs. I am confident an arrangement satisfactory to both parties will be reached.[73]

According to an agreement concluded successfully in London on 30 April 1948 between the representatives of Ceylon and the UK Government, (known as An Exchange of Letters Concerning Ceylon's Sterling Assets and Monetary Co-operation Between The Two Governments), the two Governments agreed that on 1 March 1948 the Sterling assets of Ceylon amounted to £51 million.[74] It was recognized that notwithstanding her holding of Sterling assets, Ceylon was on the balance a debtor to the UK, as the values of investments in Ceylon of the UK nationals exceeded the total of Ceylon's Sterling balances. It was also agreed that any substantial depletion of Ceylon's Sterling assets was not at that time in the interest either of Ceylon or of the UK.[75] Hence, arrangements were made to govern the use of Sterling balances by Ceylon. According to the arrangements, provision was made for the opening by the Ceylon Government of two accounts called No. 1 and No. 2 Accounts—No. 1 Account to be credited with the receipts from current transactions and No. 2 Account to be credited with the existing Sterling assets which could not be withdrawn unilaterally.[76] To No. 1 Account was to be transferred from No. 2 Account a sum of £ 3½ million to cover any deficit in Ceylon's balance of payments up to the end of the year. In addition, £4 million was released as a working balance which could be increased by a further £1 million in the event of any unforeseen substantial rise in the price of essential foodstuffs unbalanced by other sources of income. To the extent that transfers of capital from Ceylon to another scheduled territory and vice versa were permitted under Ceylon's Exchange Control Regulations, such transfers would be debited or credited to accounts other than No. 2 Accounts. Until 31 October 1948 pending the establishment of a Reserve Bank in Ceylon, interest on the Sterling assets would be credited to No. 1 Account. From 1 November 1948, interest would be credited in the first instance, to No. 2 Account and, then transferred at such times as might be agreed on between the two Governments to the No. 1 Account. It was also agreed that Ceylon as a member of the Sterling Area would co-operate with the UK in conserving and strengthening the exchange resources of its members. While maintaining this position, Ceylon had still been able to secure a release of dollars for her essential expenditure because of her large dollar earnings.[77] Nevertheless, Ceylon agreed to make efforts to see that her gross dollar expenditure did not exceed Rs. 100 million during the War[78] as against her estimated dollar earnings of 180 millions in 1948.[79]

Apart from Sterling balances, the agreement emphasised the assistance that Ceylon would receive from the UK to develop her natural resources to facilitate the entry of Ceylon into the International Monetary Fund (IMF) and the International Bank for Reconstruction and Development (IBRD).[80]

This agreement was operative only until 31 December 1948. Though it followed in broad outline, the general pattern of other Sterling Assets Agreements between the UK and other countries, it differed from them because of the UK's recognition of Ceylon's special position by virtue of her heavy food imports, her past contributions to the Sterling Area Dollar Pool, and her relationship with the UK arising from the fact that British investments in Ceylon exceeded Ceylon's total Sterling assets. Again it covered such further subjects as the promotion of economic development, the relationship of Ceylon to such institutions as the IMF and IBRD, and monetary co-operation in general. Moreover, Ceylon's agreement was more advantageous than that with India in view of the fact that while Ceylon was granted the original privilege, formerly enjoyed by the Sterling Area members of converting her earnings into any currency whatsoever, India's right to multilateral convertibility was limited to a certain amount.[81]

The agreement was subjected to criticism in both the countries. In the UK, the principal criticism was on the amount of the current account release. While most of the "austerity-type" Sterling Balance Agreements, concluded by Britain since the advent of the dollar crisis, had provided for a materially lower rate of repayment, the grant of £3½ million for a period of 10 months, which came to 8 per cent of Ceylon's total Sterling balances, was regarded as very generous on the part of the UK.[82] On the contrary, in Ceylon Parliament, the Leftist Opposition charged the Government for having obtained only a meagre amount, which restricted her dollar purchases, and for having tied Ceylon perpetually to the Sterling bloc. J. R. Jayawardene, the then Finance Minister of Ceylon, attempted to allay these apprehensions by categorically stating in the House of Representatives that "Of £51 million, even if we had full control over it, not more than half would be available for current expenditure.... We do not want to use up our reserves. The Government is trying to finance its entire current expenditure from current revenue and utilize such reserves as there are in England and India only for capital development."[83]

The second agreement arrived at on 14 Ferbruary 1949 was an extension of 1948 Agreement for a further period of 6 months with an additional release of £1-3/4 million from No. 2 Account to No. 1 Account. It was also agreed that the two Governments would meet in London before 30 June 1949 for making further agreements.[84] Pending another agreement, this agreement was extended for a further period of three months [85]

A third agreement which was signed in August 1949 provided for the release of a further £7 million to Ceylon from No. 2 Account to No. 1 Account to cover the period from 1 July 1949 to 30 June 1950. An additional £1 million was to be released in the event of an unforeseen substantial rise in the price of essential foodstuffs unbalanced by other sources of income. It was also provided that Ceylon would retain £1 million out of her net dollar earnings in order that the new Reserve Bank of Ceylon, which was in the process of formation, might have an independent reserve of gold and dollars. The UK also recognized Ceylon's right to dispose of freely her own foreign exchange earnings, while Ceylon expressed her intention to contribute her net earnings of dollars and other hard-currency to the central Sterling Area Pool, except for $1 million which she would retain as an independent reserve for the new Reserve Bank of Ceylon.[86]

This agreement received a cool reception in both countries. The aspects that attracted criticism in London were : (a) the increase in the rate of release from the Dominion's blocked Sterling balances and (b) the arrangements for the utilization of part of the country's net dollar earnings for forming a hard currency reserve of her own."[87] Some British commentators described it "as being far too generous to Ceylon, in the context of the very serious economic crisis through which the UK was passing."[88] In Ceylon, the Opposition criticised the Government for having submitted to "economic imperialism" since Ceylon, while contributing Rs. 900 million worth of dollars to the Sterling Area Pool, had been able to draw only a small fraction of that amount for her own pressing needs.[89]

This agreement under which Ceylon was granted approval for her plan to set up a gold reserve of $1 million, only a small segment of her net dollar earnings, could not be regarded as a substantial departure from the principles and practices of the Sterling Area system, because most of the central banks of other countries participating in the system did possess gold reserves of their own.[90] But it is very significant that Ceylon, the only member of the Commonwealth with a dollar surplus expressed her intention to contribute her net earnings, to the central Sterling Area Pool, although the UK had no power to insist on such a contribution to the pool from the member countries. That Ceylon had let her Sterling assets remain undrawn despite her need to finance essential imports for development is partly attributable to the Western-oriented leadership which then controlled the Ceylon Government.

At the expiry of the third agreement on 30 June 1950, the negotiations that followed for another agreement between the two countries reached a deadlock. The UK, though willing to permit Ceylon to retain part of her dollar earnings, was not eager to agree to Ceylon's demands of a much higher release of her Sterling balances and a freer use of her dollar earnings.[91] In the absence of an agreement acceptable to Ceylon the existing agreement was extended for a further period of six months.[92] There seemed to be sufficient justification in Ceylon's demand in view of the fact that Ceylon was a net-dollar-earner contributing more dollars to the Sterling bloc's common pool[93] than she needed to take out of it to organise her national economy. Ceylon was in fact subsidizing other members of the bloc with her dollar exports for which the UK acted as a banker. Under these circumstances Ceylon could create difficulties for the UK if she decided to withdraw from the Sterling bloc and utilize for herself all the dollars she earned. One pertinent question in this context is why Ceylon did not withdraw when there was reluctance on the part of the UK to agree to her demands. It is quite obvious that if Ceylon had taken that step she would have incurred the displeasure of not only the UK but also several other members of the Sterling bloc, and whatever assistance she derived from those member countries would have been denied to her. Such a step would have had very serious repercussions on political and defence matters.

In agreements entered into with the UK prior to 1950, the utilisation of Sterling balances was permitted mainly on an annual basis. Such short term agreements impeded the implementation of a long term economic development programme. Thereafter, with a view to securing an agreement under which Ceylon's expenditure of her Sterling assets should be regulated over a period substantially longer than one year, further negotiations took place in London in December 1950. It was held that such an agreement would accord with the Colombo Plan arrangements for economic development in South East Asia in which the countries concerned would carry out six year development programmes involving some expenditure of their Sterling assets. At the end of this period, Sterling balances would be at a level considered adequate for normal working reserves and the blocking of Sterling within the Sterling Area would be ended.[94]

The advantage of such an arrangement was appreciated by both the Governments. In February 1951, a new agreement was concluded between the two Governments.[95] The new agreement was for 7 years from 1 July 1950 to 30 June 1957 in which Ceylon was given the right to withdraw £ 21 million of its Sterling balances. Transfers to the No. 1 Account within this maximum would be made when the balance in No. 1 Account fell below £12 million, but in one year transfers were limited to £3 million with a provision for flexibility and for consultation. The Government of Ceylon also accepted the UK Government's proposal that a sum of £ 4 million in gold or dollars to be set aside immediately out of the central gold and dollar resources in order to provide the Central Bank with a gold reserve relatively as favourable as the corresponding resources of the Central Banks of other independent members

ECONOMIC RELATIONS

in the Sterling Area Dollar Pool. Ceylon accepted this proposal on the understanding that after experience had been gained with the arrangements which had been made between the Bank of England and the Central Bank of Ceylon regarding dollar cover, there would be, if necessary, further consultation about the disposition of Ceylon's net surplus of dollars on current account.[96]

In 1952, Ceylon receded from the position of a very favourable balance of payments not only with the dollar countries but with all the other non-Sterling area countries as well. The situation was made more difficult when she had to purchase rice and flour from dollar countries. The economic position was modified by another agreement on Ceylon's Sterling balances in September 1952, whereby it was agreed to transfer £9.4 million from Ceylon's No. 2 Account to No. 1 Account of the Central Bank of Ceylon as a currency reserve. The Ceylon Government also agreed not to draw upon that sum without previous consultation with the UK Government.[97]

In all these Sterling balance agreements the underlying factor seems to be that both the UK and Ceylon maintained that it was in the best interests of both to continue the close financial association between them.

Trade with the UK

Since independence, Ceylon's structure of trade with the UK has remained basically unchanged. Ceylon is a large importer of food-stuffs, manufactured goods and machinery etc. and an exporter of primary products. On the contrary, the UK is an exporter of manufactured goods and machinery and importer of raw materials. On the eve of independence in Ceylon's trade—both export and import—the UK was her stable customer as well as her best supplier.

Underlying the changing trend and post-war economic policy, the national government of independent Ceylon was committed to a policy of industrialisation to bring about an overall economic development of the island. In such a context it was of importance for Ceylon to have a steady market for her principal exports and a steady flow of imports of capital equipment and raw materials essential for her industries. Soon after independence, the UK figured as a big source of supply of manufactured goods as well as a stable customer for Ceylon's exports. Hence, after independence the Government was opposed to any change in the normal trade channels and practices. However, to promote rapid industrialisation certain protectionist measures like tariffs, exchange controls,[98] and quotas, were taken and an industrial Products Act was passed by the Government.[99] These measures inevitably entailed cutting back on non-essential imports and protecting important industries that could supply local consumer needs. Till 1955, her foreign trade, both import and export, was confined to Western countries in general and with the UK in particular. The only significant exception was her trade with China following the Rubber-Rice Pact in 1952.[100] By 1955, when the effects of the Government's measures in industrial development and diversification of the economy were beginning to be felt, the pattern of Ceylon's foreign trade, which had existed till then, also underwent a change. Towards the end of 1955, the diversification of trade started when the UNP Government signed Trade and Payments Agreements with Czechoslovakia and Poland which was followed in 1956 by broadly similar agreements with Rumania.

In 1956, when MEP (Mahajana Eksath Peramuna) Government came to power it continued the policy of development of trade while maintaining and expanding the traditional markets. In pursuance of this policy, the Government entered into a large number of bilateral Trade and Payments Agreements with many countries. These agreements were both of a general as well as of a specific nature. They not only provided her with new sources of imports but also new markets for her exports. For instance, at a time when Ceylon's production of the major products like tea and rubber was increasing from year to year as a result of economic development, the consumption of these products had not increased in the traditional markets due to the fact that either a saturation point had been reached in those markets or increasing competitions were faced from synthetics and substitutes. As such, if new markets were not found, it was not unlikely that the increased production would have remained unsaleable or fetched low prices. As a result of the policy of development of trade, the volume of Ceylon's external trade, particularly with the

Socialist nations of Eastern Europe, China, UAR, West Germany and Pakistan, showed upward trends, whereas the trade with traditional customers like the UK, Australia, India, Canada, Japan and USA followed a declining trend. However, the UK remained a predominant supplier and customer of Ceylon.

From the UK, Ceylon's imports of manufactured goods covered a wide variety of capital and consumer goods—manufactured goods of iron and steel, machinery of all classes especially for Ceylon's plantation industries, motor vehicles, cotton and rayon piece goods, electrical equipments and apparatus, drugs, medicines, and other chemical products.[101]

Competition from Japan and European countries was becoming much keener in respect of consumer goods, and the UK prices. were high particularly in regard to textiles constituting Ceylon's second major imports. Despite the competition, the UK's share in Ceylon's import increased from 17.25 per cent in 1948 to 22.42 per cent in 1952.[102] In 1953, the level was virtually maintained with a share of 22.34 per cent, although the value of supplies fell by Rs. 22.6 million. It was, in fact, encouraging in view of the threat of increased competition from European countries and Japan. The lower import values were spread over a wide range of class of imports. In the food and drink and raw materials group, where the UK's interest was relatively minor, Ceylon's purchase of cheaper refined sugar from Australia and British, West Indies meant a lower level of exports from the UK. A fall in imports of petroleum from the UK was due to the loss of the bunkering oil market to Italy, whose share increased from the earlier 8.2 million gallons to 44.7 million gallons in 1953. On the other hand, the loss of trade in these commodities was largely affected by a substantial increase in supplies of ammonium sulphate from the UK at the expense of the Netherlands and Belgium. As regards manufactured goods, the value of imports of machinery and vehicles from the UK fell by Rs. 13 million as compared to 1952. This was partly due to the lower unit price as in the case of motor cars, and partly due to reduced total imports as in the case of commercial vehicles. Among other manufactured articles, the fall in the imports of cement was due to her own cement output, and partly due to the successful competition from Japan which increased her supplies from 14,000 billion, to 34,000 billion.

In 1954, there was a fall in the share as well as value of imports which was due to the fall in prices and volume. There was a substantial decrease in the value of imports of sugar, textiles, mechinery and motor vehicles. In the next two years there was an increase in Ceylon's imports from the UK, both in volume and value, despite increased competition from several other countries. In 1955, Japan was one of the UK's main competitors, particularly in textiles, and in 1956 there were the Soviet bloc countries which also became exporters to Ceylon as a result of various bilateral Trade and Payments Agreements concluded towards the end of 1955 and 1956. The total value of goods supplied by the Soviet Union, Poland, Czechoslovakia, East Germany, Hungary, Rumania and Bulgaria was in the aggregate of Rs. 7.6 million (less than 0.5 per cent of Ceylon's total imports) in 1956 compared to Rs. 7.7 million in 1955. Notwithstanding the shipping difficulties owing to the closure of the Suez Canal, shipments of manufactured goods from the UK increased both by quantity and value. In some goods like iron and steel, hoop and strip, plates and sheets, chassis with engines, bicycles, electric cables, engines and electricity generating plants, the UK exclusively enjoyed Ceylon's larger purchases.[103] Substantial increases were also recorded in the UK supplies of cement, iron and steel tubes, paper and fittings, cars, sewing machines and rubber tyres. Notable items in which the UK shipments fell in 1956 were insecticides and fungicides, and iron and steel structures.[104]

In 1957, though there was a rise in the value of imports, largely in the raw materials and manufactured goods and an increase in the volume of petroleum products, fertilisers, machinery and cement, the UK,s share of Ceylon's imports fell by 1 per cent. This was mainly due to the competition from the new markets with whom Ceylon did not have a significant volume of trade till then. In 1958, there was an increase by nearly 4 per cent because of an increase in the imports of consumer goods. But the percentage share of China in the value of Ceylon's total imports also doubled to 8.8 per cent. This was owing to an increase in a wide range of other imports.

besides rice. textiles, cement electrical goods, iron and steel, and machinery.[105] In 1959, though the percentage of imports to Ceylon from the UK remained more or less the same, the value of imports increased due to a rise in prices and freight rates (by 38 per cent) in the shipping lines in Britain and the Continent because of the slow rate of discharge of cargo.[106]

The swift rise in the UK's share of Ceylon's import which started in 1958 was arrested in 1960. From 1960 to 1963 there was a downward trend in the UK's share of Ceylon's percentage as well as value of imports. The value of imports from the UK which had risen continuously since 1954 fell in 1960.[107] This was due to the imposition of stringent tariffs by the Government in the third quarter of 1960 in order to arrest the fall of foreign exchange reserves resulting from a heavy volume of imports. In 1961, the import pattern underwent a drastic change as a result of stringent import controls affecting a wide range of consumer goods. Imports of intermediate and investment goods also fell to a level lower than in 1959 or 1960.[108] Imports from the UK fell from Rs. 433.6 million in 1960 to Rs. 361.8 million in 1961. The sharp drop was due to a fall of Rs. 35 million in the value of vehicles imported, and Rs. 6 million in the value of fertilizers.[109]

Due to a further intensification of import restrictions in 1962, because of the continuing balance of payments difficulties and the unsatisfactory position of external reserves, the UK's share as well as value of imports showed a further decline in 1962. In contrast, imports from the USSR expanded sharply by Rs. 24. 5 million, which was mainly due to the import for the first time of petroleum products to the value of Rs. 14 6 million.[110] A further intensification of import restrictions in 1963, which caused a decline of Ceylon's total imports by Rs. 160 million or 9.6 per cent, also brought about further fall in Ceylon's imports from the UK. In 1964, Ceylon's imports from the UK showed a sharp decline by nearly 4 per cent though they showed an increase in value by Rs. 20.9 million. This was basically the result of an increase in volume as well as value of total imports, notwithstanding the operation of stringent import licensing control.

Ceylon's exports to the UK were accounted for largely by tea, latex rubber, and coconut products and small quantities of other products of leather, graphite, kapok, papain, citronella oil and spices. In the first two years of Ceylon's independence, 1948—1950, Ceylon's exports to the UK showed an upward trend both in the percentage and value of exports.[111] In 1950, while there was an increase in the value and total quantity of goods exported from Ceylon, there was a steep decline in UK's share of Ceylon's exports by about 8 per cent with a slight increase in value. The decline could be attributed to the fall in the quantity of tea exported to the UK from 40.5 per cent in 1949 to 32.2 per cent in 1950.[112] In 1961, Ceylon's exports to the UK showed a steep rise both in quantity as well as value. While the large rise in export value, reaching a record total of Rs. 585.2 million was due to a steep rise in prices of export goods because of the Korean War, the rise in quantity was due to the increase in export of tea with the resumption of London Auctions in 1951 after a long interval of 12 years. The next two years showed a deterioration, both in quantity as well as value, of Ceylon's exports to the UK. This could be attributed partly to lower prices and also to the competition in her rubber markets. China which imported virtually nothing from Ceylon prior to 1951, became her second most important customer as a result of her trade agreements with Ceylon. The greatest part of Ceylon's exports to China in 1953 were accounted for by sheet-rubber worth Rs. 230 million out of a total export of Rs. 242 million, and 80 million lbs. of crepe-rubber for which the UK was by far her best customer taking 25 million lbs.[113] The year 1954 showed an increase both in quantity and value of Ceylon's exports to the UK. This was mainly as a result of an increase by 3 per cent in the value of total tea exports from 35 per cent in 1953 to 38 per cent in 1954. China, which was the new customer for Ceylon's rubber and coconut oil recorded a fall in her imports from Ceylon, mainly because the average price of rubber to China was 4 per cent lower than in 1953. In 1955, the increase in the value of exports to the UK was accounted for by an increase in the price of tea (which was the highest) while the decline of quantum of exports was due to the less quantity of tea exported.

In 1956, the quantity of tea exported to the UK increased by 30 per cent more than it was in 1955 but the value fell due to a fall in the price of tea. In 1957 increased shipments of tea rose to 40 per cent and caused a record rise in exports to the UK. From 1959 the percentage of Ceylon's exports to the UK remained more or less the same with slight fluctuations from year to year. The fluctuations in value can be attributed to the price variations of the three major commodities to the UK—tea, rubber and coconut products.

But the trend of Ceylon's export trade reveals that, since 1960, shipments to the European Economic Community and the Commonwealth have been declining while the share of Eastern European countries has been steadily increasing. The percentage of total domestic exports shipped to Eastern European countries, including the Soviet Union has increased, without a break, from 0.1 in 1956 to 3.3 in 1960 and 8.7 in 1964. The pattern is much the same for imports from Eastern Europe as could be expected from the bilateral nature of this trade which rose from 0.5 per cent in 1956 to 8 per cent of the total imports in 1964.[114]

The most noteworthy feature of Ceylon's trade with the UK is the continuous favourable balance of trade, with the exception of the year 1959, though large changes in exports and imports of Ceylon have resulted in wide fluctuations in the balance of trade.[115] Her exports fetched higher prices and imports cost less over the years, and the terms of trade were generally favourable. The volume of Ceylon's total exports increased because of the economic development which boosted up her production of export products; and the volume of imports, especially in consumer goods, increased correspondingly with the population growth. The UK has shared proportionately in the increase of trade; the Ceylon-UK trade, however, took a bad turn in 1959 when it showed a deficit of Rs. 15 million, the only recorded unfavourable balance since independence. The strict policy of import control introduced by the Government restored the favourable balance of trade in 1960. The continuance of the import policy under individual import licensing by which imports were either banned or restricted lowered the UK's share in Ceylon's imports gradually. Consequently, it resulted in a further increase in the favourable balance of trade though there was no notable increase in UK's share of Ceylon's exports during 1960—1964 period.

The UK is still by far Ceylon's most important customer as well as supplier, but trade between the two countries is declining to the advantage of other Commonwealth countries, China, the USSR and Eastern Europe, and the European Economic Community mainly because of the competition from these countries.

Trade Agreements

At the time of independence. Ceylon's trade with the UK had been guided by the Ottawa Agreement of 1932 signed between the Empire countries by which mutual preference was granted for the imports of goods from one another. This Imperial preference was continued even in the post-independence period. Besides this, the system of bulk purchase contracts, started by the UK Food Minister in the post-war years with a view to stabilize the market for commodities, was also continued by Ceylon. These bulk purchase contracts were concluded in two principal export commodities from Ceylon to the UK—tea and coconut products. Under these contracts, the producers and planters in Ceylon enjoyed some security from the price fluctuations of a free market. But the significant part of these contracts was that they stipulated only one side of a trade bargain, *i.e.* they dealt with only the exports of a certain quantum of commodities from Ceylon to the UK. These contracts were renewed either annually or every alternative year, as the case was, and prices were also agreed upon.

The first contract in coconut products that was signed after independence was the Ceylon Copra Agreement between the two Governments for the purchase of copra and coconut oil from Ceylon which became effective from 1 July 1948 to 31 December 1950.[116] This agreement provided that any quantity taken by the UK during the period from 1 July to 13 December 1948 should be at the price of £50 per ton of copra f.o.b. Ceylon ports. The price for a minimum quantity of 40,000 tons of oil in 1949 was based on a price of £55 per ton of copra, f.o.b. Ceylon ports. It was also agreed that, towards the end of 1949 negotiations would start for a long term contract (possibly for 5 years) including the year 1950.[117]

In December 1949, negotiations for a new copra contract between the British Food Ministry and the Ceylon Government broke down as Ceylon asked for a higher price than the British Food Ministry's officials were willing to recommend.[118] Meanwhile, Ceylon decided to liberate her entire trade in coconut oil and copra, as prices agreed upon by bulk purchase contracts did not keep pace with the world prices. In the free market Ceylon got £110 per ton for copra, while Britain paid £55.[119] After devaluation, free Sterling prices of oils and oil seeds moved up sharply even though they had previously benefited by an exceptionally high premium over similar dollar material. Moreover, as certain "hard currency" countries were taking steps to help the movement of their exports of oils and seeds, the then existing Sterling prices were vulnerable. Under these circumstances Ceylon decided to liberate her entire export trade in copra and coconut oil by not renewing the UK contract. Since the termination of the contract with the UK Government, Ceylon's coconut oil became freely exportable to any country willing to pay the best price.

In tea also, the system of bulk purchase was continued. Under this system the quantity and price of tea exported to the UK was negotiated annually on a one-year contract with the UK Ministry of Food. But this bulk purchase contract system was discontinued in April 1951 when free London tea auctions, were resumed[120] at the continued request of planters and producers in Ceylon as they could enjoy an open market in London.

Notwithstanding the absence of any formal trade agreements between the two countries, and a series of Trade and Payments Agreements which Ceylon entered into with other foreign countries with the object of creating new markets for general expansion and diversification of her international trade, the trade between Ceylon and the UK expanded over the post-independence years.

Economic assistance from the UK

Economic assistance to developing countries, which became independent after the World War II, was not contemplated by the UK except as an emergency measure to be used in special circumstances only.[121] Although India, Pakistan and Ceylon became independent in 1947-48, the custom of giving a 'golden handshake' to newly independent Commonwealth countries was not established by the UK for another dozen years[122] due to financial difficulties she herself was facing after the World War II. In the case of these countries, their substantial Sterling balances accumulated during the war seemed to have effectively disqualified them from help at this stage. But economic assistance to overseas governments was provided in 1949 by the Export Guarantees Act of 1949 by which the Board of Trade was empowered to make loans to overseas governments. But in the case of Ceylon, this Act did not become an important channel of aid until 1958 because the British Government had given virtually no bilateral aid to the independent developing countries of the Commonwealth. Besides this, the independent countries, in common with the dependent territories, were granted access to the London Market to raise loans.[123] In 1954, at the meeting of the Commonwealth Finance Ministers in Sydney, the UK announced that the Commonwealth Governments could borrow money on the London Market not only for specific projects but also in support of general programmes of development. Accordingly, Ceylon successfully floated a loan of £5 million in March 1954.[124]

Economic assistance under the Colombo Plan

In 1950, improvement in the economic conditions of South and South East Asia assumed importance after the Communists' take over in China took place. The vital importance of economic welfare in the maintenance of political stability of the countries of the two areas in question was one of the primary themes of discussions in the Foreign Ministers' Conference at Colombo in January 1950.[125] The trend in this line was set up by D. S. Senanayake, the then Prime Minister of Ceylon, who declared : "The fundamental problem of Asia is economic and not political, and it is necessary for world peace that positive steps should be taken to tackle Asian poverty and improve the standard of living."[126] The urgency and realization of such a programme was emphasized by Hugh Gaitskell, Britain's Minister for External Affairs, at the Second Commonwealth Consultative Committee meeting in London,[127] when he exhorted the participants to address themselves to their task "in a spirit of realism and urgency" and to play their full part "in translating ideas and plans as swiftly as possible into solid achievements."[128] So, in July 1951, the Colombo Plan became operative with both political and economic objectives as it was widely recognized that economic development was closely related to the social and political stability of the two areas.[129]

Against this background it was natural for the UK to provide economic assistance to independent countries of South and South East Asia. The UK's contribution to Ceylon under the Colombo Plan has taken two forms—release of Sterling, and technical assistance.

Release of Sterling

In accordance with the agreement concluded in 1950-51 with Ceylon, provision was made for a release of £19 million from Sterling balances to finance development during the six years of the Plan. By the end of the period it was expected that the balances would be reduced to the level of reserves which Ceylon would wish to hold for the protection of her external financial position.[130]

Technical Assistance

Technical assistance from the UK under the Colombo Plan has been given to Ceylon in three forms—(a) by providing training places in the UK, (b) providing experts, and (c) by the supply of equipment for research and training. From July 1951 to June 1956, the UK provided training in Britain for 332 Ceylonese technicians and financed the provision of 81 experts in a variety of fields.[131] These experts studied local conditions in close association with the Ceylonese officials, and their advice was available to the Ceylonese Government in planning new undertakings. Acting in co-operation with the UK, the UK Territories in South East Asia accepted trainees from Ceylon in rural broadcasting.[132] This process of technical aid was of value in the further development of the country. The grants were mainly in the form of laboratory equipment for the University of Ceylon, medical equipment for the Health Department, and books and equipment for the Education Department.

From 1950 to 1956, Britain gifted to Ceylon equipments and materials to the value of £76,698.[133]

Despite a socialist government in power, Ceylon received more economic assistance—both capital and technical—from the UK during 1956—65 than she received in the pre-1956 period from the UK; more training places and equipments were provided during this period.[134] Since the inauguration of the Colombo Plan till 1958, the UK provided only technical assistance for all developing countries in the South and South East Asia, including Ceylon. The Commonwealth Economic Conference at Montreal in 1958 marked a turning point in the UK's aid-policy. This was because of the important changes that were taking place in the Commonwealth countries at that time. Since 1957, some of Britain's colonies, which had either become independent or were about to become independent, had been unable to find resources for their economic development. Moreover, as India and Pakistan had already exhausted their Sterling balances, they had reached a situation of economic crisis and their development plans were endangered without further economic aid. Faced with this situation the importance of helping them was recognised at the Montreal Conference when the intention of the UK to introduce a new policy of Commonwealth Assistance Loans under the 1949 Export Guarantees Act was announced.[135] These loans were given to enable recipient governments to place orders for capital equipment from Britain and for projects or purposes to be agreed with them after the conclusion of the loan agreements.[136]

In pursuance of this, the Government of the UK made available to the Ceylon Government a loan up to a maximum of £2,500,000 (Rs. 33.3 million) for the purchase of telecommunication equipment from Britain.[137] The loan was repayable in 5 annual instalments from the date of drawing and was subject to interest at a rate of 1/4th per cent more than the rates applicable to loans on comparative terms granted from the Consolidated Fund of Britain under Sec. 3(2) of the Export Guarantee Act, 1949. The loan was utilised for making payments in Sterling to the manufacturers in Britain for the supply of telecommunication equipment, and for the provision of services in connection with the Greater Colombo Area Telephone Development Scheme. The prices charged to the Government of Ceylon for these supplies and services would be the same as those charged for identical supplies to the British Post Office under the Bulk Supply Agreement, with a permissible addition for packing for overseas shipment. The Loan Agreement and the subsidiary agreements were signed in 1960 and 1961 respectively. The total drawings on this loan up to 30 June 1963 amounted to £1,625,000.[138]

This loan from the UK, like loans from Socialist countries, were 'tied' to secure goods and services from the UK, though they differed in the rate of interest and the repayment period.

Britain offered additional equipment worth of Rs. 4.2 million for the University of Ceylon and the Second Medical School at Paradeniya, which was exclusive of a loan of Rs. 33.3 million out of which Rs. 6.8 million were to be spent in 1963 in financing the foreign costs of the Greater Colombo Telecommunication Development.[139]

To sum up, Ceylon's economic relations with the UK remained basically unchanged during the period 1948—65. Successive Governments in Ceylon, irrespective of their ideological differences, were fully aware of the island's economic problems and her economic dependence on world markets in general and the UK in particular. It was with a view to achieve economic independence, certain measures such as Ceylonization of employment, of ownership of plantations, and of trade and commerce besides the diversification of trade, and the industrialisation, were adopted by the UNP Governments.

The Socialist Governments, under the two Bandaranaikes continued the economic policies laid down by the UNP Governments. The Socialist Governments, though they were great advocates of nationalisation of all big industries, postponed for a decade nationalisation of tea and rubber plantations in which many British nationals and British capital were involved, lest it should result in the withdrawal of British capital and discouragement of new investment from the UK. Though, under the Bandaranaike Government, Ceylon's periphery of friends whom she could depend on for trade and technical assistance was enlarged, she retained her traditional friend, the UK, in all those spheres. So, the policy of the Bandaranaike Governments on commercial relations with the UK was in contrast to their policy in political relations which brought about a break-through by the removal of basis from the island.

As far as Ceylon's economic relations with the UK were concerned, all the Governments in Ceylon were pragmatic irrespective of their ideological differences. The value of Sterling Area membership and other economic advantages accruing from the Commonwealth in general and the UK in particular were recognised by all of them. This was because of their awareness of the island's economic problems and slow pace of economic development they achieved over the years. Though considerable increase in production, particulary rice, was achieved during this period, this was negated by the rapid expansion of population. As far as the industrial development was concerned, it did not progress as it should have due to lack of capital and technical skill for which she had to depend on foreign countries. Hence, as long as she had to depend on other countries for manufactured goods and other essentials she had to have the wherewithal for financing such imports. Ceylon was primarily dependent on her plantation products, particularly tea. It was here that Ceylon's economic relations with the UK assumed importance. It is not only that the UK was Ceylon's best customer for tea, but also much UK investment and many UK nationals were involved in her tea plantations.

NOTES

1. *Ceylon Daily News* (Colombo), 14 February 1948.
2. Henry M. Oliver, Jr., *Economic Opinion and Policy in Ceylon* (London, 1957), p. 21.
3. S. Namasivayam, *The Legislatures of Ceylon* (London, 1950), p. 93.
4. *Ibid.*, pp. 93-94.
5. *Cmd.*, 3131 (London), 1928, p. 137.
6. Sessional Paper (London), 23 of 1933, p. 4.
7. Ceylon, *S. C. Deb.*, vol. I, 1933, pp. 432-3.
8. For details refer S. U. Kodikara, *Indo-Ceylon Relations since Independence* (Colombo, 1965), pp. 91-2.

9. Already in the Donoughmore period Indians' rights in other spheres of economic activity were being limited by legislative enactments bestowing preference on the 'Ceylonese'. *Ibid.*, p. 91.
10. Ceylon, *H. R. Deb.*, vol. 4, 1948, col. 4003.
11. *Administration Report of the Controller of Immigration and Emigration,* 1949-50 (Colombo), p. cc4.
12. *Ibid.*, 1954, p. cc4.
13. Ceylon, *S. Deb.*, vol. 7, 1954, col. 1042.
14. *Administration Report of the Controller of Immigration and Emigration 1953,* p. cc4.
15. *Ibid.*, 1955, p. cc3.
16. *Ibid.*, 1956, p. cc5.
17. *Ibid.*, 1961-62, p. 13.
18. *Ibid.*, 1962-63, p. 12.
19. *Ibid.*
20. C. E. Thorogood, *Overseas Economic Surveys of Ceylon* (London, 1954), p. 33.
21. *Administration Report of the Tea Controller,* 1954 (Colombo).
22. *Ibid.*, 1965.
23. *Administration Report of the Rubber Controller, 1949,* (Colombo).
24. *Ibid.*, 1964.
25. *The Financial Times* (London), 12 September 1962.
26. *Ibid.*
27. *Board of Trade Journal,* (London), March 1952, p. 556.
28. IBRD, *The Economic Development of Ceylon* (London, 1953), p. 149.
29. *The Times* (London), 25 April 1952.
30. United Nations Department of Economic Affairs, *Economic Survey of Asia and Far East, 1953* (Bangkok, 1954), p. 42.
31. *Sri Lanka Annual Progress Report, 1958,* (Colombo), p. 47.
32. *Ibid.*
33. *Ceylon Daily News,* 2 August 1958.
34. *Ibid.*
35. *Ibid.*, 14 November 1950.
36. A Double Taxation Agreement between the UK and Ceylon, which was signed on 26 July 1950, provided for the avoidance of double taxation on income and profits. *State Papers 156,* 1950

(London, 1959), p. 351. The Agreement remained in force till April 1965 when it ceased to have effect as a result of termination by the Government of Ceylon. *Board of Trade Journal* (London), 31 July 1964, p. 239.

37. Out of this amount, Rs. 25,600,000 was in lieu of transportation and insurance, and the balance Rs. 39,900,000 represented investment incomes, interests and dividends. *Ceylon Daily News*, 31 December 1951.

38. Out of the Island's receipts, from the UK Rs. 5,000,000 represented the income from transportation and insurance, and the rest incomes on investment, interests and dividends. *Ibid.*

39. *Ibid.*, 23 November 1954.

40. For details of Repatriation of UK capital from Ceylon see Appendix IV.

41. *The Times* (London), 21 October 1955.

42. *Ceylon Daily News*, 3 November 1955.

43. *Ibid.*, 12 December 1955.

44. Central Bank of Ceylon, *Annual Report, 1957* (Colombo), p. 17.

45. *The Times* (London), 4 November 1957.

46. *Ceylon Daily News*, 22 May 1958.

47. *The Times* (London), 1 October 1958.

48. *Ibid.*

49. *Ibid.*

50. *Ceylon Daily News*, 19 October 1960.

51. For several years in the past, private remittances and migrants transfers to India and Pakistan used to top the list, but in 1961 remittances to the UK exceeded those to India and Pakistan. *Ibid.*, 2 June 1962.

52. *Ceylon Today*, vol. 11, August 1962, pp. 3-4.

53. The holiday ration was allowed only once in 7 years. The maximum amount permitted was £150 per adult. *Ibid,*, pp. 3-4.

54. *The Financial Times*, (London), 11 September 1964.

55. *Ibid.*, 8 October 1964.

56. 'Advantages' in these cases were largely considerations which were taken for granted in the 1930's and, in relation to the post-war period were perhaps thought of as disadvantages of various alternatives. P. W. Bell, *The Sterling Area of the Post-war world* (London, 1956) pp. 18-19.

57. Ceylon, *H. R. Deb.*, vol. 3, 1948, col. 994.

ECONOMIC RELATIONS 141

58. At the end of World War II, Ceylon had an unfavourable balance of trade as her exports were down in price and the price of imports increased. This resulted in the Government drawing upon her Sterling assets for her unfavourable trade payments. J.R. Jayawardene, "Ceylon's Sterling Assets", *The Ceylon Trade Journal* (Colombo), vol. 13. p. 129.

59. *The Eartern Economist* (New Delhi), 2 July 1948, p. 5.

60. Bell, *n*. 56, p. 146.

61. *Ibid.*, p. 13.

62. Until September 1949, Ceylon had an Indian rupee exchange standard. Following the devaluation of the Sterling on 19 September 1949, the Ceylon Parliament enacted into Law the Currency Amendment Act, No. 40 of 1949, providing for valuation of the Ceylon rupee in terms of gold at par with Indian rupee and Sterling yet independent from any formal link with either of them. *Ibid.*

63. *Ceylon Daily News*, 19 September 1949.

64. Three quarters of Ceylon tea and half of her rubber and coconut products were taken by these countries. *Ibid.*

65. 11 countries joined the UK in immediate devaluation—Norway, Denmark, Sweden, India, Australia, South Africa, New Zealand, Ceylon, Israel, Eire and Egypt.

66. A. D. V. de S. Indraratna, *The Ceylon Economy* (Colombo, 1966), p. 81.

67. From Ceylon's exports of rubber and coconut oil to the USA during the war, she earned a steady surplus of dollars credited to the Sterling Area's dollar pool; they obtained Sterling in exchange. Elaine Gunawardene, *External Trade and the Economic Structure of Ceylon 1900-55* (Colombo, 1965), p. 171.

68. *Administration Report of the Controller of Exchange 1949*, (Colombo), p. 4.

69. Gunawardene, *n*. 67, p. 171.

70. During the war, the funds which Britain required for her military expenditure in Ceylon she secured by making use of Ceylon's monetary status to put into circulation new rupees equivalent to the amount in pound Sterling guaranteed by IOU's (signed document acknowledging debt in the favour of IOU, 'I owe you') lodged with the Bank of England. Jayawardene, *n*. 58, pp. 129-30.

71. *Ibid.*

72. *Ceylon Daily News*, 19 March 1948.

73. *Ibid.*

74. Of the £51 million, £7.4 million represented loans to the UK which

Ceylon could not draw at once; £19.6 million represented Crown Agents funds which could not be touched until her currency law was amended and her Reserve Bank came into operation; £5 million represented Banking funds which Ceylon could withdraw; £14 million represented non-banking funds, a portion of which could be withdrawn; £5 million represented commercial banking funds which Ceylon had no right to touch. Hence out of £19 million were witdrawable by Ceylon, Ceylon, *H. R. Deb.*, vol. 3, 1948, col. 992.

75. *The Financial Times* (London), 19 May 1948.
76. Ceylon, *H. R. Deb.*, vol. 3, 1948, col. 175.
77. *Ibid.*, cols, 175-6.
78. This figure was demanded by the Ceylon delegation as being the amount needed for both public and private expenditure in dollars for 1948. *Ibid.*, cd. 176.
79. *The Times* (London), 19 May 1948.
80. Ceylon, *H. R. Deb.*, vol. 3, 1948, col. 175.
81. Under India's agreement of 1947 with the UK, the whole of her Sterling in Account No. 1 was fully convertible for current transactions into any currency. But under the agreement of 1948, her right to multilateral convertibility was limited to the extent of only £10 million. *Ibid.*, col. 997.
82. *The Financial Times* (London), 19 May 1948. Also see *Ceylon Daily News*, 20 May 1948.
83. *Ceylon H. R. Deb.*, vol. 3, 1948, col, 992-4.
84. Exchange of Letters Between the Government of Ceylon and the Government of the United Kingdom, dated 2nd February 1949, concerning Ceylon's Sterling Assets and Monetary Co-operation between the two Governments. Ceylon *Treaty Series No. 2*, 1949 (Colombo), pp. 1-2.
85. *Ceylon Daily News*, 3 May 1949.
86. *Ibid.* 23 August 1949, Also see *The Times* (London), 18 August 1949.
87. *The Financial Times* (London), 23 August 1949.
88. *Times of Ceylon*, 31 August 1949.
89. *Ibid.*
90. In India's case the Central Bank had a gold reserve of £60 million. *The Financial Times* (London), 23 August 1949.
91. *Ceylon Daily News*, 22 September 1950.
92. *The Financial Times* (London), 9 October 1950.
93. In 10 years Ceylon had paid a total of 250 million dollars into

ECONOMIC RELATIONS 143

the common account. *Ceylon Daily News*, 22 September 1950.

94. *Ibid.*, 21 February 1951.

95. Exchange of Letters between the Government of Ceylon and the Government of the UK, dated 2nd February 1951, Concerning the Treatment of Ceylon's Sterling Balances During the Seven years beginning 1st July 1950 and the Independent Reserve of Gold and Dollars to be held by the Central Bank of Ceylon. Ceylon, *Treaty Series No. 1 of 1951*, (Colombo).

96. *Ibid.*

97. Ceylon, *Treaty Series No. 13 of 1952*, (Colombo).

98. In consequence of the Sterling Assets Agreement of 1948 between the Governments of Ceylon and UK, exchange control was extended to transactions within the Sterling Area. Thus her import trade control was closely linked with foreign exchange control and, was used as an experiment to rectify her adverse balances of payment. IBRD, *n.* 28, p. 146.

99. This Act was passed in May 1949 with the aim of facilitating the sale of the industrial products of Ceylon by regulating the importation of industrial commodities from abroad. Ceylon *H.R. Deb.*, vol. 5, 1949, col. 1767.

100. This Pact has been discussed in detail in Chapter II.

101. In 1948 and 1949, the UK's share in Ceylon's imports of manufactured goods was 47.6 per cent and 46.2 per cent. respectively. *Board of Trade Journal*, 3 May 1950, p. 1003.

102. See Appendix V.

103. *Board of Trade Journal*, vol. 172, 27 April 1957, p. 956.

104. *Ibid.*

105. Central Bank of Ceylon, *Annual Report 1958*, p. 19.

106. *The Times* (London), 28 April 1960.

107. See Appendix V.

108. Central Bank of Ceylon, *Annual Report 1961*, p. 62.

109. Ceylon, Ministry of Finance, *Budget Speech 1962-3*, p. 12.

110. Central Bank of Ceylon, *Annual Report 1962*, p. 54.

111. See Appendix V.

112. *International Tea Committee Annual Bulletin of Statistics*, (London) 1953, p. 1.

113. Thorogood, *n.* 20, p. 26.

114. Central Bank of Ceylon, *Annual Report 1964*, p. 62.

115. See Appendix V.

116. *Board of Trade Journal*, 21 August 1948, p. 37.
117. *Ibid*.
118. *The Financial Times* (London), 5 December 1949.
119. *Daily Telegraph*, 30 September 1949.
120. Revival of London tea auctions helped to ensure good export resources, as buyers from the continent, America, Canada, and other countries could obtain in London all the teas—Indian, Ceylon, Dutch, East Indies and China—they required. At the Colombo auctions, only Ceylon tea could be obtained and buyers had to attend each individual auctions, whereas one buyer could act in London. *The Times* (London), 26 April 1951.
121. Immediately after the war, help was given to Greece and Burma to restore economic and financial stability after their liberation from the enemy. Overseas Development Institute, *Government Finance* (London, 1964), p. 47.
122. It was customary for the British to offer a financial settlement at the time of independence and this settlement to included an amount which the country would have otherwise received as aid from Colonial Development and Welfare sources, towards its current development programme. *Aid to Developing Countries*, Cmd. 2147 (London, 1963), p. 20.
123. *Ibid*.
124. The Colombo Plan, *The Third Annual Report of the Consultative Committee on Economic Development in South and South-East Asia*, Cmd. 9336 (London, 1954), p. 103.
125. It is in this Commonwealth Foreign Ministers' meeting held at Colombo in 1950 that the Colombo Plan for Co-operative Economic Development in South and South East Asia had its origin.
126. *The Times* (London), 10 January 1950.
127. A decision had been taken at the Commonwealth Foreign Ministers' meeting in 1950, to set up a Consultative Committee with the objectives of surveying the needs of the area; of assessing the resources of capital, and technical man-power available and required; of focussing world attention on the problem; of providing the framework within which an international co-operative effort could be developed to assist the countries of South and South East Asia to raise the standard of living of their peoples. The Committee comprised initially of Australia, Canada, Ceylon, India, New Zealand, Pakistan, and the UK and her territories in Malaya and British Borneo. The Colombo Plan, *The First Annual Report of the Consultative Committee on Economic Development in South and South East Asia (Karachi, 1952)*, Cmd. 8529, (London, 1952), p. 4.

128. L.P. Singh, *The Colombo Plan: Some Political Aspects* (Canberra, 1963), p. 11.
129. The Colombo Plan for Co-operative Economic Development in South and South East Asia, *Report by the Commonwealth Consultative Committee*, Cmd. 8080 (London, 1950), p. A 3.
130. *Ibid.*
131. See Appendix VI.
132. The Colombo Plan, *The Second Annual Report of the Consultative Committee on Economic Development in South and South East Asia* (New Delhi, 1953), Cmd. 9016 (London) p. 105.
133. The Colombo Plan Technical Co-operation Scheme. *Report by the Council for Technical Co-operation in South and South East Asia*, 1956, (Ceylon) p. 57.
134. See Appendix VI.
135. *Assistance from the UK for Overseas Development* (London, 1960), Cmd. 974 (London, 1960), p. 8.
136. *Aid to Developing Countries 1963* (London), Cmd. 2147, pp. 25-6.
137. Ministry of Finance, *External Economic Assistance* (Colombo, 1964), p. 13.
138. *Ibid.*, pp. 13-14.
139. See Appendix VII.

5
SOCIO-CULTURAL RELATIONS

Ceylon-UK relations in political, constitutional and economic fields have been explained in Chapters II, III and IV. In this chapter an attempt would be made to describe Ceylon-UK cultural relations and to analyse the British impact on her culture and education during the period 1948-65.

It has already been stated earlier that the British had a profound influence on Ceylon in education as well as culture out of which emerged a neo-Westernized elite to whom power was transferred by the colonial power on the eve of independence. Though this highly influential class which had been "schooled to think British, feel British, talk British, act British and buy British"[1] constituted only 6 per cent of the total population,[2] they were socially conspicuous because of the difference in their habits of dress, speech and ways of life, from the rest of the people of the island. Their dominance over political life was so complete that they gave rise to occasional movements demanding an important status for the language of the island,[3] and state protection for Buddhism.[4] These movements indicative of linguistic and religious upsurge, were consistently ignored by the government with unfortunate consequences for the future.

Religio-cultural issues had not become important in Ceylon's politics during the UNP regime. The process of the revival of Buddhism and traditional culture had already been started by a second layer of the elite—the Ayurvedic physicians, the Sinhalese school teachers, and the *bhikkus* of the Sangha, who rose from traditional sources of power and institutions.[5] The *bhikkus* of the Sangha formed a link between independent Ceylon and pre-colonial Sinhalese kingdoms. They were dissatisfied with the attitude of the English-educated leaders towards them,[6] and the Western-oriented administration and democratic institutions which were foreign to their knowledge, religion and culture. They were also sore that while the elements of the Westernization were encouraged, their language, religion and culture were relegated to a secondary place. They found themselves in an inferior position *vis-a-vis* other communities. The Sinhalese Buddhists belonging to this section considered the then existing social system as preventing the majority of the Buddhist population from coming into close contact with the monasteries and the monks and also as estranging them from the traditional culture of a Buddhist nation; the system was also regarded as unsuited to the genius of the majority of the inhabitants of the island.[7]

These trends, grievances and emotional upsurges were accelerated by the publication of the Buddhist Commission's Report[8] which revealed the governmental discrimination against Buddhism and also the power of the Roman Catholic Church, often regarded as a continuation of Western imperialism in a religious garb.[9] It also recommended for the creation of a Buddha Sasana Council, the appointment of a minister for religious affairs, the establishment of training centres for those seeking admission to the Sangha, the declaration of Poya as public holidays, the nationalization of all assisted schools and training colleges, the banning of horse-racing, the prohibition of the sale of intoxicating beverages, and the termination of the services of nuns working in hospitals.[10]

In addition to these, the dissolution of the Parliament and the decision of the UNP government to hold the general elections before Buddha Jayanti, an event of unique and national significance,[11] were interpreted as intended for the inevitable disruption of spiritual atmosphere and for frustrating the hopes of a Buddhist revival in the island. With these developments, the Sinhalese-educated section and those who followed the Buddhist faith were easily caught up in the wave of language, religion and cultural issues which dominated the 1956 election campaign. In step with the increasing trends of Buddhist communalism of the Sinhalese, the Mahajana Eksath Peramuna (MEP) manifesto declared that it "generally approved" the recommendation of the report of the Buddhist Commission of Inquiry and that it would "reorganise the system of education to meet the fullest spiritual, cultural, social and economic needs of the country."[12] Bandaranaike's Sri Lanka Freedom Party (SLFP) in the MEP coalition emphasised the importance of Buddhism in specific terms, that "it is woven into our culture, our way of life, and our very thoughts and actions, so that in rebuilding our people in this new era of freedom, it is very essential to remedy injustices done to Buddhism and to enable the Buddhists to take the fullest advantage of their religion and culture."[13] Philip Gunawardena's Viplavakari Lanka Sama Samaja Party (VLSSP), the Marxist group in the MEP, spoke of the need for a programme of action which was consonant with national heritage, culture and civilization.[14]

The UNP manifesto also pointed out the party's recognition of Buddhism as the religion of the vast majority of the people, its assumption to active leadership in the national celebration of Buddha Jayanti and its assurance to give careful attention to the recommendations of the Buddhist Commission's Report.[15] The UNP government had already assumed an active leadership in the celebration of the Buddha Jayanti when it appointed a Buddhist Council of Ceylon which started various religious activities—translations of sacred books into Sinhalese, the preparation of a Buddhist encyclopedia, the restoration of Buddhist holy monuments and the publication of pamphlets, magazines and books on the Buddha Jayanti.[16] But, in the context of increasing Buddhist communalism and the identification of the UNP with Roman Catholicism (an alien religion)[17] the MEP election manifesto had an effective appeal to the Sinhalese group as against the UNP's.

Consequently, the 1956 elections returned the MEP into power with a large majority.

By 1956, the cultural revival brought Buddhist values into greater prominence because religion was recognised as a great moral and cultural force in the country. Many politically active people in Ceylon regarded the Buddhist culture as the preserver and carrier of national heritage. The cultural revival represented a rural reaction to the urban worldly ways, an under-privileged class's protest against the wealthy and influential elite who had been educated in the British tradition different from Sinhalese ways and religious practices. Hence, in his eagerness to respond to the popular desires for revival of Buddhist culture submerged under the impact of the West, both negative and positive steps were taken by Bandaranaike. Initially, negative steps were taken by discarding what were regarded as the insignia of Western way of life. Thus, Bandaranaike's Cabinet at its first meeting took the decision not to serve liquor[18] at state parties and to diplomatic missions in Ceylon and to close the bars at the Parliament House.[19] To substitute the Western style of breakfast with bread, butter, egg, ham and bacon, by traditional Sinhalese dishes like Kiribath[20] was another instance of turning the back on one aspect of Western culture. A few ceremonies at the inauguration of the third Parliament also reflected the replacement of Western culture by Sinhalese tradition. The ceremony started with the beating of the 'magul bera' (traditional ceremonial drums) instead of the earlier practice of blowing of trumpets. While handing over the Throne speech text, the Prime Minister made his obeisance to the Governor-General in the traditional salute. The Throne speech was read by Governor-General for the first time in three languages—Sinhalese, Tamil, and English, in that order—which established a landmark in the history of Ceylon Parliament.[21] Besides these, the presence of an unprecedented number of yellow-robed *bhikkus* and majority of the Members of the Parliament in national dress (white sarong, baniyan and shawl) instead of Western dress of trousers and coat, reflected the resurgence of traditional Sinhalese culture.[22]

During Mrs. Bandaranaike's government more symbols of Sinhalese Buddhist culture were manifested at state functions. In 1962, at the installation of William Gopallawa as Governor-General, the whole ceremony expressed the Sinhalese culture and nationalist sentiment; the function began against the background of chanting of 'pirith' by the *bhikkus*, with an offering of flowers by the Governor-General before an image of the Buddha (installed for the first time at the Queen's House); the Governor-General wearing the national dress (instead of the usual Western uniform) sat at the feet of a *bhikku* while there were also the other traditional elements like the lighting of Sinhalese oil lamps and blowing of conch shells.[23]

Another step taken by Bandaranaike's government was to stop the Christian broadcasts in the Commercial Service which were alleged to offend the religious and cultural background of the majority of the people, though the government had to suffer a considerable financial loss.[24] Besides this, while more time on National Service Radio Programme was allotted for Sinhalese service, the duration of time allotted for English service was reduced. In 1956, though the increase in time in Sinhalese service was only by 95 minutes as compared to 1955[25] it is significant to note that the fluctuation in the duration of period in English service varied from 64.30 hrs. per week at the beginning of the year to 24 hrs. per week in July and August and back to 34.30 hrs. in the last quarter resulting in an average of 50.15 hrs. per week. It is evident from the Table below that the policy set by Bandaranaike was continued by Mrs. Bandaranaike till the end of her regime. When the duration of time in Sinhalese service was increased to 94.15 hrs. per week, in English service it was reduced to 45 hrs. per week in 1964-65. It was felt that a great responsibility was cast on the Sinhalese services to ensure that an adequate broadcasting service was provided for Sinhalese listeners who looked up to Radio Ceylon as a major source of their intellectual and cultural interests.[26]

But the most important measures taken by Bandaranaike's government for the development of indigenous culture was the establishment of a Ministry of Cultural Affairs in 1957. Through this Cultural Department, both religion and culture received a new impetus. The programmes of the Department stressed the connection between Buddhism and Sinhalese culture and the promotion of Buddhism. A Minister of Cultural Affairs Department, writing in an

TABLE 1

Broadcasting time on National Service in Sinhalese and English

Year	Sinhalese Average hrs. per week	English Average hrs. per week
1956	59.10	50.15
1960	71.30	43.15
1964-65	94.15	45.00

Source : Administration Report of the Director-General of Broadcasting for 1956—1964-65.

Article "Our Religion is the Basis of our Culture", emphasised the point, "Throughout our history we find that all aspects of our culture have had Buddhism as their background".[27] The Department also took up the responsibility of the long-term projects like the publication of Buddhist encyclopedia, the restoration of Buddhist monuments etc. started by the Buddhist Council of Ceylon in the UNP period.[28] Among the activities of the Department the most far-reaching was the establishment or recognition of almost 4,000 Vihara Sasanarakshaka Societies, temple associations for the promotion of Buddhism and the organisation of Sunday Dhamma Schools on the pattern of Christian Sunday schools. Annual subsidy and grants were also given to various Buddhist organisations and associations for religious activities.[29]

The activities of the Cultural Department were directed towards the promotion of Buddhist culture in the island as also the promotion of Ceylon's cultural relation with other countries. This the Department did through various programmes and schemes like, the exhibition of paintings and photographs both at home and in other countries, the arrangement of cultural delegation both ways and the award of scholarships for study of fine arts both at home and in the countries, like the USSR, Czechoslovakia, Rumania,

Communist China, German Democratic Republic, India and the UK.[30] As far as the UK was concerned, scholarship was awarded in 1960 for 7 months to one Ceylonese for the study of the methods of teaching traditional and contemporary arts in England and Europe. To the best Ceylonese student of Painting and Sculpture section of the Ceylon College of the Fine Arts, a scholarship was awarded for two years for studying Commercial Art at St. Martin's School of Art, London. For the study of stage craft in England, Europe and Japan, another scholarship was awarded for a period of one year. On the recommendation of the Handicrafts Panel of the Arts Council, Ceylon, scholarships were awarded for the study of textile painting with a leading firm in the UK for a period of six months.[31] With a view to promote Buddhist in the UK, the Department granted an annual grant to Vihara in London, for its maintenance and subsistence of the bhikkus.[32]

The UK, on her part, to look after the cultural activities in Ceylon, appointed an Assistant Attache for Cultural Affairs in her Diplomatic Corps from 1959.[33]

Another step taken by S.W.R.D. Bandaranaike for the restoration of Buddhist culture was the establishment of two Buddhist universities, Vidyodaya and Vidyalankara, which embedded Sinhalese culture in an educational institution of a university status. These universities were empowered to make provision "for the advancement and dissemination of knowledge and for the promotion of Sinhala and Buddhist culture."[34] At the Vidyodaya University, all students were required to take Sinhala Buddhist culture as one of their subjects.

Following the trend started by Bandaranaike for the promotion of Buddhism and traditional Sinhalese culture, Mrs. Bandaranaike's government also took some measures which affected the Christian activities in the island.[35] As the stateaided Christian schools were considered as instruments of building an alien culture and proselytization at state expense, all state-aided denominational schools were taken over by the government by a legislation passed in 1960 in the teeth of Christian opposition.[36] Strangely enough state-aided Pirivenas, educational institutions operated by Buddhist monks, were excluded from the purview of the Act.[37]

In 1962, the Governor-General Sir Oliver Goonetilleke, an Anglican Christian, was replaced by William Gopallawa, a staunch Buddhist on the basis that some of the persons involved in an abortive *coup d'etat* to overthrow the Government were high-ranking Christian officers who aspired to overthrow the true guardians of Buddhism at the helm of affairs.[38]

The attempt made by Mrs. Bandaranaike's government to take over the Press was also partly based on the allegation that the Press was dominated by Westernized, anti-national, Christians who were contemptuous of Buddhism.[39] Before the Press Bill went through the House, Mrs. Bandaranaike's government was defeated over the Address of thanks on 3 December 1964.

Education

In the post-independence period Ceylon's new leadership continued with the same values and ideals they had imbibed from the British. They continued the same educational system and practices as had prevailed in the colonial era; the distinction between the government schools and the private schools on the one hand, and the English schools and the vernacular schools on the other (the two main features of education during the colonial era), and the system of holding London University examinations in Ceylon obtaining since 1880 were also continued. The language of administration continued to remain English. An English-school product was still a better candidate in getting higher positions than his compatriot from Sinhalese or Tamil medium schools.

Despite Ceylon's new Dominion status she continued to keep up her link with the UK in the field of education, and the UK on her part was ready to give all help in that field. The colonial office, through its welfare Department, was prepared to "go on giving a helping hand" for Ceylonese students' affairs in Britain.[40] The Empire Society offered to help Ceylonese students, especially, in regard to their housing difficulties.[41] But in view of the fact that Ceylonese students were likely to suffer from an arrangement resting on nothing more solid than goodwill, F. Ritcher was appointed as a part-time Education Officer at Ceylon House in London to look after the educational

arrangements for Ceylonese students.[42] At the instance of
S.W.R.D. Bandaranaike, the then Minister of Health and Local
Self-Government, three Ceylonese doctors who were undergoing
specialised training in Britain were delegated to attend the first
International Students' Clinical Conference, organised by the
British Medical Students Association, for the inter change of
knowledge and the furthering of cultural relations between the
younger doctors of different nationalities.[43] Lord Soulbury, as
Chairman of the Advisory Committee[44] to advise and assist the
Educational Officer in London, stressed the immense importance
of keeping up the cultural link between the two countries after
Ceylon became a Dominion. He also pointed out the importance of the Western tradition in the educational system of
Ceylon and also the remarkable knowledge of English possessed
by the Ceylonese.[45]

Ceylonese students who went to London were made
eligible for admission on equal terms to London House, the
Communal Hall of Residence in Bloomesbury, by an amendment of its Charter. Specialists from Ceylon visiting London
in summer 1949 were given the opportunity of attending courses,
arranged by the British Council, intended to throw light upon
the origin and significance of British Commonwealth of
Nations.[46] Two scholarships were granted to Ceylon by the
Social Activities Division of the UNO to enable two officers to
proceed to Europe and the UK to study social welfare work
and their latest developments. This offer was considered to be
very opportune as there was an urgent need to send a competent Ceylonese officer abroad, particularly to the UK, for the
purpose of studying how social insurance work was worked out
in all its details.[47] The Ministry of Health and Local Government granted twenty more scholarships to Ceylon doctors to
enable them to proceed to the UK for specialised study and
training.[48] In December 1949, the Commissioners of the
1851 Exhibition Fund made Ceylon eligible to send one scholar
in 1950 for advanced studies in England or Scotland. The
task of dealing with all the problems of colonial students was
handed over to the British Council by the Colonial Office in
December 1949.[49] The Ceylon government contributed to the
British Commonwealth Hostel Scheme sponsored by the British
government to provide the necessary accommodation and

opportunity for students to work freely with their counter-parts from other countries.[50] Under the Colombo Plan, as part of technical assistance the UK government granted scholarships and all other allowances to the Ceylonese scholars for training in the work of controlling plant pests.[51] In March 1954, Ceylon decided to establish an Institute of International Affairs which was to have links with the Royal Institute of International Affairs in London.[52] The Federation of British Industries offered three scholarships to Ceylon Engineering graduates to enable them to acquire practical experience in all branches of engineering.[53] In February 1956, by an amendment of Britain's Teachers (super-annuation) Bill, it was provided that schools in Ceylon could have British teachers to teach English.[54]

Till 1956, though educational issues had not become important in Ceylon's politics over the years, there had developed an increasing emphasis on national languages. The demand for national languages was reasonable as only 6 per cent of the population were English-educated and the remaining 94 per cent were more or less alienated from the administration of the Westernized 'power elite' in the political, economic, and cultural spheres.[55] The policy of free education and adoption of the mother tongue as the medium of instruction enforced by the Education Act of 1947 was producing Sinhalese and Tamil educated people who had no chance of getting into higher positions, if English continued to be the official language.

Moreover, the vernacular educated people like the village teachers, Ayurvedic physicians and the Sinhalese Buddhists, who also had grievances against the UNP considered as the representative of Western culture and values, clamoured for a revival of national institutions. A large majority of the Ceylonese looked upon the Christian community with suspicion as the missionaries continued to look up to the UK for inspiration, and leadership. They also resented the fact that a large segment of the education of the island, particularly the prestige institutions which prepared young people for university courses and civil services careers were controlled by the Christians who formed only 9 per cent of the population.[56] These grievances were endorsed by the Buddhist Commission when it recommended that the whole system of education should be abolished and "all assisted schools should be taken over by the State...".[57] The MEP which in its manifesto had "generally approved the recommendations of the report of the Buddhist Commission of Inquiry" and also promised particularly to "reorganise the system of education to meet to the fullest the spiritual, cultural, social and economic needs of the country," was brought to power in the general election of 1956.[58]

One of the first enactments of the MEP government was the 'Sinhala only' Act passed in June 1956 by which Sinhalese was adopted as the official language in place of English.[59] The principle that Sinhalese and Tamil should progressively become the media of instruction in Senior Secondary Schools was accepted by the government.[60] Breaking the monopoly of higher education exercised by the English-educated classes, the two Buddhist Universities, Vidyodaya and Vidyalankara Pirivenas, were started in 1959 opening the doors of the university education to the Sinhalese-educated students. In fulfilment of SLFP's July 1960 election promises that "education paid for by the State should be given by the State" and that they would provide for education by the State based on "a system of non-sectarian schools,"[61] Mrs. Bandaranaike's government took over all state-assisted denominational schools and expropriated their properties by two enactments of 1960 and 1961.[62] Thus Christian dominance in education was brought to an end. In 1961, the National Education Commission[63] was appointed to "examine and make a comprehensive review of the entire educational system" then obtaining in Ceylon and to make recommendations for the establishment of a unified system of education.[64] One of the most important recommendations of the Commission was that all the 63 private schools should be taken over by the state as they were "completely incongruous in a national system of education inasmuch as they are restrictive in their admissions and are not open to all the children who live in an area."[65] Though a White Paper (Proposals of National System of Education) embodying some of the recommendations of the Commission was presented to the Parliament in 1964, Mrs. Bandaranaike's government was defeated before a decision was taken.[66]

Despite of all these changes in the educational system, the Bandaranaike government did not completely do away with either the English system of education or English itself. Though the attitude to the study of English had changed, there was an ever increasing demand for more English and better English in schools. There was a state of universal and general dissatisfaction with the fall of standards in English.[67] Hence efforts were made to improve the quality of English taught as a second language in schools. A Committee under the chairmanship of S.F. de Silva was appointed in October 1957 to investigate into all aspects of teaching English. A special course for teachers of English was inaugurated at the Maharagama College.[68] Through the British Council services of Dr. J. A. Noonan of the London University Institute of Education were utilized for the purpose. Some teachers were sent for postgraduate training in the teaching of English at the London University Institute of Education. A series of refresher courses for English Assistants were conducted by the Education Officer attached to the British Council in Ceylon.[69] Colombo still remained the only external centre in Asia for the Primary Fellowship examination of the Royal College of Surgeons which started from 1947.[70] The London External Degree Examinations still continued.[71] The demand for these examinations from Ceylonese students was evident from the large number of students who had entered the various examinations since 1956.[72] The number of Ceylonese students who went to the UK Universities also showed an increase over the years.[73]

Since 1956, Ceylon has continued to receive educational scholarships and other facilities from the UK. In August 1956, scientific workshop and training equipment costing 55,000 sterling was made available by the British government under the Colombo Plan for the Ceylon Institute of Scientific and Industrial Research.[74] In 1959, for the first time in its history, the Cecil Rhodes Trust offered scholarships to Ceylon students for post-graduate studies at Oxford.[75] Ceylon was the recipient of a gift from Britain of equipment worth about Rs. 172,000 for the Anatomy and Psychology Department of the University of Ceylon's Second Medical School at Paradeniya.[76]

To sum up, the UK's role in educational and cultural field was enhanced rather than diminished by the evolution of Ceylon as an independent country. Despite various steps taken for the revival and promotion of Sinhalese Buddhist culture since

1956, Western social and individual values and outlook continued even after that period. In manners and customs, food and clothing, Western style still prevailed. Western music and dances continued to be popular in places like Colombo and Kandy.

There was a deliberate reorientation of national aims and ideals in the educational and cultural spheres by giving a new impulse to educational planning with the accent on the indigenous art, culture and literature and relegating English to a secondary place. Political expediency seemed to have been the motivating factor behind these changes because even advocates of these changes wanted their children to be proficient in English. For students of Ceylon, the UK was still the finishing school. Ceylonese made the journey to London in much the same spirit as before. So, both in the field of education and culture, the British influence persisted to a noticeable extent from 1948-1965.

NOTES

1. Tarzie Vittachi, *The Brown Sahib* (London, 1962), p. 54.
2. Final Report of the Commission on Higher Education in the National Languages, *Sessional Paper* 10, 1956 (Colombo) p. 8.
3. The language problem of Ceylon after independence involved two distinct but inter-related questions : (1) 'English versus Swabasha' an issue over the extent to which the languages of Ceylon, Sinhalese and Tamil, should replace English in administration, courts, and educational institutions; (2) 'Parity versus Sinhalese only' an issue about the relative status to be accorded to Sinhalese and Tamil. The rural middle class like the Ayurvedic physicians, the Sinhalese school teachers, the Buddhist priests and businessmen in the coastal areas, who resented the privileged role of the English speaking classes, advocated 'Sinhalese Only'. D. E. Smith, ed., *South Asian Politics and Religion* (Princeton, 1966), p. 467. Also see W. Howard Wriggins, *Ceylon : Dilemmas of a New Nation* (Princeton, 1960), pp. 337-42.
4. In 1950, a delegation of high-ranking Buddhist monks from Kandy met D. S. Senanayake to request state protection and support for Buddhism. In 1951, an All-Ceylon Buddhist Congress deputation of venerable elders of the Sangha and

the Colonial Office. The British Council was to make arrangements for meeting the Ceylonese students on arrival in London, to provide transit accommodation, to make arrangements for visits, discussions, study groups, week-end and vacation courses and for private hospitality and social contacts. *Ceylon Daily News*, 30 December 1949.

50. *Ibid.*, 7 November 1951.
51. *The Times* (London), 7 May 1952.
52. *Ceylon Daily News*, 12 March 1954.
53. *The Times* (London), 17 January 1955.
54. *Ceylon Daily News*, 23 February 1956.
55. *Sessional Paper 10*, 1956, p. 8.
56. Majority of well-organised schools and colleges which were known for 'their high academic standards, good discipline, strong emphasis on English, Westernized cultural atmosphere and middle and upper class values' were built up by the Christians, while only very few such institutions were developed by the Buddhists. Smith, *n*. 3, p. 480.
57. *The Betrayal of Buddhism*, p. 97. Though the Buddhist Commission urged the abolition of the whole education system, it recommended replacing it, not by the traditional Buddhist pansalas (monastery schools), but by a modern system of state schools. Under the Education (Amendment) Act of 1951, the state-aided schools were given the choice of either (1) becoming private without state aid but with the right to levy fees, or (2) joining the free-education scheme under which the Government would pay the teachers' salaries and would make grants for laboratories, libraries etc. Most of the denominational schools elected to join the free-education scheme. Smith *n*. 3, p. 463.
58. Weerawardana, *n*. 12, p. 67.
59. Ceylon, *H.R. Deb.*, Vol. 24, col. 1940.
60. *Sessional Papers* 10, 1956, p. 15.
61. Ceylon Daily News, *Parliament of Ceylon* (Ceylon, 1960), pp. 214-5.
62. Assisted Schools and Training Colleges (Special Provisions) Act of 1960 and Assisted Schools and Training Colleges (Supplementary Provisions) Act, No. 8 of 1961.
63. To appoint a commission for the revision of the scheme of studies to give a national outlook to education imparted in schools was another promise of the SLFP in July 1960 election. Ceylon Daily News, *n*. 64, p. 215.

64. Final Report of the National Education Commission 1961, *Sessional Paper* 17, 1962 (Colombo), p. 135.
65. *Ibid.*, pp. 138-41.
66. Sumathipala, *n.* 18, p. 411.
67. *Ceylon Year Book 1958*, p. 137.
68. Sumathipala, *n.* 18, p. 404.
69. *Administration Report of the Director of Education for 1957* (Ceylon, 1960), p. A95.
70. *Ceylon Daily News*, 20 August 1957.
71. *Ibid.*, 16 May 1961.
72. See Appendix VI.
73. See Appendix VII.
74. *Ceylon Daily News*, 30 August 1956.
75. *Ibid.*, 3 March 1959.
76. *Ibid.*, 4 October 1961.

6
CONCLUSION

To get a correct perspective of the Ceylon-UK relations during the period 1948-1965, we may divide it into two phases (a) 1948-1956, corresponding to the UNP rule and (b) 1956-1965, corresponding to the Bandaranaikes' rule which also covers the short period of political instability from September 1959 to July 1960. During the two phases, the processes of continuity as well as change, are clearly visible in political, constitutional, cultural, and economic relations of the two countries.

In the political field, the critical variables which determined the Ceylon-UK relations during the UNP and the SLFP eras were : (a) the British bases under the Defence Agreement, (b) Ceylon's continuing membership of the Commonwealth of Nations, and (c) the ideological orientation of the leadership. The course of Ceylon's relations with the UK in the post-independence period had already been conceived in the Defence Agreement between the two countries. Signing a military pact with an ex-colonial country was not an usual phenomenon for a newly emerging state. A newly independent country tends to be sensitively aware of her independence, suspicious of her former colonial power and fearful of the direction great power policies would take in future. That is why countries like India and Burma chose to remain non-aligned to avoid any domination either by the ex-colonial power or by the Communist countries. But, Ceylon chose to sign the Defence Agreement, partly because it was a condition precedent to her grant of independence by Britain which had both economic and strategic interests in the Indian Ocean, and mainly because it solved her own problems of national security which, her leaders imagined, she could not have undertaken with her limited resources. A Defence Agreement for mutual or identical interests was acceptable to Ceylon because a small power prefers an ally whose identical interests actually preclude it from using all its strength on behalf of the alliance. Moreover, Ceylon's Western-oriented leadership preferred to ally with Britain as usually a small power prefers to align itself on the basis of ideology to avoid an internal crisis or external reprobation. It may be argued that for Ceylon's problem of security, alternatives were possible. She could have allied with her large neighbour, India. But to earn political capital, a small power like Ceylon which is always conscious of her size, prefers a distant ally to a large neighbour like India. Another alternative could have been to ally with one of the super powers, particularly since Britain had receded to the status of a medium Western power in terms of defence capacity after the Second World War. But alliance with a super power is inherently dangerous for a small power as it may move, not from insecurity to security, but from insecurity to the status of a satellite. Hence to Ceylon, in her search for post-independence security and stability in a bipolar world of the 1940s, her ex-colonial power was a safer ally to depend upon than super powers, as long as the ex-colonial power retained the will for limited re-engagements.

To assume that Ceylon was obliged to continue her close ties with Britain by just signing a Defence Agreement may not be correct. Any country can sign a Defence Agreement with any other country and still may not keep close relationship with her. Burma, for example, signed a Defence Agreement with Britain and still opted for complete separation from the Commonwealth. So, it is not just a Defence Agreement that matters but it is the content of the agreement that it is important.

In the case of Ceylon, retention of British bases under Defence Agreement, tied Ceylon's defence to British forces. It also committed her to a military arrangement with her ex-colonial power which was one of the protagonists in the cold war. This position became definitely inconsistent with the trend of the neutralist policy as enunciated by the UNP leaders and followed by her other Asian neighbours for whom non-alignment or neutralist policy meant no military tie with any country, either bilateral or multilateral, and non-involvement in power blocs.

This pattern of relationship underwent a change with the withdrawal of bases effected by S.W.R.D. Bandaranaike. To him neutralism connoted effected independence. This was clear from his declaration that "our independence is complete" on the historic ceremony of the transfer of the Air Force Station at Katunayake to the Ceylon government on 1 November 1957. It is, however, significant to note that once the withdrawal of bases was carried out in a friendly manner, he was not opposed to continuing the Defence Agreement with Britain because the attitude he took towards the Defence Agreement was that it was more an "enabling agreement", rather than an agreement on any specific point whatsoever.[1] Hence, not only did he not take any step to abrogate it but also continued to allow the UK naval vessels to refuel at Colombo and to permit the aircraft of the UK forces to overfly and stage through Ceylon according to the "Exchange of Letters between the Government of Ceylon and the Government of the UK regarding UK Service Establishments in Ceylon", 1957. This position continued till the end of Mrs. Bandaranaike's rule in 1965, as is evident from the statement in Parliament by Felix R. Dias Bandaranaike, the then Parliamentary Secretary to the Minister of Defence and External Affairs : "So far as the Ceylon government is concerned, the existence of an agreement of this type, an agreement to agree, surely does not contravene the sovereignty of this country or its capacity to determine its own attitude on any international question independent of this agreement."[2] Thus, though the Defence Agreement was continued, the withdrawal of British bases resulted in a significant change in the nature of Ceylon's relations with the UK.

CONCLUSION

The membership of the Commonwealth of Nations was also a pre-condition for the grant of independence as it was postulated in both the Defence and External Affairs Agreements. The UNP accepted the membership and maintained it as it served a variety of purposes. Politically, it was considered as a counter-force against India about whose political ambitions the UNP was always afraid of. It also secured her prestige and international status by getting into a partnership with a bigger nation and also into the system of consultations between the Commonwealth countries on all important world problems. Economically, she derived the benefit of economic and technical assistance from the Colombo Plan.

The Bandaranaikes also maintained the Commonwealth link, but the nature of this connection underwent a substantial change. Politically, it was no more regarded as a counter-force against India as Ceylon moved closer to Asian countries. Her political alignments with the Commonwealth remained no longer the same. The Suez dispute is an instance when she strongly opposed the policy of the UK, her senior Commonwealth partner. With her membership of the UN and the consolidation of Afro-Asian Group in the UN, membership of Commonwealth became less meaningful to her. From the economic point of view, the Bandaranaikes also recognised the advantages of the Commonwealth relation, like the economic and technical assistance under the Colombo Plan, but the importance of the Sterling Area membership became less with the diversification of her trade.

Ideologically, the Western-oriented UNP had its affinity with the West, though they professed a policy of neutralism. With this ideological affinity with the West, Ceylon sometimes took a non-committal position on some international issues as the SEATO and sometimes a position which differed from that of her non-aligned Asian neighbours as in the case of the Indo-China war.

In contrast to this UNP policy, Bandaranaike followed a new policy striking an even balance in matters of Ceylon's interests and relations between the West, particularly Britain, and all other countries. He established diplomatic relations with the socialist countries. Along with other Asian non-aligned countries he was as much upright in denouncing the actions of Britain in the Suez dispute and Jordon crisis as in denouncing the Soviet intervention in Hungary. But under Mrs. Bandaranaike the balance seemed tilted against the Western countries, particularly Britain. Some of her government's policies, like the nationalization of Life Insurance and the establishment of a State Petroleum Corporation, which made the position of the foreign companies virtually untenable, discriminated sharply against foreigners, mostly the British. So, in the political field Ceylon's relationship with the UK moved from being a cordial one under the UNP regime to rather a strained one under Mrs. Bandaranaike.

In the constitutional sphere, the UNP continued the monarchical system, and retained the same judicial structure and the Judicial Committee of the Privy Council as the highest court of appeal. A significant move towards change of Ceylon's constitutional status into that of a republic was made when the issue was discussed for the first time at the UNP Parliamentary group meeting in 1955. The two Bandaranaike governments made earnest efforts in this direction by setting up various committees to consider the question of the amendment of the constitution for establishing a republic. The constitutional amendment, however, could not be carried out during the two successive regimes of the Bandaranaikes because of the then existing political set up. Therefore the constitutional tie that existed in the colonial period between the two countries continued till 1965.[3]

In the cultural and educational fields, the UNP leaders who formed the intelligentsia of the country continued to value the Western culture and system of education, and maintained close contacts with Britain, especially in the educational field. The linguistic and religious conflicts which were indicative of a revival of traditional culture were ignored by the UNP who deliberately cultivated a posture of non-interference in the religio-cultural issues. But the Bandaranaike leadership, voted to power on some domestic issues like language, religion and culture, brought about a deliberate orientation of national aims and ideals in the educational and cultural spheres. A new impulse was given to educational planning with an accent on indigenous art and culture and relegated English to a secondary position. Important steps like the establishment of two

CONCLUSION

Buddhist universities and of a Ministry of Cultural Affairs were taken by the Bandaranaike government for the revival and promotion of Sinhalese Buddhist culture. Various schemes and programmes were organised to promote Ceylon's cultural relations with other countries. Related to this religious and cultural revival was an anti-Western cultural movement discarding what were regarded as insignia of Western way of life. But the process of throwing out things Western and replacing them with things Ceylonese was highly selective. For instance, none of the traditionalists suggested the abolition of parliamentary institutions, and the concept of rule of law which are purely Western. The materialistic social and individual values of the West still continued. Western music and dances continued to be popular in some of the principal towns in the island. To look after the cultural activities in Ceylon, the UK government even appointed in 1959 an Assistant Attache for Cultural Affairs in its Diplomatic Corps in Ceylon. In the educational field, the UK remained the finishing school for Ceylonese students. Since 1956, an increasing number of students continued to go to the UK universities and other technical institutions. The London External Degree Examinations continued and they were taken by a large number of Ceylonese students. The increase in Ceylon's educational interest in the UK is evident from the increase in the number of educational officers from one to two since 1957 in the Ceylon High Commission, London.[4] The changes made by the Bandaranaike governments in the educational and cultural spheres had a pragmatic base as much as political expediency.

Ceylon's economic relations with the UK remained basically unchanged during the period under discussion. The UNP government was fully aware of the island's economic problems and its economic dependence on world markets in general and the UK in particular. As in the case of all developing countries rapid economic development was one of the national objectives of the UNP governments. To realise that objective they took many measures like Ceylonization of ownership of plantations, of trade and commerce, and of employment and the diversification of trade and industrialization. But due to their Western orientation, they restricted their source of economic assistance to Western countries. They had confined their trade also to the Western countries particularly the UK. Nevertheless in view of the exigencies of the economic situation, the UNP governments signed the Trade and Payments Agreements with China in 1952 and with some other socialist countries in the later half of their rule. Thus, the UNP governments' views on economic and commercial relations with the socialist countries were in marked contrast to their views on political and diplomatic relations with those countries.

The Socialist Governments under the Bandaranaikes continued the economic policies laid down by the previous governments. As Socialists, they professed nationalization of big industries, a political strategy which they used in their efforts to win the ballot. But they had to postpone for a decade the nationalization of tea and rubber plantations in which many British nationals and British capital were involved, lest it should result in the withdrawal of British capital and discouragement of new investments from the UK. Though diversification of trade and sources of aid enlarged Ceylon's circle of friends, on whom Ceylon could depend for trade and aid, the Bandaranaike governments retained her traditional partner, the UK, in all these spheres. This is evident from the trade figures of the UK's share in Ceylon's exports and imports from 1956-1965. As far as aid was concerned, since the inauguration of the Colombo Plan till 1958, the UK provided only technical assistance to Ceylon in pursuance of her policy to all developing countries in the South and South East Asia. But after 1958, Ceylon received more economic assistance, both capital and technical, from the UK. As such, the economic ties between the two countries continued till 1965.

Over a decade and a half since independence Ceylon's relationship with the UK seems to have come round the full circle. During this period one can discern the elements of continuity and change in Ceylon-UK relations. In the political field, it has taken an independent policy which is evident from its stand on issues like the Suez crisis. In the economic sphere, relationship between the two countries may continue to follow the set pattern because of the colonial nature of the island's economy. Ceylon, however, is caught in a dilemma in this respect. Her indigenous nationalist sentiments propel her towards autarchy, but her size and legacies make it a hazardous task. Consequently, Ceylon's 'self-sufficiency' might oscillate from industrial to agricultural sectors and vice-versa. It is in the context of this priority determination that the relative importance of the UK for Ceylon can be appraised. Ceylon has the largest market for her tea in the UK which also has the largest investments in the plantations.

NOTES

1. Ceylon, *H. R. Deb.*, Vol. 25, 11 July 1956, col. 226.
2. *Ceylon Today*, September 1964, p. 11. As the National Government of Ceylon 1965-1970 has not abrogated it, one is led to understand that the Defence Agreement of 1947 still exists; though one of its important provisions became ineffective after the removal of bases. It cannot be regarded as a dead letter, because it seems to be in operation which may be assumed from the representation of Service personnel in the Diplomatic Corps of both the countries.
3. See the post-script. Ceylon has been made a republic on 22 May 1972.
4. Ministry of External Affairs, *Diplomatic, Consular and Other Representation in Ceylon and Ceylon Representation Abroad 1954-65.* (Colombo)

7
POST-SCRIPT
MAJOR DEVELOPMENTS IN SRI LANKA-UK* RELATIONS SINCE 1965

In the general elections of 1965 the UNP, reinvigorated under the leadership of Dudley Senanayake, won 66 seats in a House of 151 as against the SLFP's 41, LSSP's 10 and CP's 4. But it failed to obtain an overall majority and hence Dudley Senanayake formed a coalition with the support of his electoral allies the Sri Lanka Freedom Socialist Party and the Mahajana Eksath Paramuna (SLFSP and MEP)[1] and the two Tamil parties to form what was called the National Government. To the credit of the National Government, it completed its full term, although in 1968 the Federal Party (FP) withdrew its parliamentary group from the National Government following a disagreement with the Prime Minister on the Konneswaram temple issue. [2]

In the general elections of 1970, the SLFP-led United Front (SLFP, LSSP and CP) won a landslide victory. Though

* For purposes of this study both the names—Ceylon and Sri Lanka—are used interchangeably.

the SLFP had a clear majority with 21 seats, its leadership shared power with LSSP and CP which had won 19 and 6 seats respectively. Notwithstanding the numerical position of the left parties in the power structure of the United Front major portfolios of Finance, Plantations, Communication and Housing were entrusted to the left parties.

It is against this background that an assessment of the Sri Lanka-UK relations since 1965, in the constitutional, cultural and economic fields, is made. As far as Sri Lanka's relations with the UK during the period 1965-72 are concerned, there seems to be an element of continuity in the policies followed by the UNP-led National Government and the SLFP-led United Front Government with the policies of these parties during their earlier terms in office. But the pattern of relationship between the two islands underwent a change during the period under review.

Constitutional relations

It is in the constitutional field that the most far-reaching changes took place in Sri Lanka affecting its relations with the UK. Among the constituents of the National Government, the UNP and the FP had no commitments in their 1965 election manifestos with regard to constitutional changes, while the SLFSP had pledged to take steps "to set up without delay a Republic composed of representatives essentially elected by the adult vote of the people"[3] and the MEP had promised "to abolish the imperialist, capitalist form of constitution which governs the country and to introduce a new constitution based on democracy, and in keeping with the cultural, political and economic needs of the nation and to make a Republic outside the Commonwealth."[4] However, the National Government took some steps in the direction of the amendment of the constitution. By adopting a realistic and conciliatory attitude in regard to constitutional changes, the Government, through a Joint Select Committee of the two Houses representing both the Government and the Opposition members, had hoped to establish a new constitution by 'revising' the existing one. Though the Opposition had originally agreed in the setting up of the Joint Select Committee,[5] when the consideration of the Joint Select Committee Motion was moved in the House in December 1965, the LSSP leader Dr. N. M. Perera felt that the Motion should be postponed in view of the new position created by the Privy Council decision which had made the Parliament a "subordinate entity."[6]

The provocation for this was, on the findings of a Bribery Tribunal which were raised before the Privy Council, Section 29(2) of the Constitution, guaranteeing certain special rights to the minority communities, was treated as an 'entrenched clause' which could not be amended with a two-thirds majority.[7]

Subsequently, when the question was brought again during 1966-67, the Opposition refused to serve on a committee empowered only to 'revise' the constitution. It maintained that the revision of the existing constitution, under which Ceylon enjoyed more or less the status of a dominion, through a "Select Committee which must function under the authority of Parliament and subject to the limitations of the Parliament itself is subject to" was inadequate. Instead a new constitution was to be made by a Constituent Assembly which would derive its authority from "the elected representatives of the people, elected not on the basis of the Ceylon (Parliamentary Elections) Order-in-Council, seated together not on the basis of Members of Parliament, not under the authority of the statute but as elected representatives of the respective constituencies to draft a constitution."[8]

In keeping with the spirit of these arguments while in opposition the three-party United Front in its Joint Election Manifesto in 1970, sought and obtained an electoral mandate "to permit the Members of Parliament to function simultaneously as a Constituent Assembly to draft, adopt and operate a new constitution which would declare Ceylon a free, sovereign and independent Republic."[9]

In the Governor-General's address on 14 June 1970 the UF Government expressed its intention to implement this electoral promise and subsequently a resolution on the Constituent Assembly was passed without division on 24 June 1970.[10] It was in terms of this mandate that Prime Minister Mrs. Sirimavo Bandaranaike convened the Constituent Assembly on 19 July 1970.

The inaugural meeting of the Assembly was convened,

not by the Governor-General who, in the constitutional sense, was the representative of the Crown, but by the Prime Minister, an elected head of the Government, and met not in the Parliament House, but at Navarangahala, the auditorium of the Royal Preparatory School. These symbolic gestures underlined the fact that both the Constituent Assembly and the Constitution which it was to draw up would derive their authority from the people of Sri Lanka and not from the power and authority vested by the British Crown and Parliament under the Soulbury Constitution

Moving the resolution to set up a Constituent Assembly, the Prime Minister, Mrs. Sirimavo Bandaranaike explained the aims and objectives of the new constitution.[11] She emphasized that "the new constitution will help to strengthen the oneness of the Ceylonese nation and overcome the stresses caused by various racial, linguistic and religious differences."[12] This sentiment was reiterated by J. R. Jayawardene, the Leader of the Opposition when he said "we are partners in a common material enterprise the purpose of which is not to secure an advantage to a political party, but to benefit the people of our country of all races and religions."[13] After it was set up on 21 July 1970 by a Motion carried unanimously[14] the Constituent Assembly met for forty-four days between July 1970 and May 1972.

On 22 May 1972, after a simple Buddhist ceremony at the Navarangahala, the President of the Consembly, Stanley Tillekaratne signed the declaration that the Constitution has been duly passed and thus "a free sovereign and independent Republic" emerged snapping the last constitutional ties with the British Crown.

With the birth of the Republic "the Lion and the Unicorn" Coat of arms of Her Majesty the Queen of England which had adorned the main entrance of the House of Parliament gave place to the new emblem of the Republic carrying the "Buddha Chakra and the Pot of Prosperity." Queen Elizabeth's photograph was replaced by that of Sri Lanka's President in all Government and public sector offices. The Queen's House which was the official residence of the Governor-General was renamed as 'Janadhipathi Medura'. The ceremonial hoisting of the National Flag of Sri Lanka by the Prime Minister, Mrs.

Bandaranaike in the quadrangle opposite the Dalada Maligawa from where it was hauled down last by the British on 2 March 1815 to mark the domination of the British Crown,[15] was another significant symbolic gesture to express the promulgation of the Republic of Sri Lanka.

With the promulgation of the new constitution, Ceylon has not only changed its nomenclature to Sri Lanka but also has departed radically from the colonial constitution in some vital respects. A hereditary monarch as the head of the State has been replaced by a nominated President for a term of four years in the new Constitution.[16] Unlike the earlier bicameral legislature which had only limited powers, a unicameral legislature, the National State Assembly has been declared to be "the supreme instrument of State power of the Republic."[17] It will be more powerful than the Contitution in the sense that it will have the power to amend the Constitution any time by a two-thirds majority of the total membership of the Assembly.

Another difference that arises from the above is that unlike the Privy Council which was vested with the authority to look into the validity of the laws passed by the Ceylon Parliament, in the new constitution no court administering justice shall have the power to enquire into or pronounce upon the validity of any law enacted by the National State Assembly.[18]

The Soulbury Constitution contained nothing corresponding to the non-justiciable Fundamental Rights and Freedoms, and Principles of State Policy which are provided in the new constitution. Finally, in contrast to the autonomous Public Service Commission that prevailed under the Soulbury Constitution, the new constitution has provided a three-member State Services Advisory Board appointed by the President for a term of four years to act as an Advisory Body to the Cabinet of Ministers in matters of appointment, transfers, promotions etc. of State Officers.[19]

Thus, with the adoption of the new constitution, the island emerged from a dominion to a republic of Sri Lanka after twenty-four years of the attainment of independence, retaining the membership of the Commonwealth. The UK welcomed the new republic of Sri Lanka within the Commonwealth. In her message Queen Elizabeth expressed her satisfaction at Sri Lanka's decision to remain within the Commonwealth and expressed her confidence that ties between the two countries would be maintained and strengthened in the coming years.[20]

Socio-Cultural Relations

In the socio-cultural spheres, the UNP-led National Government (1965-70), anxious to erase its image as a 'party of status quo'—a party dominated by the English-educated elite with an alien outlook, out of tune with the aspirations of the rural Sinhalese people—continued the trend in the promotion of traditional culture started by the Bandaranaike governments since 1956. Thus in the first Throne speech of the National Government, the Governor-General emphasized the restoration of Buddhism to the place it occupied when Lanka was free. As concrete steps in this direction, the Governor promised "to make the four Poya days holidays for the Public and Private Sectors", and "to review the national art and culture which has been the country's pride and a great heritage left to us by our ancestors".[21]

Keeping up these commitments, the National Government passed a legislation making Poya day (the weekly day of religious significance to Buddhists) as the weekly holiday replacing Sunday.[22] (The present government has again reversed the weekly holiday to Sunday.) It also announced that it would start a monk university in Anuradhapura, the ancient capital of the island.[23]

This emphasis on the promotion of indigenous culture did not interrupt the traditional UK-Ceylon links in education. In fact, since 1965 there was an upward trend in the number of Ceylonese students who went to the UK universities and other technical institutions.[24] The recognition of the Ceylon GCE (Advanced level) examinations (which has replaced the London GCE (Advanced level) examinations in Ceylon) for the purpose of admission of Ceylonese students by the universities of Oxford, Cambridge and of Wales[25] encouraged many Ceylonese students to go to the UK for higher education.

There was almost a universal clamour for the revival of external examinations of London University in Ceylon mainly for two reasons. First, it provided an opportunity to those in employment in Ceylon to obtain a University degree which was recognised throughout the world. Secondly, the leading educational institutions in Ceylon were of the opinion that the local Universities were ill-equipped to conduct the examinations on a large scale[26] unlike London University which had a specialised and organised department of conducting external examinations on a big scale. Though the London External Examinations were not revived the candidates who could not complete their London GCE (Advanced level) examination were allowed to complete it.[27]

During this period there was a noticeable change in the attitude to the study of English. There was a growing demand for more and better English teaching in schools. Since Sinhalese replaced English as the sole official language and the Swabasha became the medium of instruction in the Universities in 1956 no facilities were provided for the study of English in schools. Consequently only those who could afford private tuition were able to learn this language.

The National Council of Higher Education under the Chairmanship of Dr. G. P. Malalasekara put forward a proposal to make English compulsory in the country's four Universities by 1972 to enable graduates to pursue higher studies which most of them were precluded from doing because they were proficient in only Sinhalese or Tamil.[28] As such there was a universal demand throughout the island for more qualified teachers to teach English and more hours to be devoted to the teaching of English in all schools so that students were well-equipped to read standard text-books when they entered the Universities. Efforts were therefore made by the National Government to improve the quality of English taught as a second language in schools.

Reversing the Bandaranaike government's decision making the study of English optional, I.M.R.A. Iriyagolle, the Minister of Education announced his Government's intention of making English compulsory in all schools from the 5th Standard upwards from 1968, and to introduce a legislation to give effect to the change. Later, as more trained teachers were available, the teaching of English was to be extended to the primary level as well.[29] For the development of the second language proficiency, a series of intensive courses and training programmes in the English language for both teachers of English and pupils at different centres in the island were conducted.[30]

Some of these courses were to be organised with the cooperation of foreign educational agencies like the British Council. A language laboratory (a gift from the Asia Foundation), the first of its kind, was started in May 1969 at the Training College, Peradeniya.[31] The English language training programme in the island continued to receive the utmost co-operation and immense aid in the form of books, scholarships for specialised training abroad from the British Council, the Asia Foundation, the United States Information Service and Australian High Commission.[32]

The government's 'back to English campaign' started after the revelation that at a General Certificate of Education Examination to select students for the three Universities of Sri Lanka, only 175 out of 31,000 candidates had offered English.[33] The change in the medium of instruction had contributed to the deterioration of standards also. Though the National Government did not elevate English to the status of a compulsory language, it encouraged the study of more and better English by availing itself of all the facilities both at home and abroad.

Though the UF opposition was highly critical of this policy, it would seem that, once in power, it had to reckon with harsh realities. Soon after assuming power, the UF government decided not only to maintain but also to improve the facilities for teaching English.[34] As such the UF government would continue to provide more facilities for the teaching of more and better English in the island.

Economic Relations

The difference between the policies of the UNP and SLFP governments were pronounced in the economic field. The coming into power of the National Government led to a re-orientation of Ceylon's economic policies from left to right-wing principles. The new government had been formed at a time when the country was facing an economic crisis due to shortages of imports, rising prices, depleted level of external assets, the rising cost of living and unemployment. Mrs. Bandaranaike's government (1960-1965) had pushed through much controversial legislation which had alienated the economic interests particularly the British, both at home and abroad. Consequently, the energies of the private sector remained largely unharnessed; private foreign capital was discouraged by a dispute with the three companies over compensation by a moratorium on the remittance of profits, dividends, interests and by an unfavourable climate in general. While the public sector was functioning at a low level of efficiency, the private sector was unable to contribute its best as it was adversely affected by heavy taxation and stringent controls enforced by the previous government.

The National Government's approach in putting the country's economy in order was different from that of the SLFP. While the SLFP's emphasis was on the development of an indigenous industrial sector and state control, the UNP emphasised the 'green revolution' and mixed economy with encouragement to the private sector particularly the British-owned tea industry. Consequently the steps taken by Dudley's government were directed towards creating a favourable climate for the flow of foreign capital, technological and managerial skills.

Thus the government issued a statement welcoming private foreign investment on terms and conditions advantageous both to the island and the foreign investor. As an incentive foreign investors were guaranteed freedom to remit profits, dividends, interest on debentures and preference shares to non-residents, and the proceeds of the sale of liquidation of investments after local liabilities had been met. They were also permitted to bring in foreign managerial and technical personnel, and to remit the maintenance of families of foreign personnel employed on retirement. Non-discriminatory treatment of foreign investors *vis-a-vis* indigenous investors in matters relating to taxation, trade regulations, provision of basic facilities and other aspects of business activities constituted another important plank of official policy.[35]

The government also declared that it had no intention of nationalizing any of the private undertakings and that was to become necessary for overriding considerations in the public interest, prompt, effective and adequate payments were to be made as compensation.[36] However, it did not make the quick impact expected by the government. In spite of this liberalised approach, the UNP government did not relax the moratorium imposed by Mrs. Bandaranaike's government in 1964 till the balance-of-payments position improved, but approved foreign investments were exempted from the application of moratorium. The moratorium was formally lifted only in December 1968.[37]

To facilitate the operation of foreign banks a legislation was passed in the House of Representatives on 29 July 1968.[38] This enabled the Minister of Finance to lift the restrictions placed in 1961, on foreign banks (following the reorganisation of the Bank of Ceylon and the People's Bank), from opening new accounts for Ceylonese customers. As a matter of policy, however, the Finance Minister decided to use this legislation after taking into account the extent to which each bank was willing to co-operate with the government in the strengthening of Ceylon's external payments situation, in training and employment of local personnel, in participating in the financing of economic activities and in bringing out certain institutional changes.[39]

British Banks in Ceylon were the first to act on these conditions. They entered into an agreement with the Central Bank under which they had offered it credit to draw up to £4,000,000 and a further £2,000,000 as a stand by to be used in an emergency. They also expressed willingness to provide long-term capital for economic development either as a contribution to the Development Finance Corporation of Ceylon or as assistance to any long-term credit institutions. They gave their co-operation in running the Bankers' Training Institute (Ceylon) under the sponsorship of the Central Bank of Ceylon.[40]

To meet its financial needs further, the government attempted to get as much foreign aid as possible from other countries. One of the first steps taken by the government in this direction was to end the compensation dispute with the three foreign oil companies—Shell (British), Caltex and Esso (American)—whose assets had been largely taken over in 1961 by the State-owned Ceylon Petroleum Corporation. Through a legislation on the basis of an agreement signed between the Ceylon government and the three oil companies, a compensation of Rs. 55 million was to be paid to the oil companies (Shell to receive Rs. 33 million while Caltex and Esso Rs. 11 million each) spread over 7 years.[41] The last instalment of compensation was paid to the oil companies in July 1970 by the UF government. In actual fact, it appeared that the oil companies had climbed down from Rs. 100 million to Rs. 55 million for political reasons. The Agreement opened the doors for much-needed foreign aid particularly from America which had suspended all aid in 1963 on compensation dispute.

As a gesture towards Senanaike's government policies the Western bloc particularly the UK came forward to help Sri Lanka's immediate financial needs. An Aid-Ceylon Group comprised of Australia, Canada, France, Japan, West Germany, the UK, and the USA was organised by the World Bank to provide aid to Ceylon on a systematic basis. The Group through five aid programmes committed aid in a sum of Rs. 2,100 million between 1965 nnd 1969.[42]

In addition to the assistance obtained under these programmes of aid, considerable economic assistance was also received from many Western countries on a bilateral basis from 1965 to 1969. The UK was one of the countries which generously extended aid to Ceylon. Since 1965 the British aid committed and pledged to Ceylon totalled Rs. 12.71 million— all interest free maturing over 25 years—for the import of British goods such as fertilizers, vehicles, tractors etc. intended to increase productivity and promote its development. In addition the UK offered Ceylon £1 million of food aid under the Rome Food Aid Convention for the purchase of wheat or coarse grains other than rice.[43] Besides this, the £2.5 million Telecommunications Section 3 Loan signed in 1961 was increased by £235,000 in January 1966 to meet increased costs.[44] Under the Colombo Plan Britain's Ministry of Overseas Development provided assistance to depute four experts to Colombo to work with Air Ceylon for two years.[45]

Unlike the earlier UNP governments, the National Government also welcomed economic assistance from and maintained economic cooperation with socialist countries. Accordnig to foreign aid figures released by the Ministry of

Planning and Economic Affairs in Colombo in October 1969, the USSR commitments amounted to Rs. 142.8 million in grants and credits to Ceylon.[46] But no fresh aid came from China because of the strained relationship that had developed in the political field between the two countries during this period.

As far as trade was concerned, the major part of trade of Ceylon continued to be with the Western countries particularly the UK. In 1969 Ceylon's exports to and imports from the UK were 20.2 per cent and 17.4 per cent respectively.[47] But unlike the earlier UNP governments, the National Government did not confine Ceylon's trade with Western countries alone. On the contrary, Sri Lanka's bilateral pacts were mostly with the socialist countries like USSR and China.

It is significant to note that while political relations with China following a ban on the inflow of communist literature, was somewhat restrained, trade between the two countries continued. Rubber-rice agreements between the two countries were reviewed and renewed every year. The need to have a ready buyer for Ceylon's rubber apparently forced Dudley's government to continue the barter trade with China which had begun in 1952. This trade involved principally the exchange of 38,000 tons in 1965 to 62,000 tons in 1969 of rubber for 200,000 tons of rice every year. Though increasing production of rice had enabled Ceylon to reduce its imports of rice progressively from countries like Burma and Thailand, rice imports from China continued to be constant as that permitted the export of more rubber at a price higher than prevailing world price. Thus China not only maintained its second position in its import-export trade but even registered an increase therein.

With the return of Mrs. Bandaranaike to power as the head of left-oriented coalition in May 1970, the new government announced a radical economic policy. It had on its agenda nationalization of the banking system, of import trade in essential commodities, the control of the agency houses which were stated to be "a major vehicle through which imperialism dominates the plantation economy." In accordance to this policy, the first few months of the new government brought a series of nationalization measures. It nationalized the subsidiary companies of Shell, Caltex and Esso, manufacturing chemicals and pesticides, and took over marine banking services from the companies on 1 January 1971.[48] By passing the State Trading Corporation Bill in December 1970 to regulate internal and external trade, trade was partly nationalized and partly Ceylonized because import, export and the wholesale were largely in foreign hands.[49]

In pursuance of the government's policy to handle the import trade in all essential goods, the State Trading Corporation was to import Rs. 250 mn. worth of general goods in 1972.[50] Under the Business Acquisition Act passed on 6 May 1971, which gave the government wide powers, it took over the British Ceylon Corporation Ltd., to break the monopoly of the company in the export of coconut oil and thereby also improve the price of copra—a major foreign exchange earner.[51] Under the five-year development plan 1972-1976, the Agriculture Minister, Hector Kobbekaduwe declared on 22 July 1971 the government's decision to take over 18 tea and rubber estates in Kandy district owned by the British, Indian and Ceylonese interests covering about 15,000 acres to uplift the local peasantry.[52]

Despite these policies and measures, the economic situation in the island remained bleak. There were dislocations of economic life leading to more unemployment, shortages of food, rising prices and general hardship. This economic situation of the country was very much reflected in the statement of the Trade Minister T. B. Illangaratne on the government's trade policy on 3 February 1971, "Ceylon is facing an economic crisis of the greatest magnitude. Its existence is ship-to-mouth one. "[53]

These hard economic realities forced the government to modify its economic policy. As such many declared intentions like the nationalization of the banking system were not taken. While replying to a resolution tabled by some 54 members of Parliament, urging the government to nationalize foreign commercial banks, the Prime Minister, Mrs. Bandaranaike stated that it was not the desire of the government to embark on nationalization aimlessly. She made it clear that the government's take-over of foreign commercial banks and other ventures would be only at the opportune movement.⁵⁴

There were adequate reasons for such a cautious policy of the government. The Finance Minister N. M. Perera discovered that the foreign banks had been giving short-term credits to the government to pay for what had been termed as "ship-to-mouth existence". Commenting on the modified policy of the government, the *East African Standard* wrote on 11 August 1972 under the caption 'Sri Lanka veers over a little to the right', "The Government has now gone so far as to assure the private sector 'complete security'...." Hard economic realities have now made the Government modify its strategy to such an extent as to be accused by leftists outside the ruling alliance as "betrayers of socialism."⁵⁵

In order to meet the problem of loan repayment and also to import rice at a reasonable price, the UF government continued to seek aid from and encourage more trade with both Western and socialist countries. Under a £3 mn. loan signed on 28 August 1970, Britain was to provide Ceylon fibre glass, rayon tyre cord, motor cycles, fork lift trucks and spares for motor vehicles, locomotives and aircraft as well as earth moving, construction and agricultural machinery and telecommunication equipment. This brought total British aid to £6 mn. pledged at the Aid Ceylon Group meeting in February 1970.⁵⁶ Ceylon signed an agreement on 4 November 1972 with Britain under which it will get an interest-free loan to the tune of £1 mn. to enable it to import fertilizers, chemicals, spare parts and components, certain raw materials, engineering stocks and electrical and telecommunication equipment, etc. This loan brought the total value of Britain's interest-free loan to Ceylon since November 1965 to £25,535,000.⁵⁷ In 1971, Britain was to make available a loan of £625,000 to Ceylon to improve water supply in Galle. Britain also provided £700,000 for purchase of flour during the harvest year 1970-71.⁵⁸

To overcome its economic difficulties, Ceylon received economic assistance from socialist countries also. China has been a generous dispenser of aid to Ceylon. Under an agreement signed in Colombo on 27 May 1971, China made available an interest-free long-term loan of Rs. 150 mn. to meet the government's programme of economic development.⁵⁹

With this loan, the total economic assistance made available by China amounted to Rs. 405 mn. (Rs. 130 mn. in grants and Rs. 275 mn. interest-free loans).

As far as Sri Lanka's trade during the UF period is concerned, both the UK and China have maintained their first and second position respectively.

Political Relations

If the UNP-led and SLFP-led governments have shown proximity in their economic policies by not taking extreme steps in view of the economic difficulties of the island, they have kept almost a constant area of differentiation in their policies on political issues. This differentiation has manifested itself in the stand they have taken on some of the international issues in which the UK is directly involved. Referring to the Indonesian-Malaysian conflict Senator A. F. Wijemanne, the Minister of Justice, who represented the Prime Minister, Dudley Senanaike at the Commonwealth Prime Ministers' meeting held in London was reported to have told the conference that though Ceylon was friendly with both countries, it had to deplore Indonesia's policy towards Malaysia. He also said that the Premiers "should reassure the Malaysian Premier of their support for Malaysia's integrity. If Indonesia's grievance was the existence of the British bases in Malaysia, Indonesia's present policy could only serve to extend their life."[60] This criticism of Wijemanne at Indonesia showed that he leaned a little heavily on the side of Malaysia where the UK was involved.

The SLFP-led UF government's left-wing edge was visible in its stand on some other issues. Speaking at the Commonwealth Heads of Government Conference at Singapore, Mrs. Bandaranaike condemned the British arms sale to South Africa on the grounds that South Africa had outraged the conscience of the world by her studied defiance of U.N. resolutions, the basic conception of human rights and world opinion generally, by persisting in apartheid policies which were not approved by most governments, inculding the UK. She also strongly opposed the Anglo-American decision to establish a communication base at Diego Garcia, a British-owned island in the Indian Ocean.[61]

In Ceylon's special paper on the Indian Ocean presented

to the Commonwealth Conference by Mrs. Bandaranaike, she reiterated her earlier proposal of turning the Indian Ocean area to a 'neutral nuclear-free zone' for which she won support from Afro-Asian countries at Lusaka. The Ceylonese proposal was endorsed by all who spoke except the British Foreign Secretary, Sir Alec Douglas Home and the Australian Premier John Gorton.[62] As Mrs. Bandaranaike felt that the expansion of naval activity in the Indian Ocean, the general intensification of big power politics, and regional tensions had lent urgency to the need for giving shape to the peace zone idea, she advocated for an 'Indian Ocean Zone of Peace' in her speech in the U.N.

A resolution sponsored by Ceylon declaring the Indian Ocean area a zone of peace and calling upon the big powers to negotiate with Indian Ocean nations for the elimination of military installations, nuclear weapons or great power rivalry in the region was approved by 61 votes with 55 abstentions in the General Assembly's Political Committee. China was among the 61 nations which voted for the resolution; USSR (which had supported the idea earlier), France, USA and the UK abstained.[63] The Soviet Union had supported Ceylon's proposal earlier on the ground that "it is their lawful demand that answers the spirit and letter of the UN Charter." But when the proposal was put to vote, the Soviet Union abstained.[64] The change in the Soviet Union's attitude might be attributed to the fact that following polarization of forces in South Asia in the wake of Bangladesh events there would be increasing USA and Soviet naval presence in the region.

The UK which had not endorsed Ceylon's proposal at the Commonwealth Summit at Singapore could not accept it as it cut across the British Prime Minister's consistent contention that increasing Soviet naval presence in the Indian Ocean is a threat to the security and peace in the region. The British Foreign Secretary, Sir Alec Douglas Home's contention was that while the UK had reduced its naval strength to negligible proportions and the USA had not comparatively increased her naval strength in the area, Soviet naval strength particularly that of its sub-marine force had been doubled.[65] Moreover, Britain wanted to maintain a "minimal naval presence" in the area partly in fulfilment of the obligations it has accepted under the five-power defence agreement with South East Asian countries like Malaysia, Singapore, Australia and New Zealand, and partly to make sure of itself that its oil supply from the Persian Gulf is not jeopardised. Sir Alec Douglas also justified the British move to sell "a very limited quantity of naval arms" to South Africa as the UK needed the Simonstown base in South Africa to sustain the British naval presence in the Indian Ocean.[66]

Conclusion

In sum, looking at the trend of events in Sri Lanka, one may discern that though the dependence of Sri Lanka on the UK has been, relatively speaking, lessened, the importance in trade with the UK is likely to continue. It is evident from the fact that though the imports and exports of Sri Lanka with the UK has dwindled from 17.3 per cent in 1948 to 14.3 per cent in 1970 and 32.2 per cent in 1948 to 22.8 per cent in 1970 respectively, the UK still continues to remain first in imports as well as exports. Thanks to the economic stakes which the UK has in the island, it is understandable that whatever be the nature of political interactions, the UK's concern for stability in the island will manifest itself in economic terms. It is evident from a bird's eye-view of the pattern of the foreign economic aid and the contribution of the UK therein. Out of the net receipt of foreign assistance, UK held a lion's share as is clear from the Table below :

Net receipts for assistance *i.e.* loans and grants and share of the UK therein.

	1965-66	1966-67	1967-68	1968-69	1969-70
Total	118	208.6	190.2	353.6	259.5
UK	10.6	49.4	51.9	51.3	51.8

Source : Ceylon, Department of Census and Statistics, *Statistical Pocket Book of Ceylon*, 1971, p. III.

The prompt military assistance provided by the UK in the May 1971 insurrection reiterates the attitude further.

In the socio-cultural sphere, the place of English in Sri Lanka is analogous to what it is in India; it might not retain its earlier privileged position but will continue to be known, however, by a much larger number than before in view of the rapidly increasing number of graduates.

Sri Lanka's adoption of a new constitution but the retention of the old Commonwealth links is an indication of the importance which it has ascribed to the socio-economic advantages without supporting the UK move on issues which directly affect the national interests of Sri Lanka. While no Ceylonese government may like wholesale nationalization of the plantations, a left of the centre government like that of the present one may impose more and more stringent conditions *vis-a-vis* the repatriation of assets and the control of agency houses.

NOTES

1. The UNP had an electoral agreement with the SLFSP led by C.P. de Silva. Although the UNP had no electoral agreement with the other parties except SLFP, LSSP & CP it decided not to put any candidates against the leaders of these parties. Ceylon Daily News, *Parliament of Ceylon 1965*, (Colombo) p. 16.

2. As Senator M. Tiruchelvam, Minister of Local Government and the representative of the FP in the National Government, was asked by the Prime Minister to suspend the work of a committee which he had appointed to demarcate the area of Konneswaram temple, a venerated Hindu temple, he resigned from the National Government on September 15, 1968; but he decided to support the Government on all matters which did not adversely affect the Tamil Community. *Times of Ceylon* (Colombo), 8 February 1969.

3. Ceylon Daily News, *n.* 1, p. 183,

4. *Ibid.*, p. 190.

5. Ceylon, *H.R. Deb.*, Vol. 60, 1965, col. 2498.

6. *Ibid.*, Vol. 63 II 1965, col. 4269.

7. *Ibid.*, col. 4270.

8. Ceylon, *H.R. Deb.*, Vol. 71, I 1967, cols. 315-16.
9. Ceylon Daily News, *Parliament of Ceylon 1970* (Colombo), p. 173.
10. *Tribune* (Colombo), 2 August 1970.
11. Resolution reads as follows—"We the Members of the House of Representatives, in pursuance of the mandate given by the people of Sri Lanka at the general election held on 27 May 1970, do hereby resolve to constitute, declare and proclaim ourselves the Constituent Assembly of the people of Sri Lanka for the purpose of adopting, enacting and establishing a Constitution for Sri Lanka which will declare Sri Lanka to be a free sovereign and independent Republic pledged to realise the objectives of a socialist democracy including the fundamental rights and freedoms of all citizens and which will become the fundamental law of Sri Lanka deriving its authority from the people of Sri Lanka and not from the power and authority assumed and exercised by the British Crown and the Parliament of the United Kingdom in the grant of the present Constitution of Ceylon nor from the said Constitution and do accordingly constitute, declare and proclaim ourselves the Constituent Assembly of the people of Sri Lanka and being so constituted, appoint the 29th day of July, at 10.00 a.m. as the date and time when the Constituent Assembly shall next meet in the Chamber of the House of Representatives for carrying out the said mandate under the presidentship of Wanniarachi Don Stanley Tillekaratne, M.P. in his absence of Ibrahim Adham Abdul Cader, M.P. and to consider business introduced by or on behalf of the Minister of Constitutional Affairs." *Ibid.*
12. *Ibid.*
13. *Ibid.*
14. Ceylon, *Proceedings of a Meeting of the Members of House o, Representatives at Navarangahala and continued in the House of Representatives*, 21 July 1970, col. 508.
15. *The Indian Express* (Delhi), 23 May 1972.
16. *The Constitution of Sri Lanka* (Ceylon) 1972, Sec. 5, p. 3.
17. *Ibid.*, Sec. 5, p. 3.
18. *Ibid.*, Sec. 39.
19. *Ibid.*, Sec. III (1 & 2), p. 42.
20. *Statesman* (Delhi), 23 May 1972.
21. Ceylon, *H.R. Deb.*, vol. 60(1), 1965, col. 98-99.
22. *Times of Ceylon*, 30 January 1966.
23. Urmila Phadnis, Coalitions in Ceylon—3, The National Government of 1965. *Tribune* (Colombo), 29 August 1971.

24. See Appendix. VII.
25. *Tribune* (Colombo), 26 February 1965.
26. *Ibid.*
27. *Ibid.*, 18 April 1966.
28. *Times of Ceylon*, 30 May 1968.
29. *The Hindu* (Madras), 22 September 1967.
30. For details see Ceylon, *Administration Report of the Director-General of Education for 1968-69* (Colombo 1972), pp. 156-57.
31. *Ibid.*, p. 157.
32. *Ibid.*
33. *Tribune*, 27 April 1969.
34. Speaking at the Ananda College prize-giving on 28 July 1971, the Minister of Education, Dr. Badiuddin Mahamud said that under the proposed reform, the foundation of job-orientation in education would be laid at the junior secondary education and the National Certificate of Education would replace the present GCE. Ordinary Level examination. He also added that the teaching of English would be made compulsory from Grades six upwards in all schools and when facilities improved and with more teachers English would be made progressively compulsory from Grade three upwards. Ceylon, Ministry of Defence and External Affairs, *News Bulletin* (Colombo), 4 August 1971, p. 1.
35. Ceylon, Department of Information. *Ceylon Today*, vol. 15, no. 4, April 1966, p. 13.
36. *Ibid.*
37. *Tribune* (Colombo), December 15, 1968.
38. Ceylon, *H. R. Deb.*, vol. 79 no. (9) 1968, col. 1591.
39. *Ibid.*, vol. 79(8), 1968, cols. 1450-57.
40. *Ibid.*, cols. 1451-52.
41. *Tribune* (Colombo), 22 May 1965.
42. Ceylon, Department of Information, *Ceylon Today*, vol. 18, (7-8), July-August 1969, p. 13.
43. *Ibid.*, vol. 18 (1), January-February 1969, p. 18,
44. *Ibid.*, vol. 16(6), June 1967, p. 17.
45. *Ibid.*, vol. 18(1 & 2), January-February 1969, p. 54.
46. *Times of Ceylon*, 31 October 1969.
47. Ceylon, Department of Census and Statistics, *Statistical Pocket Book of Ceylon*, 1970, pp. 78-79.
48. *Patriot* (Delhi), 16 August 1970.

49. The Information Division, Ceylon High Commission (New Delhi) *Ceylon Newsletter*, 11 December 1970, p. 3.
50. *Ceylon Daily News*, 5 November 1971.
51. *Ibid.*, 10 March 1972.
52. *Ibid.*, 23 July 1971.
53. Institute for Defence Studies and Analyses, *India in World Strategic Environment Annual Review*, vol. 1, 1970-71, p. 339.
54. *Hindu* (Madras), 9 November 1971.
55. Institute of Defence Studies & Analyses, *News Review on South Asia*, August 1972, p. 131.
56. Institute for Defence Studies & Analyses, *n.* 53, p. 351.
57. *Ceylon Daily News*, 5 November 1971.
58. Institute for Defence Studies & Analyses, *n.* 53, p. 351.
59. *Ibid.*, p. 352.
60. *Tribune* (Colombo), June 26, 1965.
61. Ceylon, Department of Information, *Ceylon Today*, vol. 20 (1 & 2), January-February 1971, pp. 7-15.
62. *Times of Ceylon*, 12 March 1971.
63. *Statesman* (Delhi), 15 January 1972.
64. *Ibid.*
65. *Hindustan Times* (Delhi), 9 February 1972.
66. *Times of India*, 9 February 1972.

APPENDICES

APPENDIX I
UNITED KINGDOM-CEYLON DEFENCE AGREEMENT

Whereas Ceylon has reached the stage in constitutional development at which she is ready to assume the status of a fully responsible member of the British Commonwealth of Nations, in no way subordinate in any aspect of domestic or external affairs, freely associated and united by common allegiance to the Crown.

And whereas it is in the mutual interest of Ceylon and the United Kingdom of Great Britain and Northern Ireland that the necessary measures should be taken for the effectual protection and defence of the territories of both and that the necessary facilities should be afforded for this purpose.

Therefore the Government of the United Kingdom and the Government of Ceylon have agreed as follows :

(1) The Government of the United Kingdom and the Government of Ceylon will give to each other such military assistance for the security of their territories, for defence aganist external aggression and for the protection of essential communications as it may be in their mutual

interest to provide. The Government of the United Kingdom may base such naval and air forces and maintain such land forces in Ceylon as may be required for these purposes, and as may be mutually agreed.

(2) The Government of Ceylon will grant to the Government of the United Kingdom all the necessary facilities for the objects mentioned in Article I as may be mutually agreed. These facilities will include the use of naval and air bases and ports and military establishments and the use of telecommunications facilities and the right of service courts and authorities to exercise such control and jurisdiction over members of the said Forces as they exercise at present.

(3) The Government of the United Kingdom will furnish the Government of Ceylon with such military assistance as may from time to time be required towards the training and development of Ceylonese armed forces.

(4) The two Governments will establish such administrative machinery as they may agree to be desirable for the purpose of co-operation in regard to defence matters, as to co-ordinate and determine the defence requirements of both Governments.

(5) This Agreement will take effect on the day when the constitutional measures necessary for conferring on Ceylon fully responsible status within the British Commonwealth of Nations shall come into force.

Done in duplicate, at Colombo, this 11th day of November 1947.

Signed on behalf of the Government of the United Kingdom of Great Britain and Northern Ireland.

(Sd.) HENRY MOORE

Signed on behalf of the Government of Ceylon.

(Sd.) D. S. SENANAYAKE

Source : *Command Papers,* 7257 (London, 1947), pp. 2-3.

APPENDIX II

UNITED KINGDOM-CEYLON EXTERNAL AFFAIRS AGREEMENT

Whereas Ceylon has reached the stage in constitutional development at which she is ready to assume the status of a fully responsible member of the British Commonwealth of Nations, in no way subordinate in any aspect of domestic or external affairs, freely associated and united by common allegiance to the Crown.

And whereas the Government of the United Kingdom of Great Britain and Northern Ireland and the Government of Ceylon are desirous of entering into an agreement to provide for certain matters relating to external affairs.

Therefore the Government of the United Kingdom and the Government of Ceylon have agreed as follows :

(1) The Government of Ceylon declares the readiness of Ceylon to adopt and follow the resolutions of past Imperial Conferences.

(2) In regard to external affairs generally, and in particular to the communication of information and consultation,

the Government of the United Kingdom will in relation to Ceylon observe the principles and practice now observed by the Members of the Commonwealth, and the Ceylon Government will for its part observe these same principles and practice.

(3) The Ceylon Government will be represented in London by a High Commissioner for Ceylon, and the Government of the United Kingdom will be represented in Colombo by a High Commissioner for the United Kingdom.

(4) If the Government of Ceylon so requests, the Government of the United Kingdom will communicate to the Governments of the foreign countries with which Ceylon wishes to exchange diplomatic representatives proposals for such exchange. In any foreign country where Ceylon has no diplomatic representative the Government of the United Kingdom will, if so requested by the Government of Ceylon, arrange for its representatives to act on behalf of Ceylon.

(5) The Government of the United Kingdom will lend its full support to any application by Ceylon for memberhip of the United Nations, or of any specialised international agency as described in Article 57 of the United Nations Charter.

(6) All obligations and responsibilities heretofore devolving on the Government of the United Kingdom which arise from any valid international instrument shall henceforth insofar as such instrument may be held to have application to Ceylon devolve upon the Government of Ceylon. The reciprocal rights and benefits heretofore enjoyed by the Government of the United Kingdom in virtue of the application of any such international instrument to Ceylon shall henceforth be enjoyed by the Government of Ceylon.

(7) This Agreement will take effect on the day when the constitutional measures necessary for conferring on

APPENDIX II

Ceylon fully responsible status within the British Commonwealth of Nations shall come into force.

Done in duplicate, at Colombo, this 11th day of November 1947.

Signed on behalf of the Government of the United Kingdom of Great Britain and Northern Ireland.

(Sd.) HENRY MOORE

Signed on behalf of the Government of Ceylon.

(Sd.) D. S. SENANAYAKE

Source : *Command Papers*, 7257 (London, 1947), p. 3.

APPENDIX III

EXCHANGE OF LETTERS BETWEEN THE GOVERNMENT OF CEYLON AND THE GOVERNMENT OF THE UNITED KINGDOM SERVICE ESTABLISHMENTS IN CEYLON

Colombo, June 7, 1957

No. 1

From : His Excellency Sir Cecil Syers, High Commissioner for the United Kingdom in Ceylon.

To : The Honourable S.W.R.D. Bandaranaike, Prime Minister of Ceylon.

Office of the
United Kingdom High Commissioner,
Colombo, Ceylon.
7th June 1957.

My dear Prime Minister,

I write this letter to place on record the main points which the Ceylon and United Kingdom Delegations have agreed on

APPENDIX III

behalf of their two Governments in the talks which began in Colombo on 29th March regarding United Kingdom Service Establishments in Ceylon. These are as follows :

(1) In accordance with the declared policy of the Ceylon Government that United Kingdom bases in the Island (hereafter referred to as "the Bases") should be closed down, the naval base at Trincomalee and the Royal Air Force station at Katunayake will be formally transferred to the Ceylon Government on 15th October 1957 and 1st November 1957, respectively.

(2) Subject to sub-paragraphs 3 and 4 below the United Kingdom Government will continue to use certain facilities for a limited time hereafter referred to as "the rundown". Such use of some of the facilities will cease within two to three years and of all will cease by 1st March 1962, provided that, if the process of rundown is interrupted by causes outside the control of the United Kingdom Government, the period of rundown may be increased as may be mutually agreed.

(3) During the rundown the use of these facilities will be subject to the general control of the Ceylon Government and the Ceylon Government reserves to itself the right to deny such use to the United Kingdom Government if any situation arises where, in pursuance of its general international policy, the Ceylon Government finds it necessary to do so. Subject to this condition the Ceylon Government will grant the United Kingdom Government the free and uninterrupted use and operation of these facilities and the right to administer their establishments as at present. The United Kingdom Government for its part will not, in the use of the facilities, interfere with such plans of development as the Ceylon Government might undertake in the areas concerned. If any difficulties should arise in

this connection the two Governments will consult together in order to arrive at a satisfactory solution.

(4) Detailed arrangements regarding the facilities which it is intended the United Kingdom may continue to use, and arrangements which it is intended to put into operation to implement sub-paragraphs 1 to 3 above in other respects, will be made.

(5) In addition to the grant of facilities under sub-paragraph 3 above, the Ceylon Government will give to the United Kingdom Forces all necessary facilities and assistance in connection with (i) the withdrawal of the Forces and (ii) the removal or disposal by the Forces of all their stores, equipment and other movable property.

(6) The Government of Ceylon shall pay to the United Kingdom Government the sum of Rs. 22 million in five equal instalments of Rs. 4,400,000 in each of the Ceylon Government financial years 1957-58 to 1961-62 inclusive. This payment will be made in respect of the installations to be transferred to the Ceylon Government and the cancellation of certain claims between the two Governments arising out of the occupation or disposal of the bases by United Kingdom Forces. Detailed provisions regarding financial matters are contained in the Annex to this letter, which Annex shall be regarded as an integral part hereof. In each year payment will be made in rupees within the total of United Kingdom estimated governmental expenditure in Ceylon, any balance being paid in sterling at the rate of Rs. 13.3102 to £1.

(7) Installations to be transferred to the Ceylon Government in accordance with the provisions of paragraph 2 of the said Annex shall be handed over as and when vacated by the United Kingdom Forces.

(8) The United Kingdom Forces and the members thereof will continue to enjoy during the period of rundown all the immunities and privileges hitherto enjoyed by them.

(9) During the period of rundown and after its completion the Ceylon Government, in accordance with normal Commonwealth practice but subject to the requirements of the general policy of the Ceylon Government, will continue to allow (a) United Kingdom naval vessels to refuel at Colombo; and (b) aircraft of the United Kingdom Forces, and on charter to those Forces, to overfly and stage through Ceylon.

(10) The United Kingdom Delegation supplied to the Ceylon Delegation a programme of the numbers of locally recruited employees of the United Kingdom Forces who it was intended would, as a consequence of the rundown, cease to be employed by the United Kingdom. The United Kingdom authorities will furnish at regular intervals both forecasts of future redundancies and particulars of impending discharges. I should be grateful to have your confirmation that the foregoing is acceptable to the Ceylon Government as a summary of the results of our discussions and that this letter and your reply shall constitute an agreement between our two Governments.

Yours sincerely,
(Sd.) C. G. L. SYERS,
High Commissioner.

The Hon. S.W.R.D. Bandaranaike, M.P.,
Prime Minister of Ceylon,
Colombo.

ANNEX ON FINANCIAL MATTERS

The detailed provisions regarding financial matters (referred to in sub-paragraph (6) of the letter to which this forms the annex) are as follows:

1. The claims of each Government arising out of the occupation or disposal of the Bases were made known to the other Government and were discussed at the talks mentioned in the said letter. These claims are cancelled and the Ceylon Government undertakes the settlement of outstanding balances on existing claims and of any future claims by third parties in respect of damage compensation relating to requisitioned property occupied by the United Kingdom Forces.

2. Ceylon will take over all the United Kingdom Forces installations (including any United Kingdom interest in the land) as vacated, except—

   (a) The fuel tanks at Colombo and Trincomalee.
   (b) The present Royal Air Force site at Colpetty including Steuart Lodge and Coolgardie.
   (c) Trenchard House.
   (d) Two Naval Residences in Gregory's Road, Colombo.
   (e) Thirty prefabricated houses at Trincomalee.

The installations taken over will include fixed fans, all water plant, the generators and electrical systems at Royal Naval Yard, Trincomalee, Diyatalawa, and Royal Air Force Station, Katunayake, and refrigerating equipment at Lotus Road Cold Stores but not movable refrigerating units at Mud Cove, Trincomalee. All other fiixtures, fittings, equipment, machinery, cranes, hoists, plant and stores other than normal landlords' fixtures will be excluded.

3. During the period of the rundown the following arrangements shall apply :

APPENDIX III 205

(a) The United Kingdom Forces will make no payment in respect of rates payable to local authorities and maintenance of public roads.

(b) The United Kingdom Forces, who will be paying the operating costs of the water and electrical systems at the Bases, will charge for all supplies made either to the Ceylon Forces or to non-service users, and will not make any payment to the Ceylon authorities for the supplies used by themselves or in respect of the use of any facilities still operated by them.

(c) If the United Kingdom authorities should wish to dispose of installations, other than those to be transferred to the Ceylon Government under this agreement, the Ceylon Government will be consulted and will give sympathetic consideration to the grant of such facilities as may be necessary to enable the United Kingdom authorities to obtain a fair price for the installations concerned. If the United Kingdom authorities wish to dispose of freehold properties other than those to be transferred to the Ceylon Government under this agreement the Ceylon Government will be consulted.

(d) At the Royal Ceylon Air Force stations no charges against the Royal Air Force will be made for the use enjoyed by the Royal Air Force of common user facilities operated at no appreciable extra cost by the Royal Ceylon Air Force, *e.g.* air traffic control, fire and crash services, navigation aids. Similarly in the case of common user facilities operated by the Royal Air Force no charges against the Royal Ceylon Air Force will be made provided no appreciable extra cost is involved. So long as any common user facilities at Katunayake are operated by the Royal Air Force or the Royal Ceylon Air Force, the cost of maintenance, to standards which will be mutually agreed, of runways, aprons, taxi tracks, and roads will be shared equally between the Royal Air Force and the Royal Ceylon Air Force. Until this maintenance work can be performed by the Royal Ceylon Air Force it will be undertaken as an agency service by the

Air Ministry Directorate General of Works. In the event of the airfield at Katunayake being used by international civil air traffic the agreement of the Royal Air Force to accept a liability for paying half the cost of airfield & c. maintenance would require revision.

(e) After 1st November 1957, the Royal Ceylon Air Force will assume responsibility for any rent payble to private land owners in respect of land occupied by the Royal Air Force. The Royal Air Force will reimburse the Royal Ceylon Air Force in respect of the said land as the area of land occupied by the Royal Air Force bears to the total of the area of the said land. The proportion of rent to be reimbursed will be adjusted at intervals as and when the Royal Ceylon Air Force progressively takes over land and buildings at present occupied by the Royal Air Force.

(f) The Royal Ceylon Air Force will assume complete responsibility for the cost of operation and maintenance of facilities transferred to them.

(g) Each Air Force will be responsible for the cost of maintaining buildings occupied by it.

4. The procedure for the disposal of surplus equipment and stores will be as follows :

(a) The Ceylon Government will be given the first option to purchase equipment and stores of which the United Kingdom authorities may wish to dispose during the rundown period.

(b) The United Kingdom authorities will notify the Ceylon Government of equipment and stores available for purchase, together with the prices proposed, and the Ceylon Government will within 21 days of such notification state whether they desire to purchase the equipment or stores and if so the price they are prepared to pay.

(c) If the Ceylon Government's offer is acceptable as regards price and other terms to the United Kingdom authorities the equipment or stores will be handed over on payment.

(d) If the Ceylon Government does not make any offer in accordance with paragraph (b) above, or if their offer is not acceptable to the United Kingdom authorities, the equipment or the stores concerned will be removed by the United Kingdom authorities or offered for sale by auction or otherwise without further reference to the Ceylon Government provided that in exceptional cases by mutual agreement the equipment or stores shall not be offered for sale.

(e) The Ceylon Government will subject to its normal regulations and practices regarding visas issue any necessary visas and permits to residents of other countries who apply to visit Ceylon for the purpose of purchasing equipment or stores of which the United Kingdom authorities may wish to dispose. In the case of purchases of equipment or stores by such residents of other countries, the Ceylon Government will so far as possible grant any export licences which may be necessary for the removal of the equipment or stores from Ceylon.

(f) Customs duty on equipment and stores sold will be payable by the United Kingdom authorities at the rate of 20 per cent of the sale price for all items other than cars and imported furniture, to which the normal rates will apply, except that no duties will be payable in respect of equipment and stores which are sold to the Ceylon Government or which were purchased locally by the United Kingdom authorities. In the case of equipment or stores purchased by residents of countries other than Ceylon, the Ceylon Government will grant to the exporter drawback of duty at the time of export on production of evidence that the articles exported were disposed of by the United Kingdom authorities.

(g) The above procedure shall not apply in the case of equipment and stores transferred to the Ceylon Government as part of facilities transferred for operation by them, payment for which shall be on the basis of United Kingdom Services vocabulary rates plus departmental expenses less depreciation.

No. 2

From : The Honourable S.W.R.D. Bandaranaike, Prime Minister of Ceylon.

To : His Excellency Sir Cecil Syers, High Commissioner for the United Kingdom in Ceylon.

Colombo, 7th June 1957.

My dear High Commissioner,

I refer to your letter of 7th June 1957, setting out the results of discussions which began in Colombo on 29th March 1957 regarding the United Kingdom Service Establishments in Ceylon, which reads as follows :

"I write this letter to place on record the main points which the Ceylon and United Kingdom Delegations have agreed on behalf of their two Governments in the talks which began in Colombo on 29th March regarding United Kingdom Services Establishments in Ceylon. These are as follows :

(1) In accordance with the declared policy of the Ceylon Government that United Kingdom Bases in the Island (hereafter referred to as the "Bases") should be closed down, the naval base at Trincomalee and the Royal Air Force Station at Katunayake will be formally transferred to the Ceylon Government on 15th October 1957, and 1st November 1957, respectively.

(2) Subject to sub-paragraphs 3 and 4 below, the United Kingdom Government will continue to use certain facilities for a limited time hereafter referred to as "the rundown". Such use of some of the facilities will cease within two to three years and of all will cease by March 1, 1962, provided that if the process of rundown is interrupted by causes outside the control of the United Kingdom Government, the period of rundown may be increased as may be mutually agreed.

APPENDIX III 209

(3) During the rundown the use of these facilities will be subject to general control of the Ceylon Government and the Ceylon Government reserves to itself the right to deny such use to the United Kingdom Government if any situation arises where, in pursuance of its general international policy, the Ceylon Government finds it necessary to do so. Subject to this condition the Ceylon Government will grant the United Kingdom Government the free and uninterrupted use and operation of these facilities and the right to administer their establishments as at present. The United Kingdom Government for its part will not, in the use of the facilities, interfere with such plans of development as the Ceylon Government might undertake in the areas concerned. If any difficulties should arise in this connection the two Governments will consult together in order to arrive at a satisfactory solution.

(4) Detailed arrangements regarding the facilities which it is intended the United Kingdom Government may continue to use, and arrangements which it is intended to put into operation to implement sub-paragraphs 1 to 3 above in other respects will be made.

(5) In addition to the grant of facilities under sub-paragraph 3 above the Ceylon Government will give to the United Kingdom Forces all necessary facilities and assistance in connection with (i) the withdrawal of the Forces, and (ii) the removal or disposal by the Forces of all their stores, equipment and other movable property.

(6) The Government of Ceylon shall pay to the United Kingdom Government, the sum of Rs. 22 million in five equal instalments of Rs. 4,400,000 in each of the Ceylon Government financial years 1957-58 to 1961-62 inclusive. This payment will be made in respect of the installations to be transferred to the Ceylon Government and the cancellation of certain claims between the two Governments arising out of the occupation or disposal of the bases by United King-

dom Forces. Detailed provisions regarding financial matters are contained in the Annex to this letter which Annex shall be regarded as an integral part hereof. In each year payment will be made in rupees within the total of United Kingdom estimated governmental expenditure in Ceylon, any balance being paid in sterling at the rate of Rs. 13.3102 to £1.

(7) Installations to be transferred to the Ceylon Government in accordance with the provisions of paragraph 2 of the said Annex shall be handed over as and when vacated by the United Kingdom Forces.

(8) The United Kingdom Forces and the members thereof will continue to enjoy during the period of rundown all the immunities and privileges hitherto enjoyed by them.

(9) During the period of rundown and after its completion the Ceylon Government, in accordance with normal Commonwealth practice but subject to the requirements of the general policy of the Ceylon Government, will continue to allow (a) United Kingdom naval vessels to refuel at Colombo; and (b) aircraft of the United Kingdom Forces, and on charter to those Forces, to overfly and stage through Ceylon.

(10) The United Kingdom Delegation supplied to the Ceylon Delegation a programme of the numbers of locally recruited employees of the United Kingdom Forces who it was intended would, as a consequence of the rundown, cease to be employed by the United Kingdom. The United Kingdom authorities will furnish at regular intervals both forecasts of future redundancies and particulars of impending discharges.

I shall be grateful to have your confirmation that the foregoing is acceptable to the Ceylon Government as a summary of the results of our discussions and that this letter and your reply shall constitute an agreement between our two Governments."

2. I am pleased to confirm that your letter is acceptable to the Ceylon Government as a summary of the results of the discussions and that your letter, together with this reply, shall constitute an agreement between our two Governments.

Yours sincerely,
(Sd.) S.W.R.D. BANDARANAIKE

His Excellency Sir Cecil Syers, K.C.M.G., CVO,
High Commissioner for U.K. in Ceylon.

Source : *Treaty Series* No. 4 of 1957 (Colombo) pp. 1-6.

APPENDIX IV

REPATRIATION OF UK CAPITAL FROM CEYLON

Rs. Million

Year	Private remittances and migrants' transfers	Interests, dividends, profits and other investment means
1951	21.4	74.5
1952	17.4	51.2
1953	20.7	47.2
1954	18.2	54.8
1955	17.7	82.4
1956	25.6	85.3
1957	21.3	80.6
1958	28.1	67.0
1959	20.8	58.8
1960	16.8	61.2
1961	17.8	49.1
1962	15.8	42.1
1963	13.0	44.9
1964	13.1	28.9
1965	11.8	9.0
1966	13.7	30.6
1967	11.0	34.0
1968	12.6	31.5
1969	9.0	55.3
1970	9.0	49.4
1971	10.3	58.0

Source: Central Bank of Ceylon Annual Reports, 1951—1971.

APPENDIX V

CEYLON'S TRADE WITH THE UK 1948—1970

Year	Import Percentage	Value (Rs. m.)	Export Percentage	Value (Rs. m.)	Balance of Trade (Rs. m.)
1948	17.25	171.4	32.20	301.2	+ 129.9
1949	18.01	185.3	33.50	335.3	+ 150.0
1950	19.72	230.0	24.57	365.9	+ 135.9
1951	21.95	342.1	32.18	585.2	+ 243.1
1952	22.42	381.8	29.39	413.5	+ 31.7
1953	22.34	359.2	25.91	384.7	+ 25.5
1954	20.97	293.1	28.87	494.8	+ 201.7
1955	21.02	306.9	26.89	501.8	+ 194.9
1956	21.15	344.7	30.24	498.3	+ 153.6
1957	20.46	369.0	28.91	458.3	+ 89.3
1958	24.26	416.4	34.29	565.2	+ 148.8
1959	24.71	495.4	28.39	479.6	− 15.8
1960	22.12	433.6	28.28	502.0	+ 68.4
1961	21.25	361.8	29.20	490.5	+ 128.7
1962	20.64	342.5	29.98	529.4	+ 186.9
1963	20.08	301.1	30.53	520.3	+ 219.2
1964	16.30	322.0	28.57	531.7	+ 209.7
1965	17.90	263.7	26.37	505.2	+ 241.5
1966	16.77	340.1	24.75	414.9	+ 74.8
1967	15.75	273.8	29.02	473.4	+ 199.6
1968	14.70	319.1	24.7	488.8	+ 169.7
1969	17.40	443.0	20.2	378.5	− 64.5
1970	14.30	329.8	22.8	454.7	+ 124.9
1971	Not available				

Source: *Statistical Abstract of Ceylon*—1948—1971.

APPENDIX VI

NUMBER OF STUDENTS WHO ENTERED THE VARIOUS LONDON EXTERNAL EXAMINATION (1) 1949—1963

Year	No. of Students
1949	2790
1950	2694
1951	2675
1952	3663
1953	3647
1954	4175
1955	4385
1956	6188
1957	5200
1958	8603
1959	9939
1960	10283
1961	10171
1962	8769
1963	8857

Various examinations were :
(a) London Matriculation or General Certi fic te of Education (Advanced level).
(b) Intermediate in Arts, Science, Law, Commerce & Engineering.
(c) Diploma on Education, Public Administration & Geography.
(d) B.A., B.Sc., B.Com., LL.B. & B.A. (Hons.).
(e) M.A., M.Sc., LL.M.
(f) Technical.
(g) Professional.

Source : Compiled from *Statistical Abstract of Ceylon* 1949—1964.

APPENDIX VII

NUMBER OF CEYLONESE STUDENTS IN THE UNIVERSITIES OF THE UK 1948—1970

Year	No. of Students
1948-49	171
1949-50	158
1950-51	184
1951-52	160
1952-53	186
1953-54	208
1954-55	191
1955-56	257
1956-57	233
1957-58	234
1958-59	221
1959-60	224
1960-61	248
1961-62	251
1962-63	227
1963-64	203
1964-65	220
1965-66	222
1966-67	270
1967-68	295
1968-69	306
1969-70	402
1970-71	Not available

Sources: 1. *Uninersities Year Book* 1948—1950.
2. *Commonwealth Universities Year Book* 1951—1971.

SELECT BIBLIOGRAPHY

PRIMARY SOURCES

i. Official Documents

Agreement between the Government of Ceylon and the Government of the Union of Soviet Socialist Republics for the Promotion of Cultural Co-operation, Treaty Series No. 1 of 1958 (Colombo).

Agreement between the Government of the United Kingdom of Great Britain and Northern Ireland and the Government of Ceylon for the Avoidance of Double Taxation and the Prevention of Fiscal Evasion with respect to Taxes on Income, Treaty Series No. 9 of 1950 (Colombo).

Aid to Developing Countries, Cmd. 2147 (H.M.S.O., London, 1963).

Assistance from the UK for Overseas Development. Cmd. 974 (H.M.S.O., London, 1960).

Bandaranaike, S.W.R.D., *The Foreign Policy of Ceylon : Extracts from Statements* (Colombo, 1961) edn. 3.

———, *The Government and the People : A Collection of Speeches* (Colombo, 1959).

———, *Speeches and Writings* (Colombo, 1963).

———, *Towards a New Era : Selected Speeches...made in the Legislature of Ceylon, 1931—1959* (Colombo, 1963).

Bandung 1955 : Addresses to the Asian-African Conference and Statements to the Press by the Rt. Hon. Sir John Kotelawala, Prime Minister of Ceylon (Government Press, Ceylon, 1955).

Between Two Worlds : The Collected Speeches of the Rt. Hon. Sir John Kotelawala, Prime Minister of Ceylon, November-December 1954 (Government Press, Ceylon n.d.).

SELECT BIBLIOGRAPHY

Central Bank of Ceylon, *Annual Reports of the Monetary Board to the Minister of Finance, 1950—1970* (Colombo).

Ceylon, *Administration Reports of the Commissioner of Labour 1948—1965* (Colombo).

————, *Administration Reports of the Director of Industries for 1955—1958* (Colombo).

————, *Administration Reports of the Controller of Immigration and Emigration for 1949—1965* (Colombo).

————, *Administration Report of the Controller of Exchange 1949* (Colombo, 1950).

————, *Administration Reports of the Director-General of Broadcasting for 1955—1965* (Colombo).

————, *Administration Reports of the Director of Cultural Affairs for 1958—1965* (Colombo).

————, *Administration Reports of the Director of Education for 1955—1957* (Colombo).

————, *Administration Report of the Director-General of Education for 1968—1969* (Colombo, 1972).

————, *Administration Reports of the Rubber Controller for 1954—1965* (Colombo).

————, *Administration Reports of the Tea Controller for 1954—1965* (Colombo).

————, *Chamber of Commerce, Annual Reports and Accounts 1949—1964* (Colombo).

————, Department of Census and Statistics, *Census of Ceylon 1946* (4 Vols.) (Colombo, 1951).

————, Department of Census and Statistics, *Ceylon Year Book 1950—1970* (Colombo).

————, Department of Census and Statistics, *Statistical Abstracts for 1949—1970* (Colombo).

————, Department of Census and Statistics, *Statistical Pocket Book of Ceylon*, 1970.

————, Department of Commerce, *Thirty Years of Trade Statistics* (Colombo, 1956).

―――, House of Representatives, *Parliamentary Debates, 1947—1971* (Colombo).

―――, *The Independence of Ceylon,* Sessional Paper XXII—1947 (Colombo).

―――, Ministry of External Affairs, *Diplomatic Consular and Other Representation in Ceylon and Ceylon Representation Abroad 1950—1965* (Colombo).

―――, Ministry of Finance, *Budget Speeches 1962—1972* (Colombo).

―――, Ministry of Finance, *Economic and Social Development of Ceylon (A Survey) 1926—1954* (Colombo, 1955).

―――, Ministry of Finance, *Government Policy in respect of Private Foreign Investment in Ceylon* (Colombo, 1955).

―――, Ministry of Finance, *External Economic Assistance : A Review from 1950—1964* (Colombo, 1964).

―――, Ministry of Finance, *Foreign Economic Aid : A Review from 1950—1962* (Colombo, 1962).

―――, Ministry of Planning and Economic Affairs, *Foreign Aid* (Colombo, 1966).

―――, Planning Secretariat, *Six Year Programme of Investment 1954/1955 to 1959/1960* (Colombo, 1955).

―――, *Proceedings of a Meeting of the Members of House of Representatives at Navarangahala and continued in the House of Representatives, 21st July 1970* (Colombo).

―――, *Proposals for the Establishment of District Councils under the Direction and Control of the Central Government* (Government Press, Ceylon, 1968).

―――, *Reform of the Constitution,* Sessional Paper XVII, 1943 (Colombo, 1943).

―――, *Report of the Joint United Kingdom and Australian Mission on Rice Production in Ceylon—1954.* Sessional Paper II—1955 (Colombo).

―――, *Report of the Select Committee on the State Council on Sinhalese and Tamil as the Official Languages,* Sessional Paper XXII—1946 (Colombo).

SELECT BIBLIOGRAPHY

———, *Report of the Special Committee on Education*, Sessional Paper XXIV—1943 (Colombo).

———, Senate, *Parliamentary Debates 1954—1969* (Colombo).

The Colombo Plan for Co-operative Economic Development in South and South East Asia, *Report by the Commonwealth Consultative Committee*, Cmd. 8080 (London, 1950).

The Colombo Plan Technical Co-operation Scheme, *Reports for 1955—1970* (H.M.S.O. London).

Commonwealth Economic Committee, *Commonwealth Trade 1949—1965* (H.M.S.O., London).

The Constitution of Ceylon, Sessional Paper III—1948 (Government Press, Ceylon).

The Constitution of Sri Lanka (Ceylon, 1972).

Exchange of Letters between the Government of Ceylon and the Government of the United Kingdom dated 2nd February 1949, concerning Ceylon's Sterling Assets and Monetary Co-operation between the Two Governments, Treaty Series No. 2 of 1949 (Colombo).

Exchange of Letters between the Government of Ceylon and the Government of the United Kingdom dated 2nd February 1951, concerning the Treatment of Ceylon's Sterling Balances during the Seven Years beginning 1st July 1950 and the Independent Reserve of Gold and Dollars to be held by the Central Bank of Ceylon, Treaty Series No. 1 of 1951 (Colombo).

Exchange of Letters between the Government of Ceylon and the Government of the United Kingdom concerning Ceylon's Sterling Assets, Treaty Series No. 13 of 1952 (Colombo).

Exchange of Letters between the Government of Ceylon and the Government of the United Kingdom regarding United Kingdom Service Establishments in Ceylon, Treaty Series No. 4 of 1957 (Colombo).

Exchange of Letters dated 17th March 1961, between the Government of Ceylon and the Government of the United Kingdom regarding the Loan of £2.5 million to finance Greater Colombo Telephone System, Treaty Series No. 2 of 1961 (Colombo).

Final Report of the Commission on Higher Education in the National Languages (Sinhalese and Tamil), Sessional Paper—1956, (Government Press, Ceylon).

The Final Report of the Official Languages Commission, Sessional Paper XXII—1953 (Government Press, Ceylon).

Finance Act, No. 65 of 1961 (Government Press, Ceylon).

Indonesia, Ministry of Foreign Affairs, *Asia—Africa Speaks from Bandung* (Djakarta, 1955).

Official Records of the General Assembly of the United Nations, *Eleventh Session, 590th Plenary meeting, 1956* (New York).

————, *Eleventh Session, 663rd Plenary meeting, 1957* (New York).

————, *Eleventh Session, 677th Plenary meeting, 1957* (New York).

————, *First Emergency Special Session, 561st Plenary meeting, 1956* (New York).

————, *Second Emergency Special Session, 571st Plenary meeting, 1956* (New York)

————, *Third Emergency Special Session, 742nd Plenary meeting, 1958* (New York)

Proposals for conferring on Ceylon fully Responsible Status within the British Commonwealth of Nations, Cmd. 7257 (H.M.S.O., London, 1947).

Report on Indian Constitutional Reforms (Calcutta, 1918).

Report on Lieutenant-Colonel Colebrooke upon the Administration of the Government of Ceylon to the Rt. Hon. Viscount Godrich (London, 1831).

Report of the Special Commission on the Constitution. Cmd. 3131 (H.M.S.O., London, 1928).

Report of the Commission on the Constitutional Reform. Cmd. 6677 (H.M.S.O., London, 1945).

Thorogood, C. E. *Overseas Economic Survey of Ceylon* (H.M.S.O., London, 1954).

SELECT BIBLIOGRAPHY

Trade Agreement between the Government of Ceylon and the Government of the Czechoslovak Republic, Treaty Series No. 3 of 1956 (Colombo).

Trade Agreement between the Government of Ceylon and the Government of the People's Republic of Hungary, Treaty Series No. 5 of 1956 (Colombo).

Trade and Payments Agreements between the Government of Ceylon and the Government of the Polish People's Republic, Treaty Series No. 2 of 1956.

Trade and Payments Agreement between the Government of Ceylon and the Government of the People's Republic of Bulgaria, Treaty Series No. 6 of 1956 (Colombo).

Trade and Payments Agreements between the Government of Ceylon and the Government of the People's Republic of Rumania, Treaty Series No. 8 of 1956 (Colombo).

United Kingdom, Board of Trade, *The Commonwealth and the Sterling Area : Statistical Abstract 1949—1965* (H.M.S.O., London).

————, Central Statistical Office, *Annual Abstract of Statistics 1956—1965* (H.M.S.O., London).

————, Central Office of Information, *The Pattern of Commonwealth Trade*, No. R. 3927 (London, July 1958).

————, Central Office of Information, *Trade and Payments 1957-58*, No. R. 3941 (London, July 1958).

————, Central Office of Information, *The Sterling Area*, No. R. 3949 (London, August 1958).

————, House of Commons, *Parliamentary Debates*, Fifth Series, Vols. 438-609 (1947—1964).

————, Overseas Development Institute, *Government Finance* (London, 1964).

————, *State Papers 156, 1950* (H.M.S.O., London, 1959).

United Nations, Department of Economic Affairs, *Economic Survey of Asia and Far East, 1953* (Bangkok, 1954).

UNP Journal 1951—1959 (Colombo).

United National Party, *The Manifesto and Constitution of the United National Party* (Colombo, 1947).

ii. Other Documents

Ceylon Association in London, *Reports and Accounts* (London, 1965).

Eden, Sir Anthony, *The Memoirs of Anthony Eden : Full Circle* (Boston, 1960).

International Tea Committee, *Annual Bulletin of Statistics 1953—1965* (London).

Kotelawala, Sir John, *An Asian Prime Minister's Story* (London, 1956).

Mahajana Eksath Peramuna, *Joint Programme of the M.E.P.* (Colombo, 1956).

The Planters' Association of Ceylon, 1854—1954 : A centenary issue (The Times of Ceylon Ltd., Colombo, 1954).

The Planters' Association of Ceylon, *Planters' Association Review*, Vols. 15-32, 1948—1965 (Colombo).

Sri Lanka Annual Progress Report 1957—1958 (Colombo).

SECONDARY SOURCES

i. Books

Abeyasinghe, Tikiri, *Portuguese Rule in Ceylon 1594—1612* (Colombo, 1966).

Almond and Coleman, *The Politics of the Developing Areas* (Princeton, 1960).

Amarasingam, S. P., *Rice and Rubber : The Story of China-Ceylon Trade* (Colombo, 1953).

Arasaratnam, S., *Ceylon* (New Jersey, 1964).

Ariyapala, M. B., *Society in Medieval Ceylon* (Colombo, 1956).

Bailey, Syndney D., *Ceylon* (New York, 1952).

————, *Parliamentary Government in Southern Asia* (New York, 1953).

Bell, P. W., *The Sterling Area in the post-War World* (London, 1956).

Benett, G. (ed.), *The Concept of Empire : Burke to Attlee 1774—1947* (London, 1953).

SELECT BIBLIOGRAPHY

Black Joseph E. & Thompson Kenneth W., *Foreign Policies in a World of Change* (New York, 1963).

Brock, W. R., *Britain and the Dominion* (Cambridge, 1951).

Bryant, Arthur, *A Choice for Destiny : Commonwealth and Common Market* (London, 1962).

Buddhist Committee of Inquiry, *The Betrayal of Buddhism* (Balangoda, 1956).

Burch, Betty B. and Cole, Allan B. (ed.), *Asian Political Systems* (Melborne, 1968).

Calvocoressi, Peter, *Survey of International Affairs 1954* (London, 1957).

Catholic Union of Ceylon, *Education in Ceylon according to the Buddhist Commission Report* : A Commentary (Colombo, 1956).

Carrington, Charles Edmund, *The British Overseas : Exploits of a Nation of Shopkeepers* (Cambridge, 1950).

Ceylon Daily News, *Parliament of Ceylon, 1947* (Colombo, 1947).

―――, *Parliament of Ceylon, 1956* (Colombo, 1956).

―――, *Parliament of Ceylon, 1960* (Colombo, 1960).

―――, *Parliament of Ceylon, 1965* (Colombo, 1965).

―――, *Parliament of Ceylon, 1970* (Colombo, 1970).

Cherry, J., *All the Cards on the Table : Foundations of British Foreign Policy* (London, 1948).

Codrington, H. W., *A Short History of Ceylon*, (London 1947).

Collins, Sir Charles, *Public Administration in Ceylon* (London, 1951).

Commonwealth Universities Year Book 1951—1971 (London).

Cook, Elsie K., *Ceylon, Its Geography, Its Resources and Its People* (London, 1951).

Corea, Harindra, *Freedom What Then* ? (Colombo, 1960).

Crane, Robert I., and Burton Stein, *Aspects of Economic Development in South Asia* (New York, 1954).

de Silva, Colvin R., *Ceylon ander the British Occupation, 1795—1833*, 2 Vols. (Colombo, 1962).

Eayrs James, *The Commonwealth and Suez*, (London, 1964).

Eckles, Robert, B., *Britain, Her Peoples and the Commonwealth* (Toronto, 1954).

Economist Information Unit, *If Britain Joins : The Economic Effects of Membership* (London, 1961).

Emerson, Rupert, *Representative Government in Southeast Asia* (Cambridge, 1955).

Farmer, B. H., *Ceylon : A Divided Nation* (London, 1963).

————, *Pioneer Peasant Colonization in Ceylon* (London, 1957).

Fernando, J. L., *Three Prime Ministers of Ceylon* (Colombo, 1963).

Fifield, R. H., *The Diplomacy of Southeast Asia, 1945—1958* (New York, 1958).

Folliot, Denise (ed.), *Documents on International Affairs, 1954* (London, 1957).

Frankel, S. H., *The Economic Impact on Under-developed Societies* (Oxford, 1953).

Franks, Oliver S., *Britain and the Tide of World Affairs* (London, 1955).

Goonewardene, Leslie, *L.S.S.P. Manifesto* (Colombo, 1951).

Goonewardena, K. W., *The Foundation of Dutch Power in Ceylon* (Amsterdam, 1958).

Gunasekera, H. A. de S., *From Dependent Currency to Central Banking in Ceylon* (London, 1962).

Gunawardane, Elaine, *External Trade and the Economic Structure of Ceylon 1900-1955* (Colombo, 1965).

Hamilton, W. B., Robinson Kenneth, and Goodwin, C.D.W. (eds.), *A Decade of the Commonwealth 1955-1964* (Durham, 1966).

Harvey, Heather J., *Consultation and Co-operation in the Commonwealth* (London, 1952).

Henderson, William, *Pacific Settlement of Disputes—The Indonesian Question 1946—1949* (New York, 1954).

Hoffmann, Stanley H. (ed.), *Contemporary Theory in International Relations*, (New Delhi, 1964).

SELECT BIBLIOGRAPHY

Hulugalle, H.A.J., *Ceylon* (Colombo, 1957).

Indraratna, A.D.V. de S., *The Ceylon Economy* (Colombo, 1966).

International Bank for Reconstruction and Development, *The Economic Development of Ceylon* (Baltimore, 1953).

Jansen, G.H., *Afro-Asia and Non-alignment* (London, 1966).

Jayasuriya, A.P., *Sri Lanka Freedom Party—First Anniversary Number* (Colombo, 1952).

Jayasuriya, J.E., *Some issues in Ceylon Education* (Peradeniya, 1964).

Jeffries, Sir Charles, *Ceylon—The Path to Independence* (London, 1962).

———, *Transfer of Power* (London, 1960).

———, *" 'O.E.G.', A Biography of Sir Oliver Earnest Goonetilleke"* (London, 1969).

Jennings, Sir Ivor, W., *The Approach to Self-Government* (Cambridge, 1956).

———, *The Commonwealth in Asia* (Oxford, 1951).

———, *The Constitution of Ceylon* (London, 1949), edn. 3.

———, *The Economy of Ceylon* (London, 1951), edn. 2.

———, *Problems of the New Commonwealth* (Durham, 1958).

Kahin, George M., *The Asian-African Conference, Bandung, Indonesia, April 1955* (Ithaca, 1955).

Kearney, Robert N., *Communalism and Language in the Politics of Ceylon* (Durham, 1967).

———, *Trade Unions and Politics in Ceylon* (California, 1971).

Keuneman, Pieter, *The Fight for Left Unity* (Colombo, 1951).

Kodikara, S.U., *Indo-Ceylon Relations since Independence* (Colombo, 1965).

Levi Werner, *The Challenge of World Politics in South and Southeast Asia* (New Jersey, 1968).

Liska George, *Alliances and the Third World* (Baltimore, 1968).

Ludowyk, E.F.C., *The Modern History of Ceylon* (London, 1966).

——, *Story of Ceylon* (London, 1962).

——(ed.), *Robert Knox in the Kandyan Kingdom* (London, 1948).

Mansergh, Nicholas, *The Commonwealth and the Nations* (London, 1948).

——, *Documents and Speeches on British Commonwealth Affairs 1931-1952*, 2 Vols. (London 1953).

——, *The Multi-racial Commonwealth* (London, 1954).

——, *Survey of British Commonwealth Affairs* (London, 1958).

Mason, Philip (ed.), *India and Ceylon : Unity and Diversity* (London, 1967).

Mehden, Fred R. Von Der, *Politics of the Developing Nations* (New Jersey, 1964).

Mende, Tibor, *South-East Asia between Two Worlds* (London, 1955).

Mendis, G.C., *Ceylon Today and Yesterday* (Colombo, 1957), edn. 2.

——, *Ceylon under the British* (Colombo, 1952), edn. 3.

——, *The Early History of Ceylon* (Calcutta, 1954).

—— (ed.), *The Colebrooke—Cameroon Papers, Documents on British Colonial Policy in Ceylon 1796-1833*, 2 Vols. (London, 1956).

Miller, J.D.B., *The Commonwealth in the World* (London, 1958).

——, *Britain and the Old Dominions* (London, 1966).

Mills Lennox, A., *Ceylon under the British Rule 1795-1932* (Colombo, 1964).

Muelder, Wallace R., *Schools for a New Nation* (Colombo, 1962).

Mukerji, K.P., *Madame Prime Minister Sirimavo Bandaranaike* (Colombo, 1960).

Myrdal, Gunnar, *Asian Drama : An Inquiry into the Poverty of Nations* (Toronto, 1968).

Namasivayam, S., *The Legislatures of Ceylon 1928-1948* (London, 1950).

Nicholas, C.W. and Paranavitana, S., *A Concise History of Ceylon* (Colombo, 1961).

Northedge, F.S., *British Foreign Policy* (London, 1962).

―――(ed.), *The Foreign Policies of the Powers* (London, 1968).

Oliver Henry, M. Jr., *Economic Opinion and Policy in Ceylon* (London, 1957).

Pakeman, S.A., *Ceylon* (London, 1964).

Panikkar, K.M., *Asia and Western Dominance* (London, 1953).

―――, *India and the Indian Ocean* (London, 1951), edn. 2.

―――, *The Strategic Problems of the Indian Ocean* (New Delhi, 1944).

Perera, S.G., *A History of Ceylon by Schools* (Ceylon, 1949), edn. 4.

Pieris, Ralph (ed.), *Some Aspects of Traditional Sinhalese Culture* (Peradeniya, 1956).

Political and Economic Planning, *Colonial Students in Britain— A Report* (London, 1955).

Ponnambalam, G G., *Presidential Address, First Plenary Session, The All Ceylon Tamil Congress* (Colombo, 1944).

Radhakrishnan, Sarvepalli, *East and West : Some Reflections* (London, 1954).

Rahula, W., *History of Buddhism in Ceylon : The Anuradhapura Period* (Colombo, 1956).

Ramachandran, N., *Foreign Plantations Investment in Ceylon 1889-1958* (Central Bank of Ceylon, 1963).

Rao, P.R. Ramachandra, *India and Ceylon : A Study* (Bombay, (1954).

The Revolt in the Temple (Sinha Publications, Colombo, 1953).

Robertson, Sir Dennis H., *Britain in the World Economy* (London, 1954).

Robert-Wray, Sir Kenneth, *Commonwealth and Colonial Law* (London, 1966).

Rothstein, R. L., *Alliances and Small Powers* (New York, 1968).

Royal Institute of International Affairs, *Documents on International Affairs 1949-1950* (London, 1953).

―――, *Outline of British Foreign Policy in East and South-East Asia, 1945-1950* (London, 1950).

Rustow, D. A., *Politics and Westernization in the Near East* (Princeton, 1956).

Ryan, Bryce, *Caste in Modern Ceylon : The Sinhalese System in Transition* (New Brunswick, 1953).

Sabaratnam, N., *National Education—Its Concept and Content* (Jaffna, 1961).

Sarkar, N. K. and Tambiah, S. J., *The Disintegrating Village* (Colombo, 1957).

Singh L. P., *The Colombo Plan : Some Political Aspects* (Canberra, 1963).

Singer, Marshall, R., *The Emerging Elite : A Study of Political Leadership in Ceylon* (Massachusetts, 1964).

Smith, D. E., *South Asian Politics and Religion* (Princeton, 1966).

Smith, F. Harold, *The Buddhist Way of Life* (London, 1957).

Snodgrass, Donald R., *Ceylon: An Export Economy in Transition* (Illinois, 1966).

Stanley, Eugene, *The Future of Underdeveloped Countries; Political Implications of Economic Development* (New York, 1954).

Story Francis, *Buddhism Answers the Marxist Challenge* (Rangoon, 1952).

Sumathipala, K.H.M., *History of Education in Ceylon 1796-1965* (Dehiwala, 1968).

Tennent J. Emerson, *Ceylon*, Vol. II (London, 1860).

Thompson, V. and Adloff, R., *Minority Problems in Southeast Asia* (Stanford, 1955).

The Times, *Common Market and Commonwealth* (London, 1962).

SELECT BIBLIOGRAPHY

Underhill, Frank H., *The British Commonwealth* : *An Experiment in Co-operation among Nations* (Durham, 1956).

Varma, S. P. and Misra, K. P., *Foreign Policies in South Asia* (New Delhi, 1969).

Vittachi, Tarzie, *The Brown Sahib* (London, 1962).

――――, *Emergency '58* ; *The Story of the Ceylon Race Riots* (London, 1958).

Weerawardana, I. D. S., *Ceylon General Election 1956* (Colombo, 1961).

――――, *Government and Politics in Ceylon 1931-1946* (Colombo, 1951).

――――, *The Senate of Ceylon at Work* (Colombo, 1955).

Weerawardana, I. D. S., and M. I., *Ceylon and Her Citizens* (Madras, 1956).

Wheare, K. C., *The Constitutional Structure of the Commonwealth* (London, 1960).

Wickramaratne, G.E.P. de S. (ed.), *Ceylon and Kotelawala* (Dehiwala, 1964).

Wickremasinghe, S. A., *The Economic Crisis* (Colombo, 1953).

――――, *The Way Ahead* : *An Economic Policy for Ceylon* (Colombo, 1955).

Wiener, Myron, *Political Changes in South Asia* (Calcutta, 1963).

Wijesekera, O. H. de A., *Buddhism and the Moral Problem* (Colombo, 1945).

Williams, Harry, *Ceylon Pearl of the East* (London, 1963), edn. 2.

Wint, Guy, *Spotlight on Asia* (London, 1955).

Wittfogel, K. A., *Oriental Despotism* : *A Comparative Study of Total Power* (New Haven, 1957).

Woodhouse, C. M., *British Foreign Policy since the Second World War* (Hutchinson, 1961).

Woodward, Calvin A., *Growth of a Party System in Ceylon* (Brown University Press, 1969).

Wriggins, W. Howard, *Ceylon : Dilemmas of a New Nation* (Princeton, 1960).

———, *The Ruler's Imperative* (New York, 1969).

Woolf Leonard, *Diaries in Ceylon, 1908-1911 and Stories from the East* (London, 1963)

Zinkin, M., *Asia and the West* (London, 1951).

———, *Movement of Free Asia* (New Jersey, 1956).

ii Articles in Periodicals

"Authoritarianism in Ceylon", *The Round Table* (London), September 1961, pp. 379-86.

Bandaranaike, S.W.R.D., "Ceylon and the Commonwealth", *Asian Review* (London), Vol. 52, 1956, pp. 217-21.

B.M., "A People's Government : Social and Political Trends in Ceylon", *The World Today* (London), Vol. 12, 1956, pp. 281-91.

Cardew, John, "Ceylon's Trade with China : The Economic Background", *New Commonwealth* (London), Vol. 25, 1953, pp. 377-78.

Carrington, Charles Edmund, "A New Theory of the Commonwealth", *International Affairs* (London), Vol. 31, 1955, pp. 137-48.

Carter, Gwendolen M., "The Asian Dominions in the Commonwealth", *Pacific Affairs* (New York), Vol. 22, 1949, pp. 367-75.

"Ceylon's Austerity hits UK Exports", *The Financial Times* (London), March 1963, p. 1.

"Ceylon : Asianism and the Commonwealth Connexion", *The Round Table*, March 1951, pp. 193-99.

"Ceylon's Best Customers", *The Financial Times* and *News of Ceylon* (Colombo), September 1961, pp. 1-2.

"Ceylon's Pattern of Trade", *The Financial Times* and *News of Ceylon*, April 1962, pp. 1-2.

"Ceylon : Problems and Prospects", *Pakistan Horizon* (Karachi), Vol. 16, 1963, pp. 242-58.

"Ceylon's Shifting Pattern of Trade", *The Financial Times* and *News of Ceylon*, September 1963, p. 7.

"Ceylon Today", *The Round Table*, June 1964, pp. 262-70.

"China is still the Best Customer", *The Financial Times* and *News of Ceylon*, August 1963, p. 4.

Conan, A.R., "Re-structing the Sterling Area", *The Banker* (London), May 1968, pp. 429-36.

Farmer, B.H., "The Social Bases of Nationalism in Ceylon", *Journal of Asian Studies*, Vol. 25, 1965, pp. 431-39.

Fernando, M., "The S.L.F.P., Capitalist or Socialist?", *Ceylon Economist* (Colombo), Vol. 5, 1961, pp. 165-177.

Harney, R.M., "The Foreign Policy of Ceylon under Two Premiers", *Australian Outlook* (Melbourne), Vol. 14, 1960, pp. 69-81.

Gunawardana, Philip, "Nationalisation of foreign-owned tea plantations", *Ceylon Economist*, Vol. 4, 1958, pp. 131-148.

Hudson, G.F., "How Unified is the Commonwealth", *Foreign Affairs* (New York), Vol. 33, 1955, pp. 679-88.

Indraratna, A.D.V. de. S., "The development problems of under-developed countries", *Ceylon Economist*, Vol. 4, 1958, pp. 191-214.

Jayawardene, J.R., "Ceylon's Sterling Assets", *The Ceylon Trade Journal* (Colombo), Vol. 13, 1948, pp. 129-30.

———, "D.S. Senanayake's Foreign Policy", *Ceylon Historical Journal* (Dehiwala), Vol. 5, 1955, pp. 49-61.

Jennings, Sir Ivor W., "Crown and Commonwealth in Asia", *International Affairs*, Vol. 32, 1950, pp. 137-47.

———, "The Dominion of Ceylon", *Pacific Affairs*, Vol. 22, 1949, pp. 21-23.

———, "Nationalism and Political Development in Ceylon", *Ceylon Historical Journal*, Vol. 3, 1953, pp. 62-84, 197-206.

———, "Politics in Ceylon since 1952", *Pacific Affairs*, Vol. 27, 1956, pp. 338-52.

Jones, P.H.M., "Peking's Trade Offensive IV—Ceylon", *Far Eastern Economic Review* (Hongkong), Vol. 27, 1959, pp. 45-47.

Kanesthasan, S., "Foreign capital in the economic development of Ceylon", *The Ceylon Journal of Historical and Social Studies*, Vol. 6, 1963, pp. 84-98.

Kearnery, Robert N., "Sinhalese Nationalism and Social Conflict in Ceylon", *Pacific Affairs*, Vol. 37, 1964, pp. 125-36.

King, John Kerry, "Rice Politics", *Foreign Affairs*, Vol. 31, 1953, pp. 453-60.

Kodikara, S.U., "Ceylon's Relations with Communist Countries", *South Asian Studies* (Jaipur), Vol. 2, 1967, pp. 103-30.

Kotelawala, Sir John, "Ceylon as Switzerland-in-Asia", *New Commonwealth*, Vol. 29, 1955, pp. 315-17.

Meegama, S.A., "The Demand for Consumer Imports in Ceylon 1947-1959", *The Ceylon Journal of Historical and Social Studies*, Vol. 7, 1964, pp. 88-96.

Miller, J.D.B., "Britain, the Commonwealth and European Integration", *Australian Outlook*, Vol. 13, 1959, pp. 3-18.

"The New Ceylon", *Eastern Economist*, July 1956, p. 39.

Palmer, Norman D., "Organizing for Peace in Asia", *The Western Political Quarterly* (Utah), Vol. 8, 1955, pp. 1-43.

Perera, A.B., "Plantation Economy and Colonial Policy in Ceylon", *Ceylon Historical Journal*, Vol. 1, 1951, pp. 46-58.

Phadnis, Urmilla, "Ceylon and the Sino-Indian Border Conflict", *Asian Survey* (California), Vol. 3, 1968, pp. 189-96.

———, "Federal Party in Ceylon Politics : Towards Power or Wilderness?", *Economic & Political Weekly*, May 17, Vol. 4, 1969, pp. 839, 841-43.

———, "Neo-Buddhists in India & Ceylon", *Economic & Political Weekly*, Vol. 4, 1969, pp. 1897-98.

———, "Non-alignment as a Factor in Ceylon's Foreign Policy", *International Studies* (New Delhi), Vol. 3, 1962, pp. 425-42.

———, "Prophets of Power", *Far Eastern Economic Review*, Vol. 64, 1969, pp. 379-80.

Reynolds, P.A., "British Foreign Policy since the Second World", *International Studies*, Vol. 1, 1959, pp. 137-153.

Senanayake, D.S., "Speech delivered over the B.B.C. on 'The Middle Way' of moderation as a path to Peace", *Ceylon Historical Journal*, Vol. 5, 1955-1956, pp. 110-14.

Senanayake, Maitripala, "Our Religion is the Basis of our Culture", *The Buddhist*, Vol. 31, 1961, pp. 4-7.

Sheen Vincent, "The People of Ceylon and their Politics", *Foreign Affairs*, Vol. 28, 1949, pp. 68-74.

Shetty, K.P., "Ceylon's Foreign Policy : Emerging Patterns of Non-alignment", *Political Science Review* (Jaipur), Vol. 5, April 1966, pp. 1-32.

Sirimavo R.D. Bhandaranaike, "Message", *Ceylon and World Affairs* (Colombo), October 1960, p. 3.

Stephen, Ian, "Report on Ceylon", *New Commonwealth*, Vol. 27, 1954, pp. 329-33.

Taussig, H.C., "Ceylon in the New World", *Eastern World* (London), March 1957, pp. 18-19.

Tsou Szu-I, "Trade between China and Ceylon", *People's China* (Peking), Vol. 20, 1956, pp. 9-11.

Tung, S.Y., "Ceylon—A Firm Trading Base", *Far Eastern Economic Review*, Vol. 31, 1961, pp. 53-55.

Vanden Driesen, I.H., "Some trends in the economic history of Ceylon in the 'modern' period", *Ceylon Journal of Historical and Social Studies* (Peradeniya), Vol. 3, 1960, pp. 1-17.

Wheare, K.C., The Nature and Structure of the Commonwealth", *American Political Science Review* (Wisconsin), Vol. 47, 1953, pp. 1016-28.

Wijesena, P.K.D., "Ceylon-USSR Economic Relations", *Eastern World*, September 1964, pp. 28-30.

Wilson, A.J., "Ceylon's Foreign Policy since Independence", *Young Socialist* (Colombo), Vol. I, 1961, pp. 27-34.

————, "The Crewe-McCallum Reforms, 1912-1921", *Ceylon Journal of Historical and Social Studies*, Vol. 2, 1959, pp. 84-115.

————, "The Governor-General and the state of Emergency, May 1958—March 1959", *The Ceylon Journal of Historical and Social Studies*, Vol. 2, 1969, pp. 160-81.

Wilson, A.J., "The Governor-General and the two dissolutions of Parliament, December 5, 1959 and April 23, 1960", *The Ceylon Journal of Historical and Social Studies*, Vol. 3, 1960, pp. 187-207.

————, "The Tamil Party in Ceylon Politics", *Journal of Commonwealth Political Studies* (Leicester), Vol. 4, 1966, pp. 117-35.

Woodward, Calvin A., "The Trotskite Movement in Ceylon", *World Politics* (Princeton), Vol. 14, 1962, pp. 307-21.

Wriggins, W. Howard, "Impediments to unity in new nations: The Case of Ceylon", *American Political Science Review*, Vol. 55, 1961, pp. 313-20.

Yershov, Y, "Six Years of Soviet-Ceylonese Trade", *Financial Times and News of Ceylon*, April 1964, p. 9.

iii Newspapers

Ceylon Daily News (Colombo)
Ceylon Daily Mirror (Colombo)
Ceylon Observer (Colombo)
Ceylon Newsletter (Ceylon High Commission, New Delhi)
Daily Express (London)
Daily Telegraph (London)
The Eastern Economist (Delhi)
The Hindu (Madras)
The Hindustan Times (Delhi)
Manchester Guardian (Manchester)

Morning Times (Colombo)
New York Herald Tribune (New York)
New York Times (New York)
Observer (Colombo)
The Scotsman (Edinburgh)
The Statesman (Delhi)
Sunday Times (Colombo)
Times of Ceylon (Colombo)
The Times (London)

INDEX

A.F. Jones & Co. Ltd. 111
Adult suffrage 5
Afro-Asian Conference, Bandung 38, 39, 41, 85, 86, 92
Agreement on Public Services (Ceylon-U.K.) 7, 8, 9, 10
Aid-Ceylon Group 182, 185
Air base, British 25, 27, 36, 69, 78
Air Transport Agreement (Ceylon-China) 86
All-Ceylon Buddhist Congress 158, 159
Almond, Gabriel A. 16
American flotilla
  Harbour facilities 37, 48, 49
American Missionary Society 20
Anuradhapura 177
Arasaratnam, S. 20
Armed forces
  Training 8, 24
Arts Council, Ceylon
  Handicrafts Panel 152
Asia Foundation 179
Asian-African Conference 85
Asian Conference, New Delhi, 1948 45, 46
'*An Asian Prime Minister's Story*' 56
Asian Switzerland 68
Attlee, Lord 47
Australian High Commission 179

Baily, Sydney D. 16
Balance of payment 115, 120, 121, 122, 124, 125, 134, 135, 181
Balfour Declaration 30
Bandarnaike, F.R.D. 88, 166
Bandarnaike, S.W.R.D. 18, 46, 64, 66, 92, 95, 96, 98, 99, 137, 148, 149, 150, 152, 153, 166, 167, 177,
200, 204, 208, 211 ; Assassination 66; Crossed floor 64-5; Neutral policy 67-78; On British bases 71-2, 73, 74, 75, 76, 78, 93; On Commonwealth 79-80; On communism 85; On economic development 104-5; On Hungarian uprising 90-1; On nationalisation 81; On socialism 68; On Suez dispute 89; On trade policy 84
Bandarnaike, Mrs. Sirimavo 66, 71, 87, 88, 95, 98, 149, 152, 153, 156, 161, 166, 168, 174, 176, 180, 181, 183, 184, 187; Government defeated 66, 153; Neutral policy 68; On India-China dispute 87-8; On nationalisation 82, 84; Visit to Czechoslovakia 88; To U.S.S.R. 88
Bandung Conference, *See* Afro-Asian Conference
Banes, Edward 11
Bangladesh 187
Bank for Reconstruction and Development 121
Bank of Ceylon 83, 181
Bankers' Training Institute 181
Banks 113
  Nationalisation 183
Banks, Central 117, 124
Banks, Foreign 83, 181, 185
Barter 11
Battle Act 39
Bell, P.W. 140
Bentham, Jeremy 3
Beverages, Intoxicating 147
Bhasa Peramuna 64
Bhikkus 147, 149, 150, 152
"Bloodless Arena" 70

Board of Trade 134
Bogor Conference 38
Boleshevik-Leninist Party 19
Bonstead, R.C. 110
Bribery Tribunal 174
British bases 25, 26, 36, 56, 68, 69, 71-8, 89, 93, 94, 166, 186
　Letters exchanged 200-11
British Broadcasting Corporation 70
British Ceylon Corporation Ltd. 184
British Commonwealth Hostel Scheme 154-5
British Council 154, 157, 161, 162, 179
British Guiana
　Prime Minister 38
British Medical Association 86
British Medical Students Association 154
British Peace Committee 37
Brock, W R. 17
Buddha, Impage of 150
Buddha Jayanti 147, 148
Buddha Sasana Council 147
Buddhism 14, 20, 66, 146, 147, 177
Buddhist Commission of Inquiry 147, 148, 155, 156, 159
Buddhist Council of Ceylon 148, 151
Buddhist encyclopedia 151
Buddhist revival 147-8, 149, 151, 169
Buddhist universities 152, 156, 169
Bureaucracy, Indigenous 2
Burma
　Independence 7, 9-10
Business Acquisition Act, 1971 184

Cabinet 9, 69
Cader, I.A.A. 190
Caltex Oil Company 83, 181, 182, 184
Cambridge University 177

Canada
　British bases 25
Cardew, John 61
Cecil Rhodes Trust 157
Census and Statistics Department 19
Central Bank of Ceylon 125, 181
Ceylon
　Area 1
　British rule 2-10; Educational impact 13-15; Socio-economic impact 11-13
　Dutch rule 2, 11
　Independence 7, 9-10, 21
　Portuguese rule 2
　Rebellion, 1797 2
　Strategic importance 1, 23, 24
Ceylon Association in London 110
Ceylon-China Friendship Association 86
Ceylon College of the Fine Arts 152
Ceylon (Constitution) Order-in-Council, 1946 10
Ceylon Copra Agreement 132
Ceylon Currency Ordinance 117
Ceylon Daily News 22, 26, 54, 77
Ceylon GCE (advanced level) examination 177
Ceylon House, London 153
Ceylon Independence Act, 1947 10, 34
Ceylon Independence Bill, 1947 9, 22
Ceylon Independence (Commencement) Order-in-Council, 1947 10
Ceylon Institute of Scientific and Industrial Research 157
Ceylon Insurance Corporation 82
Ceylon Muslim League 9, 18
Ceylon National Congress 5, 9, 18, 35
Ceylon Observer 54
Ceylon Order-in-Council, 1946 6
Ceylon (Parliamentary Elections) Order-in-Council 174

INDEX

Ceylon Petroleum Corporation 181
Ceylon Port Cargo Corporation 81
Ceylon Reform League 5
Ceylon University 135, 137, 157
Ceylonization 105-11, 169, 184-5
China
  Goodwill Mission 37
  Recognition 28, 29, 37
  Relations with Ceylon 37, 40, 41, 84, 85, 86, 183
Chou En-lai 38, 53
  Visit to Ceylon 85
Christian Sunday Schools 151
Civil service 12, 15, 20
Coconut industry 13, 39, 105
Coffee crash, 1847 12
Coffee industry 12, 14
Cold war 85
Cole, G.D.H. 14
Colebrooke-Cameron Commission, 1820 4, 11, 13-14, 16, 105
Coleman, J.S. 16
Collins, Charles 17, 19, 76
Colombo Academy 20
Colombo Municipal Council 27
Colombo Plan 32, 78, 124, 155, 157, 167, 182
  British economic assistance 134-5
Colombo Plan Exhibition, 1957 70
Colombo port 81
Colombo Powers 51, 52, 54
Colombo Powers Conference 38
Colombo Powers Meeting, New Delhi, 1956 90
Colonial administration 2-10
Colonial economy 105
Colonial Office 154, 162
Colonial students 154
Cominform 38
Commission on Higher Education 158
Commissioner of Commodity Purchase 111
Commonwealth Consultative Committee Meeting, Second 134
Commonwealth Correspondents Association 79
Commonwealth Economic Conference, Montreal, 1958 136
Commonwealth Finance Ministers' Conferences 28, 134
Commonwealth Foreign Ministers' Conferences 28, 144
Commonwealth High Commissioners' Conference 29
Commonwealth of Nations 7, 8, 9, 10, 15, 22, 28, 49, 54, 56, 72, 78, 79, 84, 85, 90, 93, 94, 134, 154, 173
  Burma's membership 30, 165
  Ceylon's membership 23, 30-1, 74, 164, 167, 176, 177, 189
  India's membership 30
  Pakistan's membership 30
Commonwealth Prime Ministers' Conferences 27, 28, 30, 33, 74, 85, 87, 186
Commonwealth Relations Office 28
Communal Hall of Residence, Bloomesbury 154
Communal representation 5
Communism 35, 51, 54, 55
Communist colonialism 38
Communist countries
  Relations with Ceylon 35-42, 84-8, 167-8, 182-3
Communist Party of Ceylon 19, 35, 37-8, 90, 172, 173
Communist Party of China Congress 86
Communist Party of the U.K. 37
Conference on Trade and Employment, Havana, 1948
  Final Act 30
Consolidated Fund of Britain 136
Constituent Assembly 174-5
Constitution Bill, 1944 6
Constitution of Ceylon 176, 189
Constitutional conventions 33
Constitutional relationship 23,

30-5, 94, 168, 173-7
Corea, Claude 34, 85, 89, 93
Corporation of London 35
Cotton Spinning and Weaving Mill 87
Crewe-McCallum Reforms 4
Crown 2-10, 33
Cultural Affairs Ministry 150-1, 152, 169
Cultural delegations 151
Cultural relations 146-63, 168, 169, 173, 177-9, 189
  China 86
  U.S.S.R. 86-7, 88

Dahanayake, W. 66
Daily Mail 69
Daily Telegraph 77
Dalada Maligawa 176
Declaration of 1943 6
Defence Agreement (Burma-U.K.) 165
Defence Agreement (Ceylon-U.K.) 7, 8, 9, 10, 18, 23-7, 50, 56, 71, 73, 76-7, 164, 165, 166, 167, 195-6
Defence Ministry 77
Democratic republic 78-80, 94, 168, 173, 174, 175, 176
Devaluation, 1949
  Implications on Ceylon 117-19
Development Finance Corporation 181
Diego Garcia 186
Dien Bien Phu 49
Disarmament 74
Dodds-Parker fact-finding mission 52
Dominion status 6, 7, 8, 15, 29, 71, 153, 154
Donoughmore Commission 106
Donoughmore Constitution, 1931 5, 17, 18, 106
Double Taxation Agreement (Ceylon-U.K.) 112, 139
Driesen, I.H. Vanden 19
Duke of Edinborough 35
Duke of Glouchester 34

East African Standard 185
East India Company 2, 11
Eastern World 67
Eayers, Jumeo 102
ECAFE Conference, Colombo 38
Economic aid 88, 181, 182, 185, 188-9
Economic aid, American 39, 40
Economic aid, British 133-5, 167, 170, 182, 188-9
Economic aid, Chinese 86, 87, 183, 185-5, 188-9
Economic aid, Russian 183
Economic Aid Agreement (Ceylon-China) 86, 87
Economic development 104, 125, 185
  Intra-Commonwealth consultation 28
Economic imperialism 123
Economic policy 70-1, 82, 179, 184
Economic relations 104-45, 169, 170, 173, 179-86
  Communist countries 182-3
Eden, Anthony 50, 51
Education 148, 153-8, 168
  British impact 13-15, 146
  Dutch system 13
Education Act, 1947 155
Education Department 135
Egypt-Israel conflict 89-90
Elizabeth II, Queen 34, 177
Empire Society 153
Employment
  Ceylonization 105-8, 169
English language 14, 153, 157, 178-9, 189
English schools 13, 14, 153
Esquimalt base 25
ESSO Oil Company 181, 182, 184
Examinations
  Cambridge system 14, 20
Executive Committee 5
Executive Council of Senior Officers 4
Exhibition (1851) Fund 154
Export Guarantees Act, 1949

INDEX

134, 136
External Affairs Agreement (Ceylon-U.K.) 7, 8, 9, 10, 18, 23, 27-30, 167, 197-9
External Affairs Ministry 41, 77

Farmer, B.H. 76, 99
Federation of British Industries 155
Federal Party 74, 172, 173
Fernando, J.L. 96
Fetch, Master Ralph 16
Fisheries Ordinance, 1940 106
Five Principles of Peaceful Co-existence 53, 85, 86
Football team, Russian 38
Foreign commerce 11, 13, 39, 126-7, 129
   Ceylonization 109-11, 166-70, 183-4
   U.K. 125-32, 170, 213
Foreign exchange 114-15, 116, 117
Foreign investment 180, 181
Foreign investment, British 111-16, 137, 170, 212
Foreign Ministers' Conference, Colombo, 1950 134
Foreign relations 186-9
   China 37, 40, 41, 84, 85, 183
   Communist countries 35-42, 84-8, 167-8, 182-3
   Non-alignment 64-103
   Representatives abroad 29
   Poland 87
   USSR 30, 35-6, 57, 74, 84, 86, 88
   U.K. 21-63
   U.S.A. 74, 78
Formosa 48
Four-Power Conference, Berlin, 1954 49
Fundamental Rights 176

Gaitskell, Hugh 134
General Certificate of Education Examination 179
General elections, First 8-9
   1956 64, 65, 147-8, 149, 156

1960 66
1965 172
1970 172-3
General import licences 110
General insurance 82
Geneva Agreement on Indo-China 50
Geneva Conference, 1954 50
Goderich, Viscount 16
Goonetilleke, Oliver 7, 8, 18, 21, 24, 31, 44, 107, 119, 153
Goonasinha, A.E. 55
Goonewardane, Leslie 80
Gopallawa, William 149, 153
Gorton, John 187
Government Banking Corporation 83
Governor 3, 4
Governor-General 33, 36, 65, 68, 71, 82, 149, 150, 153, 174, 175, 177
Greater Colombo Area Telephone Development Scheme 136
Greater Colombo Telecommunication Development 137
Green revolution 180
Growther, J.G. 37
Gunawardene, Elaine 141
Gunawardene, Philip 64, 66, 81, 114, 148
Gunawardene, R.S.S. 39, 91
   On neutrality 43
Gunawardene, Senarath 69

Halifex base 25
Health Department 135
Henry, *Mrs.* D. 38
High Commissioners 28, 33, 34
High Commissioners Office 28
Hinduism 14, 20
Hindustan Times 54
Home, Alac Douglas 187, 188
Home, Lord 69
Horse-racing 147
House of Commons (U.K.) 7, 9, 22, 47
House of Representatives 8-9, 23, 24, 27, 32, 36, 38, 42, 45, 48, 55,

69, 71, 73, 75, 79, 81, 122, 153, 172, 181
   Motion on independence 9-10
Hulugalle, H.A.J. 16, 20
Hungarian uprising
   Ceylon's attitude 90-2, 168

Illangaratne, T.B. 83, 184
Immigrants and Emigrants Act 106-7, 108
Immigration 106-7, 114
Immigration and Emigration Department 107
Imperial Conferences 28
Imperial Honours 69
Imperialism 1, 46
Import and Export Control Department 110
India
   Independence 7
   Montague-Chelmsford Report, 1918 5
India-China dispute, 1962 77, 87
Indian Council of World Affairs 80
Indian labour 12, 13
Indian National Congress 18, 64, 66
Indian Ocean 1, 7, 23, 24, 69, 73, 165, 186-7
Indigenous culture 150, 177
Individual import licences 110
Indo-China war
   Ceylon's attitude 43, 49-51, 52, 167
Indonesian question
   Ceylon's attitude 43, 44-7
Indonesian-Malaysian conflict
   Ceylon's attitude 186
Indraratna, A.D.V. de S. 141
Industrial Products Act 126
Industrial Revolution 3
Industrialisation 125, 126, 169
Institute for Defence Studies and Analyses 192
Institute of International Affairs 155
International Medical Students Association 154
International Monetary Fund 121
Intra-Commonwealth Consultation 28-9, 56
Iriyagolle, I.M.R.A. 178

Jagan, Cheddi 38
Janadhipathi Medura 175
Jansen, G.H. 62
Jayawardene, J.R. 48, 60, 74, 96, 116, 122, 141, 175
Jefferies, Charles 16, 17, 18
Jennings, Ivor 8, 17, 18, 19, 20, 58, 59, 63
Jessup, Philip 45
Jinadasa, J.P. 29
Joint Committee to amend the Constitution 80, 173
Jones, Creech 7
Jordan crisis
   Ceylon's attitude 92-4, 95, 168
Judicial structure 35, 168

Kandy Kingdom 1, 2, 33, 160
Kandyan Chiefs 2-3
Kandyan Provinces 3
Katunayake base 71, 73, 74, 75, 76, 77, 166
Kem Amendment Legislation 39
Keuneman, Pieter 48, 92
Kirbath 149, 160
Kobbekadowe, Hector 184
Kodikara, S.U. 58, 138
Konneswaram temple 172
Korean war 37, 39
   Ceylon's attitude 43, 47-9
Kotewala, John 26, 34, 37, 56, 61, 62, 63, 65, 66, 73, 96; At Bandung "Conference 38; Middle-way" policy 43; On China 53; On Commonwealth 32; On Defence Agreement 27; On flag and anthem 35; On Korean war 50; On SEATO 51-2, 53, 54, 55-6

Labour 11
Labour, Migratory 12

INDEX

Labour Ministry 107
Labour Party (U.K.) 7, 17
Land Development Ordinance, 1935 106
Language laboratory 179
Lanka Sama Samaja Party 19, 25, 172, 173
Laski, Harold J. 14
Leftist Parties 35, 37, 48, 57, 66, 122
Legislative Council 4, 5, 17
Life insurance
  Nationalisation 82-3, 84, 95, 168
Linguistic nationalism 66
Liquor Serving 69, 149
Loan Agreement (Ceylon-U.K.), 1960 137
Loan repayment 185
Local government services
  Ceylonization 106
London Conference, 1956 89
London External Degree Examination 169, 178
London GEC (advanced level) examination 177, 178
London House 154
London Market 134
London Missionary Society 20
London University 178
  Institute of Education 157
London University Examinations 153, 177-8
Ludowyk, E.F.C. 98
Lusaka Conference 187

Magul bera 149
Mahajana Eksath Peramuna 57, 64, 126, 149, 160, 172, 173
  Election manifesto 66, 81, 148, 156
Mahamud, Badiuddin 191
Maharagama College 157
Mahavamsa 159
Malabar Officers 2
Malalasekara, G.P. 159, 178
Maldives 94
Malik, Jacob 36

Mansergh, Nicholas 25, 58
Marikkar, C.A.S. 69
Marine insurance 82
Maritime Provinces 3, 11
Maritime Transport Agreement (Ceylon-China), 1963 88
Mendis, G.C. 16, 19
'Middle way' 36, 43, 68, 85
Military assistance, British 8, 24, 164, 189
Military co-operation 28
Military service 12
Mill, James 3
Mills, Lennox A. 16
Missionary schools 13
Mixed economy 180
Monarchy 33, 34, 35, 56, 168, 176
Monk University 177
Moscow University 86
Moore, Henry 9, 196, 199
Morning Times 26
Moscow World Youth Festival 88

Naganathan, E.M.V. 74
Namasivayam, S. 58, 138
National anthem, British 35
National Assembly 176
National Council of Higher Education 178
National dress 149, 150
National Education Commission 156, 163
National flag 175
National Government 172
National languages 155
National movement 4-5, 14, 21, 35
National Service Radio Programme 150
Nationalisation 80-4, 137, 170, 180-1, 183, 189
Naval base, British 25, 36, 69, 78
Navarangahala 175
Nehru, Jawaharlal 44, 45, 52, 53, 67, 69, 70
Netherland
  Indonesian 'police action' 44-7
Neutrality 43, 56, 64-103, 165,

166, 167
New York Times 71
Non-aligned policy
  British reaction 64-103
Noonan, J.A. 157
North, Frederick 16
Nuns 147

The Observer 53
Official language 156, 178
Omnibus Service Licensing Ordinance, 1942 106
Oliver, Henry M. 138
Opposition leader 64
Opposition parties 9, 10, 25, 27, 38, 40, 48, 50, 51, 52, 74, 122, 123, 174, 175
Order-in-Council, 1920 5
Oxford University 157, 177

Pakeman, S.A. 17
Parliamentary delegation
  Visit to USSR 86
Payments Agreement between Ceylon and Japan 29
People's Bank 83, 181
People's Front 35
People's United Front 64
Perera, N.M. 19, 25, 48, 83, 115, 174, 185
Perera, S.G. 19
Perera, William A. 85
Permanent residence permits 108
Petroleum industry nationalisation 83-4, 95, 181-2, 184-5
Phadnis, Urmila 190
Pirith 150
Planning and Economic Affairs Ministry 183
Plantation industry 11-12, 20, 105, 108, 111, 169
  Nationalisation 68, 80-1, 82, 93, 189
Poland 38, 42, 57
Political parties 9, 66, 89, 90
  Defection 64-5
Politt, Henry 37
Pound Sterling 116, 117

Poya 147, 177
President 176
Press Bill 153
Press Commission 161
Principles of State Policy 175
Privy Council 174, 176
  Judicial Committee, 35, 168
Public Service Commission 175
Public Services 8
  British obligations 7
  Ceylonization 105-6

Queen
  Visit to Ceylon 34, 65
Queen Elizabeth, The Queen Mother 70
Queen's House 150, 175
Queen's titles 34, 59-60

Radio Ceylon 150, 151
Rajakariya 11, 19
Rajasingh, Wickrama 2
Rees-William, D.R. 22
Religio-communal conflict, 1915 4-5
Representative government 5
Ritcher, F. 153
Roman Catholic Church 147, 148
Rome Food Aid Convention 182
Rose, Alan 96
Royal College of Surgeons, 157
Royal Dutch Air Lines (KLM) 44
Royal Institute of International Affairs 155
Royal Preparatory School 175
Royal Title Act, 1953 34
Rubber export 39-40, 41
Rubber industry 13, 39 40, 105
  Nationalisation 70, 137, 170
Rubber Replanting Programme 86
Rubber-Rice Pact (Ceylon-China) 126, 183
Rupee companies 109
Rural broadcasting 135

Sabbath 67
St. Matint School of Art, London

152
Sayers, Cecil 41
Scholarships 151-5
Scholarships, British 154, 155, 157
Scholarships, Russian 86
Scholarships, UN 154
School Commission 14
Schools
   Nationalisation 147, 156
Secretary of State for the Colonies 3, 7, 8, 106
Senanayake, D.S. 6, 7, 8, 9, 17, 18, 22, 44, 59, 62, 64, 65, 73, 95, 96, 158, 159, 182, 196; BBC address, 1951 42; Death 65; Dislike of communism 35-6, 37; On British relations 22, 23, 42; On China 37; On Commonwealth 30-3; On Defence Agreement 23-4, 26; On economic assistance 134; On Korean war 47, 48; On monarchy 33; Visit to New Zealand 32
Senanayake, Dudley 6, 26, 37, 40, 41, 55, 57, 66, 96, 172, 180, 183, 186; Became Prime Minister 65; On British relations 42-3; On Queen's position 34, 65
Senanayake, R.G. 40, 55, 96
   Defection 65
Senanayake, Maitripala 160
Service Establishments
   Exchange of letters 200-11
Shaw, Bernard 14
Shell Petroleum Company 83, 84, 181, 182, 184
Silva, C.P. de 66, 98
Silva, Coluin R. de 19, 74, 92, 189
Silva, Mrs. Joe de 38
Silva, K.M. de 161
Silva, S.F. de 157
Simhala Mahasabha 9, 18
Simontown base 24
Simpston base 74
Singapore 72
Singh, L.P. 145

'Sinhala only' Act, 1956 156
Sinhalese dishes 149
Sinhalese language 13, 14, 153, 156, 178
Smith, Adam 3
Smith, D.E. 158, 159, 160, 162
Solar eclipse, 1955 38
Soulbury, Lord 96, 154
Soulbury Commission 6, 18
Soulbury Constitution 6, 9, 176
South Africa
   British bases 25
South East Asian Prime Ministers' Conference, Colombo, 1954 49, 50, 51
South East Asian Treaty Organisation
   Ceylon's attitude 43, 51-6, 73, 167
   Colombo Powers' attitude 52, 54
Sri Lanka Freedom Party 64, 66, 82, 148, 156, 160, 164, 172, 173, 179, 180, 186
Standard Vacuum Oil Company 83
State Council 5, 6, 9, 17, 106
State Petroleum Corporation 95, 168
State Services Advisory Board 176
State Trading Corporation 184
State Trading Corporation Bill 184
Sterling Area 78, 79, 116-7, 121, 167
Sterling Area Dollar Pool 125
Sterling Area Pool 123
Sterling Assets Agreements 121-2
Sterling Balance Agreements 118-25
Sterling companies 109, 115
Students abroad
   U.K. 153, 157, 158, 169, 177, 214-15
Suez Canal 75, 80, 128
Suez Canal dispute
   Ceylon's attitude 89-90, 94, 95,

167, 168, 170
Sumathipala, K.H.M. 160, 163
Sunday Dhamma Schools 151
Suntharalingam 27
Supreme Commander of the Allied Powers in Japan 29
Swabasha 178
Syers, Cecil 200, 203, 208, 211

Tambiah, H.W. 59
Tamil labour 12
Tamil language 13, 14, 153, 178
Taussig, H.C. 97
Tea industry 13, 39, 105, 108, 180
 Nationalisation 70, 137, 170
Teachers (Superannuation) Bill, U.K. 155
Technical assistance 88, 155
Technical assistance, British 135-7, 167, 170
Temporary Residence Tax Act, 1961 108
Temporary Resident Permits 107, 108
Tennent, J. Emerson 3, 16
Thorogood, C.E. 139, 143
Three-Man Political Mission (Hungary) 92
Tillekaratne, Stanley 175
Tillekaratne, W.D.S. 190
The Times 34, 70
Times of Ceylon 47, 55
Tiruchelvam, M. 189
Trade Agreements 132-3
Trade and Payment Agreement with China 86, 170
Trade relations
 China 39, 40, 41, 57, 84, 86, 87, 110, 126, 128, 130, 183
 Communist countries 39, 42, 57, 126-7, 129, 183
 Czechoslovakia 84, 110, 126
 Poland 84, 110, 126
 Rumania 84, 111, 126
Training College, Peradeniya 179
Trincomalee base 71, 73, 74, 75, 77
Trine 65

Trotsyite Party 74
Truman, 48

U Nu 53
Union Jack 35
United Front 179, 182
United Front, 1970 172
 Election manifesto 174
 Government 173-89
U.K.
 Consul-General in Peking 29
 Food Ministry 133
 Ministry of Health and Local Government 154
 Ministry of Overseas Development 182
 Strategic interests 7
United National Party 9, 18, 64, 66, 70, 74, 84, 104, 126, 137, 147, 148, 151, 155, 160, 164, 167, 168, 170, 172, 173, 179, 180, 183, 186
 No-confidence motion 27, 38
 Parliamentary Group 34, 168
 Relations with Communist countries 35-42
 Relations with U.K. 21-63
United Nations 91
 Afro-Asian Group 94, 167
 Ceylon's membership 28, 30, 31, 36, 45, 46, 57, 167
 China's membership 85, 87
 Egypt-Israel conflict 90
 Essentials of Peace Resolution 93
 Hungarian question 91-2
 Indian Ocean 187
 Indonesian question 45, 46
 Korean war 37, 39, 47
 Peace through Deeds Resolution 93
 Social Activity Division 154
 South African question 196
 Special Investigation Committee on Hungary 91-2
 Suez question 89
U.N. Emergency Force 90
Unites States Information Service

179
U.S. News and World Report 71, 78, 84

Vernacular schools 13, 14
Vidyalankara University 152, 156
Vidyodaya University 152, 156
Viet-Minh 49, 51
Vihara Sasanarakshaka Societies 151
Viplavakati Lanka Sama Samaja Party 64, 148
Vittachi, Tarzie 158
Voice of America 69

Wales University 177
Weekly holiday 177
Weerawardena, I.D.S. 19, 97, 159, 162

Wells, H.G. 14
Western music 158, 169
Westernization 147, 155
Wheare, K.C. 58, 59, 60
Wickremasinghe, S.A. 19
Wijemanne, A.F. 186
Wijewardane, *Mrs.* Vimla 86
Wilson, A.J. 16, 161
Woolf, Leonard 20
World Bank 182
World war, First 4
World war, Second 6, 7, 21, 116, 119, 121, 133, 134
Wray, Kenneth Robert 60
Wriggins, H. Howard 18, 60, 95, 96, 97, 158, 159

YMCA, Colombo 92